KILTER LEADERSHIP

Alan Rogers

Copyright © Alan Rogers, 2025

ISBN 978-1-915962-95-9

Published by Compass-Publishing UK 2025

Cover artwork by © Alexa Whitten - The Book Refinery

Edited and designed by The Book Refinery
www.TheBookRefinery.com

All rights reserved. This book or any portion thereof may not be reproduced or used in any manner whatsoever without the express written permission of the publisher except for the use of brief quotations in a book review.

This book contains material designed to assist your business. While the author has made every effort to verify that the information provided in this book is correct and up to date, the author assumes no responsibility for any error, inaccuracy or omission.

The advice, examples and strategies contained herein are not suitable for every situation. The materials contained herein are not intended to represent or guarantee you will achieve your desired results, and the author shall not be liable for damages arising there from. Success is determined by a number of factors beyond the control of the author, including but not limited to market conditions, the capital on hand, effort levels and time. You understand every individual business carries an inherent risk of capital loss and failure.

Dedicated to Lisa-Anne - who thinks of everything and everyone, so I can pursue adventures like this book.

Contents

Introduction   13
The four levels of the Kilter Leadership Taxonomy   14
The balance, craft and path of leadership   17

LEVEL 1

1 – Self-Awareness   21
The foundation of leadership   21
Science, strengths and frustrations   23
Four preference types: Understanding what drives or drains you   25
Leveraging preferences to mitigate frustrations and lead effectively   27
   Health warning: Preferences not competences   32
The problem of over-reliance on strengths   33
   Case study: The creative leader's dilemma   34
Managing frustrations to prevent burnout   35
   Case study: Preventing burnout through delegation and collaboration   36

2 – Responsibility   39
Responsibility: No blame, no excuses   39
What responsibility in leadership is   40
When not to take responsibility   43
Delivering feedback as a skilled leader: Steps to consider   44
   Example in practice: Responsibility in feedback   46
   Ensuring lasting solutions: Preventing issues recurring   47
   Example in practice: Finding the root of the issue   48
How responsibility assists ambition   48

    Scenario comparison: Blaming vs taking responsibility   48
    Timeline comparison: Blame vs responsibility   50
  The challenges of responsibility: Holding people to account   53
  Responsibility at a cultural level: When everyone takes ownership, amazing things happen   54
    A school-trip debrief: Collective ownership for future success   55
    Health warning: Responsibility vs legal accountability   57

3 – Relationships   59

  The importance of relationships in leadership   60
  Delivering on your role and responsibilities   62
  Ego is the enemy (yours and theirs)   65
  Conflict resolution and empathy in relationships   68
  Building trust through tough conversations   70
  Competition without clarity: *The silent poison within teams*   70
  Balancing relationships with decision-making   73
    The final challenge: The 'beyond the Wall' task   75

4 – Communication   79

  Communication as a leadership foundation   79
  Vision and clarity   80
  Adapting communication styles   82
  Empathy in communication   83
  Communication as a continuous process   84
  The power of listening in leadership   85
  Communicating through actions   87
    Case study: Leading by example   88
  Matching courage with compassion in leadership communication   90
    Example in Practice: Missed deadlines   90
  Techniques for identifying the core issues in communication   92
    Communication: Everyone's responsibility   95
    Reflection Exercise for Self-Improvement   98

LEVEL 2

5 – Developing Others — 103

The three dimensions of development — 106
- Health warning: Avoiding manipulation — 109
- Case study: Misguided and manipulative motivation — 110
- Situational Leadership: Blanchard's model — 114
- Example: Driving instruction — 116

The difference between mentoring and coaching — 117

Understanding the drama and empowerment triangles in leadership — 119
- The Drama Triangle: Toxic roles that hinder growth — 119
- The Empowerment Triangle: A blueprint for resilience and accountability — 120

6 – Delegation — 129

The role of delegation in leadership — 130

Situational Leadership and delegation — 131
- Example in practice: Reorganising the shop floor — 132

The benefits of delegation — 133

Fear of letting go – 'Yes, Chef!' — 134

Balancing feedback with leadership growth — 135

Developing others while retaining standards — 135
- Example in practice: Head-chef mode — 136

Delegation as a tool for stability and success — 136

The power of delegation in managing rebellious behaviour — 138

Avoiding the pitfalls of unskilled delegation — 139

Techniques for effective delegation — 140

Using delegation experiences to become a better team member — 141

7 – Creating Advantages — 145

- The dual reality: Problems and opportunities in every situation — 146
- Golden opportunities (problems) — 148
    - Health warning: Balancing problem recognition with opportunity focus — 153
- The Kilter Problem-to-Opportunity Framework — 155
    - Example in practice: Big opportunities in low-profile jobs — 156

8 – Turning Work into Results — 161

- Success aspects — 162
    - Example in practice: Using nudges to increase parking ticket compliance — 165
    - Health warning: The critical skill of balance — 166
    - Process vs outcome: The leadership balancing act — 166
    - Example in practice: Mastering process and outcome — 167
    - Two schools: A tale of purpose and currency — 171
- Monitoring and messaging: Shaping team culture — 172
- Selecting and building the right currency — 172
    - The Walsh–McCullum approach: Let the scoreboard look after itself — 173
    - Health warning: Avoiding the pitfall of humiliation — 176
    - Building leadership currency: Demonstrating respect and accountability — 178

LEVEL 3

9 – Managing Emotions — 183

- Stage 1: Separation — 184
    - The power of choice: Aligning with the you you're proud of — 190
    - More power of choice: Aligning with the ideal situation you want to create — 191

Stage 2: Work through — 193

   Example in practice: The normalising skill — 196

   Expectation and acceptance: The role of perspective – fairy tale vs reality — 199

   Scenario: Managing unrealistic expectations in the workplace — 203

   Example in practice: Managing anxiety vs stress — 206

Stage 3: Plan and action — 208

   Mind-system dynamics: How we can get our systems to work together — 215

10 – Decision-Making Under Pressure — 219

The realities of decision-making under pressure — 220

Key factors that cause pressure in leadership — 221

The SODA loop: A practical decision-making tool — 222

Organisational agility: Failing fast and failing safely — 226

Managing emotions during decision-making — 227

Building confidence in decision-making — 228

Learning from high-pressure decisions: The role of experience in the SODA loop — 228

The cycle of continuous improvement — 231

   Putting the SODA loop into action: Ensuring a high-quality, professional meeting — 231

11 – Team Dynamics — 239

The importance of understanding team dynamics — 242

   exercise: Vision creation for smaller teams — 246

Identify your norms and build your culture — 250

Tool for finding your team's strengths — 251

Aligning team members with the right roles — 252

Fostering collaboration and managing conflict — 256

Adapting leadership style to team dynamics — 258

LEVEL 4

12 – Strategic Leadership — 263
- Strategy defined — 264
- From reactive to proactive and from proactive to strategic — 266
- Kilter Strategic Framework — 274

13 – Culture Creation — 281
- Every action is a brick in the wall — 281
- What organisational culture is — 283
  - *Exercise: Vision creation* — 285
  - *Example in practice: Cycling team vision* — 287
- The leader's role in shaping culture through communication — 289
- What's measured and monitored becomes culture, so focus on processes — 290
  - *Example in practice: sales team at work* — 291
- Strategic culture creation: Building an inclusive and values-driven organisation — 292
- Addressing challenges in culture creation — 294
- The impact of added pressure and the importance of the *why* in culture — 295
- Handling conflict and toxic behaviours — 297
- How culture impacts long-term success — 300
- Setting personal visions or smaller-team visions — 301

14 – Leadership Structure and Pathways — 303
- The importance of leadership pathways — 304
- Creating leadership pathways based on strengths and commitment — 305
  - *Example in practice: The impact of promotion decisions in a school context* — 306

Front-loading skills to avoid the Peter Principle   307
   Scenario: A chain of incompetence   308
   Preventing the Peter Principle:
   A strategic leadership pathways approach   309
The three replacements rule   310
Building a strong, future-ready team   311
Creating opportunities for leadership development   312
Aligning leadership development with organisational strategy   314
Leadership structures   315
   Health warning: Potential consequences of neglecting
   core-subject standards   317
Creating strategic leadership structures   317
   Example in practice: Strategic creation of a technologies
   lead role in a primary school   320
Balancing role creation with organisational sustainability   323

Final Reflection: From Natural to Skilled and Balanced Leadership   327
About the Author   329
References
  330

Introduction
The Purpose of the Kilter Leadership Taxonomy

Leadership isn't a singular skill but a series of balanced abilities: courage and compassion; discipline and flexibility; and forethought and action. The **Kilter Leadership Taxonomy** addresses leadership as a structured developmental journey that builds from a personal contribution to making a broader organisational impact. Leadership is a constant balancing act, and mastering it requires intentional development and continuous refinement. Despite its universal importance across industries and sectors, leadership remains one of the least formally taught skills.

The Kilter Leadership Taxonomy views leadership as a craft. As with any craft, some aspects will come naturally to us, while others may feel like a challenge, a frustration or a drain. Yet, like all crafts, both our natural strengths and areas of struggle can be developed through focused attention and deliberate practice. Embracing this mindset allows leaders to view each element of their development as an opportunity for growth and mastery, rather than as an obstacle.

The Kilter Leadership Taxonomy has been designed to address this gap in formal leadership education by offering a structured, practical approach to leadership development. It provides a clear pathway that guides individuals from merely having an immediate impact to engendering a strategic and cultural influence.

At its heart, the Kilter Leadership Taxonomy is a hierarchical structure that organises key leadership skills into four distinct levels. It begins with the foundation – personal leadership – and builds progressively toward broader, future-focused decision-making. This approach allows leaders to move from understanding and managing themselves to impacting and inspiring others, managing performance under pressure, and, ultimately, guiding the strategic direction of teams, departments or entire organisations.

This taxonomy not only provides a roadmap for leadership growth but also serves as a flexible toolkit that leaders can return to whenever needed. The goal isn't to create a fixed, one-size-fits-all model; instead, it offers a dynamic framework that adapts to different leadership styles, challenges and contexts. As a leader, whether you wish to refine your self-awareness, hone your communication skills, or navigate the complexities of handling pressure or strategic decision-making, the Kilter Leadership Taxonomy is designed to support your leadership journey. This book doesn't dive deeply into every area of the taxonomy; rather, it's designed to help you, as a leader, to assess your own strengths and areas to develop and to give you ideas to explore further.

The four levels of the Kilter Leadership Taxonomy

Level 1: Personal leadership and professional skills

At this foundational level, leaders develop *self-awareness, responsibility, relationships* and *communication* – all of which are essential skills for effective and balanced leadership. These abilities – often referred to as 'soft skills' – are frequently overlooked or undervalued in favour of technical or disciplinary expertise. However, this is a significant oversight, because these foundational skills are crucial; even the most advanced technical expertise will prove ineffective if a leader lacks the abilities to understand themselves, take ownership of outcomes, build strong relationships and communicate effectively.

Self-awareness helps leaders to identify their strengths and limitations, which allows them to leverage their capabilities while managing areas where they may struggle. Responsibility is about owning outcomes – whether that's success or failure – and leading with accountability. Strong relationships create trust and collaboration, and effective communication ensures leaders can articulate their vision, provide clarity and inspire action. Together, these skills deliver the core capabilities needed for personal mastery and prepare leaders to guide and influence those around them.

Level 2: Impacting others

Once leaders have personal leadership skills in place, Level 2 focuses on expanding their leadership outward into *how you influence, guide and develop others*. This level equips leaders with the skills required to extend their influence beyond their personal impact and thus support their wider teams effectively. At this stage, leaders move from self-mastery to fostering an environment where others can thrive, which is achieved through inspiring, guiding and elevating the performance of those around them.

Level 2 emphasises developing essential interpersonal skills such as problem-solving, delegation, and the ability to nurture and develop talent within the team. It helps leaders gain the skill set needed to see problems not as obstacles but as opportunities to build trust, nurture creativity and convert challenges into meaningful results. Delegation, meanwhile, is elevated from the simple act of assigning tasks to a leadership skill that empowers others, fosters autonomy and makes certain standards are upheld.

This level also focuses on improving a leader's ability to select actions that cause meaningful results. By learning to prioritise and focus their efforts on high-impact activities, leaders enhance their efficiency and effectiveness. Moreover, Level 2 helps leaders develop and protect a reputation built on outcomes and integrity.

Level 3: Performance under pressure

Level 3 outlines the tools available to help while leading under pressure, when a leader's ability to remain composed, decisive and focused is tested. This stage emphasises a leader actively developing the skills to manage their emotions and ego, ensuring these don't disrupt their ability to lead effectively. By cultivating emotional intelligence, resilience and perspective, leaders can protect both themselves and their teams during high-stress situations.

A key aspect of Level 3 for a leader is harnessing their team's strengths and leveraging team dynamics to achieve extraordinary results. Effective leaders understand at this stage how to bring together individuals' talents and create a cohesive unit that accomplishes far more than the sum of its parts. This involves recognising and balancing the diverse strengths within the team, cultivating collaboration, and creating an environment in which everyone's contributions are valued and aligned toward shared goals. This level also focuses on making decisions under pressure, which is a critical skill for any leader. When a leader develops their ability to remain calm, assess situations objectively and act decisively, they can maximise their natural skill set while also addressing any inherent biases.

Level 4: Strategic Leadership

At the highest level of the Kilter Leadership Taxonomy, leadership becomes about *vision, influence* and *long-term impact*. Thus Level 4 involves thinking strategically – beyond the immediate team or project – and shaping the future direction of the organisation. Strategic leadership requires foresight, a deep understanding of the broader business environment and the ability to navigate complexity.

Leaders at this level must make both decisions that drive performance and ones that influence the culture, growth and sustainability of their teams or organisations. Strategic leadership is about seeing the bigger picture: aligning daily actions with long-term goals, making sure resources are allocated effectively, and guiding the team or organisation toward its objectives.

This level builds on all the skills learned in previous levels. It's about balancing short-term needs with long-term strategy, leading with both empathy and authority, and fostering a culture in which teams can innovate, collaborate and thrive. Strategic leaders also serve as role models who set the tone for leadership within their organisations and empower the next generation of leaders to emerge.

The balance, craft and path of leadership

Throughout the Kilter Leadership Taxonomy, one theme remains consistent: *balance*. Leadership is the dynamic skill of navigating competing priorities, responsibilities and forces, which requires flexibility, resilience and continuous refinement. Effective leaders must know their strengths without overreaching or becoming blind to their limitations, must develop others without lowering standards, and must balance personal responsibility with holding others accountable. This needs to be achieved with a no-excuses mindset that raises a culture of shared responsibility in which leaders set high standards for themselves and their teams, driving both performance and growth. It's equally important that leaders embrace humility, reflection and adaptability, so as to navigate the complexities of ever-changing situations with clarity and confidence. The Kilter Leadership Taxonomy provides a structured approach to developing these essential skills, which enables leaders to maintain equilibrium as they face challenges, to empower their teams and to inspire long-term success.

Leadership is one of the most transferable and necessary skills in today's world, and yet it's rarely taught with the same rigour as technical or academic expertise. The Kilter Leadership Taxonomy has been designed to change that through its comprehensive roadmap to mastering leadership.

By using the Kilter Leadership Taxonomy, leaders can solve more problems, empower more people and unlock more potential – both in themselves and in those around them. The taxonomy offers a structured approach to leadership that grows with the leader, enabling them to develop the competencies needed to lead in any context.

At its core, leadership is about making a difference: in the leader themself, in others and in the organisation. The Kilter Leadership Taxonomy equips leaders with the tools and strategies needed to make that difference, assisting them to lead with balance, adaptability and confidence. Every area of this taxonomy represents a distinct skill set, each of which can be practised and developed. While some aspects will feel more natural to individual leaders, based on their inherent tendencies and experiences, this framework is designed to help leaders, make the most of their natural strengths while also fostering growth in less-familiar areas.

Its ultimate goal is to develop you into a skilled, balanced leader who's capable of excelling in any context.

LEVEL 1

1
Self-Awareness

The foundation of leadership

Leadership isn't just about setting strategies or making decisions; as a leader, it's also about you understanding yourself and how you affect those around you. **Self-awareness** is fundamental to effective leadership, and it's the seed from which all personal and professional qualities grow. Having a clear understanding of yourself allows you to capitalise on your natural strengths and talents, while mitigating frustrations and weaknesses. As a self-aware leader, you're able to guide your teams with clarity and consistency, but the benefits extend much further.

Being self-aware deepens your appreciation of your team members, which allows for more efficient collaboration. It enables you to see that those who may frustrate or even irritate you are potentially offering insights into your blind spots and also providing balance to your own abilities. Leaders who lack self-awareness can quickly fall into burnout, frustration and imposter syndrome. They may unconsciously fill their teams with yes-people or recruit those who complement their own skills, only to resent how these individuals push back against them later on.

A lack of self-awareness hinders all areas of leadership. It can lead to ineffective communication, poor decision-making and strained relationships. Conversely, having a high degree of self-awareness enhances every other aspect of the leadership taxonomy, from responsibility to communication and to developing others. Leaders who are self-aware understand not only their own needs and emotions but also how to harness the diverse strengths of their teams.

Self-awareness has a strong link to emotional intelligence, which is considered one of the most critical predictors of personal success. This chapter explores how self-awareness, combined with emotional intelligence, shapes leaders into better decision-makers, problem-solvers and motivators.

The nuanced and essential skill of developing self-awareness requires far more than applying fixed labels to yourself or others. It involves understanding the unique interplay of your nature – the innate tendencies handed to you or shaped in your early experiences – and your character, which evolves over time through your choices and experiences. These elements together influence how you perceive the world, respond to challenges and relate to others.

Self-awareness is inherently complex because each person is shaped by a distinctive blend of experiences, beliefs and traits that can't be fully replicated or categorised. This individuality means no single method or framework will apply universally. While there are fundamental principles – such as recognising strengths, addressing blind spots and seeking feedback – each individual must explore and adapt these tools to align with their personal journey.

A critical element of the Kilter Leadership Taxonomy is its focus on understanding the interplay between how the brain functions and how this influences our leadership behaviours. This framework uses our understanding of neuroscience at a root level to help guide the development of the leadership skill set and its application. While this approach is designed to assist in personal and professional development, it doesn't profess to be an authoritative source on neuroscience. Instead, it provides broad insights that you, as a leader, can use to generalise patterns while recognising the deeper truth: each of us is entirely unique, having been shaped by individual experiences beliefs and traits that can't be fully replicated.

As Marcus Buckingham puts it in his book *Love + Work*:

> We have one hundred billion neurons in our brains that link up to form a network of one hundred trillion unique connections. Since there are approximately four hundred billion stars in the Milky Way galaxy, and there are a thousand billions in one trillion, your brain has more connections within it than five thousand Milky Ways.[1]

He goes on to suggest that the complexity of the connections in our brains are so vastly varied that they'll only exist in our lifetime.[2] Rather than simply seeking definitive answers, self-awareness is a continuous process of reflection and learning. By understanding your nature and actively shaping your character, you can better navigate relationships, better lead with authenticity and better cultivate empathy. This approach allows you to grow as both an individual and a leader, which will foster stronger connections with people and a clearer sense of purpose.

Science, strengths and frustrations

Understanding your natural strengths and frustrations isn't just a practical necessity in leadership; it's one of the most valuable outcomes of self-awareness. At its core, this process will reveal why certain tasks energise you while others drain you; this will enable you, as a leader, to operate with higher impact, authenticity and resilience.

This concept builds on the works of some renowned thinkers who have shaped our understanding of the mind. Carl Jung – one of the earliest contributors to this field – explored personality archetypes and natural tendencies, and he concludes that our preferences influence how we work, lead and connect with others. Sigmund Freud, in parallel, explored the subconscious factors shaping behaviour, which laid the groundwork for modern approaches to self-awareness.

Contemporary thinkers, such as Donald Clifton and Steve Peters, have expanded these ideas to offer practical tools to apply in leadership contexts. Donald Clifton's strengths-based framework (CliftonStrengths®) focuses on identifying and developing innate talents, emphasising that, by leaning into our strengths, we can unlock confidence and productivity. In contrast, Steve Peters' *The Chimp Paradox* highlights the interplay of the brain's alarm (chimp), rational (human) and memory-based (computer) systems.[3] His work gives leaders a pathway to managing impulses and bringing their emotional drives into line with their long-term goals. Marian Diamond's groundbreaking research on neuroplasticity further deepens this understanding; it demonstrates that, although we're born with inherent tendencies and preferences, the brain's structure can adapt and grow throughout its life. Her studies reveal that enriched environments and experiences can physically alter the brain, allowing individuals to continuously develop a character and capabilities that are well beyond their initial nature.[4]

These theories converge on their shared assertion that our natural preferences are both strengths to be harnessed and sources of frustration when misaligned. Jung's archetypes, Clifton's strengths, Peters' neuroscience and Diamond's insights on neuroplasticity collectively highlight that our innate drivers influence how we respond to challenges, build relationships and pursue growth. Importantly, they also emphasise that development isn't fixed: our capacity to learn, adapt and evolve remains central to leadership success.

To make these insights actionable, these preferences can be categorised broadly and simply into key groups. This book's practical framework allows you, as a leader, to better understand your strengths, identify areas of potential frustration, and apply these learnings effectively to your leadership skill set, while keeping in mind the ongoing potential for growth and change through intentional effort and enriched experiences.

Four preference types: Understanding what drives or drains you

This lens of psychological preferences, in its simplest form, allows individuals to be broadly categorised into four key types, with each representing different strengths and potential frustrations: the **Red** (task-oriented), **Yellow** (social and creative), **Green** (considered and harmony-oriented), and **Blue** (organisational and detail-oriented) preferences. Each of these preferences represents something that's both a strength to be harnessed and a potential area of frustration when it's out of alignment. This colour coding was popularised by the DiSC® (dominance, influence, steadiness and conscientiousness) preference testing in 1958.

Red: Driven by action and results

Leaders with a strong Red preference are naturally task-focused and action-oriented. They thrive in environments with clear objectives and opportunities to achieve tangible results. They're often energised by challenges and quick decision-making. However, this drive can also be their frustration: if tasks are delayed or if others aren't keeping up with the same pace, these leaders can become frustrated and feel as if progress is being hindered.

For Red-preference leaders, the key to managing frustrations lies in learning to collaborate with others, who may approach tasks differently, and in valuing their input while maintaining forward momentum. Delegating to others with complementary strengths (such as Green- or Blue-preference leaders) those tasks that require careful deliberation or teamwork can help balance the Red-preference leaders' approach.

Yellow: Driven by possibilities and social energy

Leaders with a Yellow preference are socially driven and excel in creative environments that require innovation and collaboration. They're energised by brainstorming, ideation and connecting with others. Their strength lies in bringing new ideas to life and inspiring those around them; however, their frustrations often emerge when they're confined to routine or to isolated work that stifles their creativity.

It's crucial for Yellow-preference leaders to recognise when they're feeling boxed in by routine tasks or excessive structure. These leaders thrive when they can motivate and engage others, but they can delegate organisational or detail-heavy responsibilities to team members with stronger Blue preferences, so as to maintain their focus on vision and innovation.

Green: Driven by considerations and harmony

Leaders with a Green preference seek harmony and are driven by thoughtfulness and stability. They function best in balanced, supportive environments that prioritise collaboration and cohesion. Their strength lies in their ability to consider all perspectives carefully before making decisions. Nonetheless, this desire for harmony can also become a source of frustration, especially when such a leader is faced with conflict, disruption or time-sensitive tasks that require immediate action.

Green-preference leaders must learn to balance their need for peace with the demands of leadership, which often involve difficult conversations or quick decisions. Partnering with Red-preference leaders, who excel at taking decisive action, can provide a powerful complement to the Green-preference leaders' more considered approach, which can therefore ensure both action and reflection are accounted for.

Blue: Driven by organisational logistics and detail

Leaders with a Blue preference are naturally inclined toward structure, order and organisation. They thrive on processes, precision and clear guidelines. Their natural strength lies in their ability to bring structure to chaotic environments and make certain that details are handled meticulously. However, they can become irritated when they're forced into ambiguous or fast-paced situations that lack clear direction or when they're dealing with teams that don't follow structured processes.

Blue-preference leaders should recognise when a situation calls for flexibility and adaptability, which can help them to step outside their comfort zone. When faced with creative or visionary work, they can involve Yellow-preference individuals. Their high degree of natural focus on processes will often facilitate innovation flourishing in the team.

Leveraging preferences to mitigate frustrations and lead effectively

As a leader, recognising your preferences and how they impact your leadership style allows you to not only leverage your strengths but also to mitigate your frustrations. A self-aware leader understands when to delegate tasks that drain their energy and when to lean into their strengths for maximum impact. Surrounding yourself with team members who complement your preferences can help you create a balanced leadership approach that will capitalise on the strengths of each individual.

For example, a leader with strong Blue organisational preferences might struggle with the creative ambiguity of a new project. Instead of becoming frustrated, they can delegate the main weight of the brainstorming phase to their Yellow-preference colleagues while focusing on creating the detailed structures that will bring the ideas to life. Similarly, a Yellow-preference leader who feels drained by routine tasks can empower a Blue-preference team member to handle the organisational aspects while focusing on creative leadership.

In this way, self-awareness becomes the foundation on which all professional and personal qualities grow. It lets leaders appreciate their team members more deeply, work together more efficiently and see those who frustrate them as complementary partners who help fill in the leader's blind spots.

As with all the other components in this taxonomy, however, self-awareness must be balanced; a leader with an unskilled approach can drive limiting beliefs about themself and others, which may have highly detrimental effects on team cohesion and personal growth.

Misconceptions about leadership preferences:
No one is one colour

It's a common misconception in leadership that people are either strictly Red or Blue: task-oriented and driven by action (Red), or detail-oriented and highly structured (Blue). In reality, many leaders have a blend of preferences that draw from various strengths, depending on the context. This mixture of traits allows leaders to be adaptable in their approaches, combining the best aspects of each preference while balancing their potential frustrations. For example, a leader may display strong Red tendencies when a project demands quick, decisive action, but they may revert to their Blue characteristics when overseeing complex systems that require meticulous attention to detail. Pigeonholing individuals as purely one type misses the complexity of their full capabilities, which often lie at the intersections between preferences.

As we explore each category in turn, it's essential to remember that these mind-profiling theories highlight combinations of preferences rather than fixed identities; our leading preference is simply one component of a larger, dynamic blend.

We'll now look at how different preference combinations manifest in leadership styles, starting with the Red–Blue pairing.

Red followed by Blue: The strategic executor

Leaders with a dominant Red preference that's followed by Blue are highly effective at executing complex strategies. Their Red preference ensures they're action-oriented, decisive, and always pushing their team toward goals and quick wins. However, their Blue side adds a layer of structure and precision that allows them to perform these tasks systematically and efficiently.

Strengths: These leaders excel in fast-paced environments that necessitate both decisive action and detailed execution. They're strategic and combine the ability to set a clear course (Red) with the precision to see it through efficiently (Blue). They thrive in leadership roles that require both vision and the ability to guarantee that no details are overlooked.

Frustrations: These leaders may become frustrated by team members who are less organised or who don't follow the structures they've set. The Red drive for speed can also clash with the Blue need for perfection, which can cause internal tension when tasks are rushed at the expense of thoroughness.

Red followed by Yellow: The inspirational visionary

Leaders who are primarily Red with a secondary Yellow preference are natural visionaries. Their Red preferences drive them to take action and lead from the front, while their Yellow side adds elements of creativity, enthusiasm and social engagement. This combination allows them to inspire their team to not only achieve but also innovate along the way.

Strengths: These leaders are dynamic, motivational and capable of rallying the team around a shared vision (Yellow), while ensuring progress is made through action and results (Red). They perform best in environments that require both rapid decision-making and the ability to inspire creativity and collaboration.

Frustrations: The primary challenge for these leaders is balancing their Red drive for results with their Yellow love of creativity and social engagement. They may become frustrated when their team's enthusiasm for brainstorming overshadows the need to execute actions swiftly. Additionally, they might struggle to manage tasks that require long-term planning or meticulous detail, as they prefer to keep the momentum going rather than getting bogged down in minutiae.

Yellow followed by Red: The creative driver

Leaders with a Yellow-Red combination are creative drivers who thrive in environments where innovation and action go hand in hand. Their Yellow side fuels their ability to think outside the box and inspire their team with bold ideas, while their Red side makes certain those ideas are swiftly put into action.

Strengths: These leaders excel in environments that demand both creativity and fast results. They're adept at launching new initiatives and getting their team excited about fresh ideas. They have the ability to bring people together with their enthusiasm (Yellow) and then lead them toward a fast project execution (Red).

Frustrations: Their biggest frustration may come when they're forced to stick to rigid plans or when their creative ideas are met with resistance from those who prefer more-structured approaches. They might also struggle with follow-through, as their Red preference for immediate action can clash with the need for long-term strategy and detail management.

Yellow followed by Green: The harmonious innovator

Leaders who are primarily Yellow but followed by Green combine creativity with a deep focus on relationships and harmony. They're socially adept and draw people together with their ideas (Yellow), while their Green side makes sure they maintain strong, collaborative relationships.

Strengths: These leaders thrive in roles that require both innovation and diplomacy. They can bring fresh perspectives to the table (Yellow) while ensuring their team members work together in a harmonious and supportive way (Green). They're natural team builders who inspire collaboration through creativity and empathy.

Frustrations: These leaders may become frustrated when they need to take quick, decisive actions, as their Green preference for harmony may cause them to hesitate in making difficult decisions, which could disrupt team dynamics. They may also find it challenging to impose structure or hold team members accountable if it risks upsetting the group's balance.

Green followed by Yellow: The collaborative idealist

Leaders with a Green–Yellow combination work best in environments where harmony and creative collaboration are paramount. Their Green preference helps them build deep relationships and foster a sense of community, while their Yellow side brings creativity and optimism to their leadership.

Strengths: These leaders are fantastic at cultivating teamwork and making their team feel valued and included. They focus on creating a supportive environment (Green) at the same time as pushing for innovation and new ideas (Yellow). Their leadership style is inclusive, which ensures everyone has a voice and which encourages creative problem-solving.

Frustrations: Their frustration often lies in environments that need fast decision-making or where conflict is inevitable. They may avoid necessary confrontations so as to maintain harmony, which can lead to issues remaining unresolved. Their preference for collaboration may also slow down decision-making processes, especially when working with more-action-oriented team members.

Green followed by Blue: The considered organiser

Green–Blue leaders are thoughtful, organised and harmony-oriented. Their Green preference drives their desire for collaboration and balance, while their Blue side makes certain they bring structure and order to their leadership.

Strengths: These leaders excel in creating well-organised, harmonious environments in which everyone knows their role and feels supported. Their planning is detailed (Blue), and they're careful to consider the emotional and social needs of their team members (Green). Their ability to create structured, collaborative spaces makes them invaluable in teams that require both order and empathy.

Frustrations: Green–Blue leaders may find themselves frustrated in chaotic or fast-paced environments in which they can't take the time they need to ensure both harmony and structure are in place. They may also struggle when their team members don't follow processes or when conflict arises, as both their preferences lean toward maintaining peace and order.

Blue followed by Green: The structured diplomat

Blue–Green leaders are meticulous and detail-oriented, but they also have a strong focus on maintaining harmony within their team. Their Blue preference engenders them creating order and clear systems, while their Green side helps them build collaborative relationships.

Strengths: These leaders are effective at ensuring both tasks and relationships are managed well. They create structured, organised environments (Blue), while they're considerate of their team's emotional and social needs (Green). Their combination of structure and empathy makes them well-suited to leadership roles that require both precision and diplomacy.

Frustrations: Their frustration arises when they're forced to make swift, unstructured decisions or when their focus on order is disrupted by conflict. They may also struggle when asked to be more flexible or when working in highly dynamic, creative environments in which structure is less valued.

Blue followed by Red: The tactical leader

Blue-Red leaders combine structure and decisive action. Their Blue preference makes them organised and meticulous, while their Red side gives them the drive to act decisively and lead from the front.

Strengths: These leaders are highly effective in implementing plans with precision (Blue) and making certain tasks are completed swiftly and efficiently (Red). They're strategic, action-oriented and capable of leading their teams toward clear, well-structured goals.

Frustrations: They may become frustrated when others don't follow processes or when their need for structure is disrupted by unpredictable events. Their desire for speed (Red) may also clash with their need for order (Blue), which creates internal tension when they have to balance these two preferences under pressure.

> **HEALTH WARNING: PREFERENCES NOT COMPETENCES**

One key detail that's often misunderstood with these types of preference-based frameworks – such as the Red, Yellow, Green and Blue leadership styles – is that they identify preferences, not abilities. These tests reveal where a leader might feel most comfortable or may most instinctively be inclined to act, but they don't automatically indicate having skill or competence in those areas.

For example, a leader who has a dominant Red preference might instinctively want to take charge, make quick decisions and lead from the front. However, this doesn't mean their decisions are always good or well thought out. Their preference for action and decisiveness might cause them to overlook important details or rush into decisions without considering all the variables. Such leaders who lack the self-awareness to recognise this tendency can make poor choices, especially in situations that need more deliberation or collaboration.

Similarly, someone with a strong Blue preference may instinctively want to organise things, create detailed plans, or structure information into tables and spreadsheets. However, this doesn't guarantee their organisational efforts are relevant, helpful or even clear to others. Being inclined toward structure is a preference, but it doesn't automatically translate into effective systems or processes. A highly organised spreadsheet is only valuable if it serves a clear purpose and is understandable to those who need to use it.

This is why self-awareness is critical, as discussed earlier. It allows leaders to not only recognise their own preferences but also assess where their strengths align with real-world effectiveness. A Red leader can learn to temper their impulse for rapid decision-making through getting others' input, while a Blue leader can seek feedback to ensure their detailed planning is truly useful and relevant.

Ultimately, understanding these preferences helps leaders determine where they naturally excel and where they might need to develop or seek complementary skills from others on their teams.

The problem of over-reliance on strengths

Although leveraging strengths is key to leadership success, over-relying on them can become a significant limitation. Leaders who focus too heavily on their natural preferences – such as being creative, harmonious, decisive or organised – may miss growth opportunities or overlook crucial aspects of leadership that necessitate a different approach. By relying blindly on their strengths, leaders can neglect the areas that need development and fail to adapt their style to different team dynamics and challenges.

Blind spots: What we don't see but others do

Blind spots arise when a leader overuses their strengths to the point they become weaknesses. For instance, a leader with a strong Yellow preference, who's driven by creativity and enthusiasm, may generate many ideas but struggle with following them through or may fail to focus on the operational realities of execution. Similarly, a Green-preference leader, who values harmony and balance, may avoid conflict or difficult conversations, which could prevent necessary changes being made or constructive feedback being taken on board.

It's a common misconception that if a leader is strong in a particular area, they'll always perform well there. However, without balance, strengths can create vulnerabilities. For example, a Yellow leader might instinctively generate new ideas and cultivate a positive, creative environment, but that doesn't mean every idea will be practical or be in harmony with the organisational goals. Similarly, a Green leader may intuitively strive to create harmony and avoid tension, but this could cause conflicts to remain unresolved and suppress critical feedback.

CASE STUDY: THE CREATIVE LEADER'S DILEMMA

Consider a Yellow-preference leader who excels at generating creative ideas and fostering an energetic, collaborative team culture. Although this strength drives innovation and team enthusiasm, it can also create a blind spot: this leader may fail to recognise the importance of structure or the details necessary for project implementation. Over time, this can result in unfinished projects and a lack of progress toward strategic goals. By becoming aware of this tendency, the leader can consciously focus on execution or bring in a more organised Blue team member to make sure ideas are realised and aligned with the overall vision.

This highlights the importance of understanding your strengths, recognising when they may have become overused, and adapting to meet the needs of the situation and the team. Effective leaders strike a balance between leveraging their strengths and growing in areas that complement those strengths, which helps to keep their leadership adaptable and holistic.

Managing frustrations to prevent burnout

Leaders inevitably face tasks that exasperate them, which is often due to misalignment with their natural strengths or preferences. Managing these frustrations effectively is critical to maintaining balance, avoiding stress and preventing burnout. If leaders consistently ignore or push through these frustrations without addressing the underlying causes, they risk becoming emotionally and physically exhausted, which can severely impact their well-being and leadership effectiveness.

The link between frustrations and burnout

Research consistently highlights the strong connection between burnout and working in areas misaligned with personal strengths. A notable study by Gallup reveals that employees who don't utilise their strengths at work are *three times more likely to experience burnout*.[5] This finding underlines the importance of bringing work tasks into line with individual strengths, not only for maintaining high performance but also for preserving emotional and mental health.

In leadership, irritations often arise when tasks fall outside a leader's natural preferences. For example, a leader with a strong Yellow preference (creativity and people-focus) may feel drained by repetitive, detail-oriented tasks. Similarly, a Green-preference leader (harmony and support-focus) may struggle with having to make a series of high-pressure decisions, which could lead to prolonged stress if not addressed.

Recognising and addressing frustrations

The key to managing frustrations is self-awareness: recognising which tasks drain your energy and understanding their impact on your performance. However, while it's essential to work within your strengths, no leader can entirely avoid tasks that don't meet their preferences. The goal is therefore to manage time and energy efficiently so work involving your strengths remains part of your routine, thus maintaining motivation and performance.

It's important that leaders never fall into the trap of saying, 'I can't do that because I'm high Yellow or low Green.' Leadership is about using strengths to *overcome* weaknesses. To be a truly skilled leader, you must stretch beyond your natural tendencies when necessary and find ways to grow in areas that don't come as easily to you. Your natural strengths must not be an excuse to avoid uncomfortable tasks; they should be a resource you can leverage to tackle challenges outside your comfort zone.

Leaders should ask themselves these questions:

» What tasks drain my energy consistently, and how can I balance them with tasks that energise me?

» Am I pushing through frustrating work without seeking support?

» How can I reframe these tasks or delegate them to someone better suited to doing them?

CASE STUDY: PREVENTING BURNOUT THROUGH DELEGATION AND COLLABORATION

Consider a senior marketing executive who thrives on creative thinking (Yellow preference) but struggles with administrative tasks, such as budget management and reporting, which are more in harmony with a Green preference. Over time, their constant juggling between creative and operational work leads to exhaustion as the executive feels drained by tasks that are a mismatch with their strengths.

On recognising the misalignment, the executive delegates the administrative duties to a team member who excels in operations. This delegation frees up the executive to focus on their creative strengths and empowers the team member to shine. The result is a more balanced workload, reduced stress and improved job satisfaction for both parties.

This example illustrates how having *self-awareness of frustrations* and implementing *strategic delegation* can prevent burnout. By acknowledging any areas of frustration and finding practical solutions – whether that's through delegation, collaboration or time management – leaders can maintain a healthy balance and sustain their long-term effectiveness.

CONCLUSION

Self-awareness is a vital foundational block of effective leadership and the one on which all other leadership skills are built. By understanding your strengths, frustrations and preferences, you'll gain the ability to lead with authenticity, clarity and resilience. Self-aware leaders are better equipped to manage their emotions, navigate challenges and build meaningful relationships with their team members. This awareness raises a deeper appreciation for the diverse strengths and perspectives of others, which enables leaders to create collaborative and high-performing teams.

Developing self-awareness isn't about limiting yourself with labels or rigid categories; rather, it's about gaining a clearer understanding of your natural tendencies and how they influence your leadership style. It's about embracing both your unique capabilities and your areas for growth, alongside recognising how others complement your blind spots. Balancing introspection with action means self-aware leaders are better able to adapt to changing circumstances, make thoughtful decisions and harness the strengths of their teams to achieve shared goals.

2
Responsibility

Responsibility: No blame, no excuses

There's no more impactful skill set in leadership than **responsibility**. Responsibility in leadership is about more than simply accepting blame or taking credit; it's about *taking ownership* in a way that moves our focus beyond blame. This skill set encourages leaders to examine every situation through the lens of potential solutions and growth, which might mean considering better preparation, building stronger relationships, offering more comprehensive training or communicating more clearly.

Leaders (such as Jocko Willink in *Extreme Ownership*[6]) emphasise the value of this approach by encouraging leaders to own every part of their mission; that is, acknowledging both the successes and areas for improvement. This is reinforced by Stephen Covey's principle of proactivity in *The 7 Habits of Highly Effective People*, which urges leaders to focus on what they can control to drive positive change.[7]

This approach creates a culture in which leaders are committed to solutions and positive results, rather than focusing on blame. By continuously reflecting on their role in every outcome, leaders empower themselves to build a resilient, proactive environment that's geared toward stability, continuous improvement and meaningful impact. Leaders who embrace responsibility at a fundamental level create an environment in which both successes and failures are shared by all members of the team.

Embracing responsibility involves forming a culture that doesn't tolerate excuses. Leaders must be vigilant; if they find themselves or members of their team blaming external factors or feeling powerless, they must return to the principles in this chapter. The first principle of leadership is focusing on what you can control, constantly striving for better outcomes and driving progress even in the face of setbacks. We'll now examine the leadership skill of responsibility, its profound impact on results and relationships, and how leaders can nurture a culture of ownership while balancing accountability, empowerment and continuous growth.

What responsibility in leadership is

Responsibility in leadership comprises more than just doing your job. It's about being accountable for outcomes, regardless of whether they're positive or negative. As a leader, you're not only responsible for your actions but also for the performance, behaviour and development of the team you lead. Taking responsibility means looking at situations and asking yourself, 'How could I have contributed to the outcome? And what can I do to raise the probability of getting better results in the future?'

In *The 7 Habits of Highly Effective People's* chapter on proactiveness, Stephen Covey emphasises the importance of taking the initiative and focusing on what you can control, rather than what you can't.[8] Covey's principle aligns with Jocko Willink's *Extreme Ownership*, in which he argues that leaders must own every aspect of their mission, even those they can't control directly.[9] This means comprehending that no success or failure rests on one person alone; instead, it's the result of the entire team's efforts, but it's the leader's responsibility to steer the ship and ensure the team is functioning at its best.

Developing responsibility as a leadership skill

To embody this form of responsibility, leaders must do the following:

- **Go first:** When something doesn't meet the standard, they must be the first to ask, 'What could I have done differently? How could I have adapted my approach, practice or systems to improve the outcome?' This is a powerful character trait that raises the probability others will follow the leader's example.

- **Focus on solutions:** When a problem arises, leaders must ask themselves, 'What solutions can I control?' This keeps them from becoming disempowered by things outside their influence.

- **Anticipate and resolve issues before they occur:** Recognise that part of effective leadership involves stepping up proactively to address potential issues. Identifying and resolving challenges early allows leaders to minimise disruptions and exemplify accountability. This readiness reflects a mindset of considering their own contributions first, ensuring both they and their team are positioned for success.

Shifting from blame to solutions

One of the biggest challenges for any leader is resisting the instinct to assign blame when things go wrong. In a blame-driven culture, people fall into the traps of trying to protect themselves, avoiding risks and hiding mistakes. This creates a toxic environment in which fear dominates and innovation is stifled. Instead, responsible leaders shift their focus from 'Who's at fault?' to 'What can we do to fix this?' and 'What was in my control that could have helped avoid this?'

In *Extreme Ownership*, Jocko Willink famously explains that leaders must own everything in their world.[10] This doesn't mean you personally take the blame for every failure; rather, it means you recognise that, as the leader, you're responsible for creating an environment in which your team can succeed. If they fail, you should ask yourself what decision, support, communication or resources you could have provided to avert the issue.

Why you should take the blame when it isn't your fault

A leader might ask, 'Why should I take the blame when it isn't my fault?' The answer lies in the nature of leadership. Success is rarely due to the work of one individual, and failures aren't either. A team thrives when every member reflects on what they could have done to avert an issue. It's not about blame; it's about responsibility and improving outcomes.

As the leader, you have the ultimate opportunity to influence your team's direction. You taking responsibility sets a powerful example that inspires others to do the same. This leads to a culture of accountability in which every team member considers how they can contribute to success, rather than deflecting responsibility. And when leaders focus on finding solutions, instead of blaming others, they create an environment in which problems are solved more quickly and trust is built.

No excuses – learn to control the weather

In leadership, making excuses is the opposite of taking responsibility. Skilled leaders recognise that, even when factors outside their control affect outcomes, their role isn't to deflect blame but to assess, adapt and improve for the future. For instance, consider a leader who's meticulously planned an event only to have an unexpected storm disrupt it. Instead of blaming the weather – which many would argue is out of the leader's control – for them not meeting their goals, a responsible leader contemplates how they might have anticipated this challenge and mitigated its impact. They approach this setback as a lesson, as they know simply blaming the weather won't help them achieve better future outcomes.

A leader excelling in responsibility would anticipate the possibility of poor weather and plan a backup option – perhaps by securing an indoor venue or adjusting the agenda to accommodate indoor activities if needed. Although it might seem like a minor detail, this level of foresight is what differentiates skilled leaders. Over time, these proactive measures accumulate and effect more reliable outcomes and more respect from their teams.

LEVEL 1: CHAPTER 2 – RESPONSIBILITY

If two leaders each plan 20 events, and one of them regularly attributes failures to external factors such as the weather, but the other continually reflects on outcomes and adapts to potential challenges, their results and reputations will diverge significantly. The leader who takes responsibility by anticipating issues and preparing contingencies will be better positioned to achieve success; however, the one who makes excuses will find themself limited in the solutions available and facing repeated setbacks. This dedication to accountability, even in tough circumstances, is the essence of responsibility in leadership.

When not to take responsibility

There's a point at which a leader should stop taking responsibility – and that's when things go well. When outcomes are positive, leaders should shift the spotlight on to their team to recognise and celebrate their contributions. By reserving taking responsibility for challenges and by directing praise toward others for successes, leaders create an environment of trust, accountability and collaboration. This approach may seem to be forgoing personal recognition, but its impact is far more significant. Leaders who prioritise their team's successes build loyalty and boost morale, thus establishing a culture in which individuals feel genuinely valued. Over time, this enhances the leader's reputation and influence, as they're seen as someone who empowers others to excel. As a result, leaders who focus on enabling team achievements are often granted greater responsibilities and more future opportunities – not because they claimed credit for every success, but because they cultivated a cohesive, high-performing team that gets results.

Why taking responsibility doesn't add stress

Leaders also often ask, 'Won't taking responsibility add more stress and thus damage my mental health?' The truth is that it's the opposite. Contemplating what you can control and taking responsibility for solutions is *empowering*, not stressful.

Here's two examples to illustrate this. Imagine two leaders who both experience the same challenging day. They're having issues with their line manager, their teams are facing performance difficulties, the equipment they rely on has been unreliable, and they've handled a series of customer complaints.

When one leader drives off the car park blaming their boss, their team, the technology or their customers, they're focusing on what they can't control. This might feel good in the moment, but it ultimately creates stress and helplessness.

However, when the second leader reflects on what they can control – how they can improve relationships with their boss, adapt their practices to the strengths of their team, or make better use of the tools at their disposal – they're concentrating on things they can actually change. This mindset shift – when it's practised day after day, week after week – makes leaders who are far more effective, less stressed and more resilient.

Delivering feedback as a skilled leader: Steps to consider

An essential yet often challenging aspect of leadership responsibility is delivering feedback in a way that fosters growth, accountability and trust. Skilled, responsible leaders don't simply highlight areas for improvement in others; they start by acknowledging their role in the situation. By doing so, they're setting a foundation of mutual respect and shared ownership, and they're therefore encouraging team members to contemplate their own actions without them feeling singled out or defensive.

Leaders approaching feedback with this mindset are creating an environment in which team members feel valued and supported, rather than criticised. The most powerful impact of openly communicating your responsibility is that it demonstrates the very attitude you want your team to emulate. When leaders take clear, authentic ownership of their part, they set a compelling example that shows accountability is not about blame but about commitment to the team's success. This transparency encourages the team members to adopt a similar approach, which makes them more likely to take responsibility for their own actions moving forward. By modelling this accountability commitment, they'll build a culture in which responsibility is shared and every team member is inspired to bring their best, reflecting the standard they exemplify as their leader.

Begin with self-reflection

Before offering feedback, responsible leaders pause to consider their own role in the situation.

They might reflect in this way:

- » 'I realise I could have provided the necessary resources and guidance for this task.'
- » 'I see I could have communicated my expectations and goals more clearly.'
- » 'I acknowledge there may have been ways I could have intervened earlier to prevent this outcome.'

Beginning with self-reflection means you're leading the conversation with the very actions and behaviours you hope to encourage in others: humility, openness and a solution-focused approach. This sets a constructive tone and shows you're accountable, collaborative and respectful. In contrast, using language that appears to be or is interpreted as attacking may direct the conversation down a negative path that furthers defensiveness and even dismissiveness (which may occur behind your back, even if not openly). Responsible leaders guide the feedback process by modelling a respectful, proactive stance that invites the same from their team.

Frame feedback as performance analysis, not criticism

If feedback isn't heard in the constructive way it's intended, a skilled leader won't blame the team member for becoming defensive. Instead, they might consider how best to frame the feedback as performance analysis rather than criticism. The goal isn't to highlight flaws but to identify opportunities for refinement, much like the world's top performers do. Consider the best football team in the world, which may have won a match 4–0. Even after such a successful performance, they review the footage, focusing on areas to tighten up on for an even stronger showing next time. Similarly, a world-renowned singer will revisit the footage of a sold-out live show to find places where the experience could be made smoother or more engaging for fans.

By approaching feedback as being part of a high-performance review process, leaders normalise the practice of reflecting and refining. Just as elite athletes and performers look at both their wins and losses as part of continuous improvement, team members can come to view feedback as a tool to achieve their best possible performance. This approach helps shift the mindset from one of fault-finding to one of growth and excellence, which allows team members to feel supported in their journey to be the best they can be with the resources they have.

In addition, a responsible leader can further demonstrate that this process is genuine by offering insights into their own areas of focus and improvement. When leaders share openly what they're working on, they're modelling an environment in which growth is constant, attainable and part of everyone's journey.

Cultivate open dialogue by minimising defensiveness

Starting feedback conversations with self-reflection can help reduce defensiveness. When leaders acknowledge their challenges in their role openly, it sets a humble and courageous tone that signals feedback isn't punitive but developmental. This approach effects more-open dialogue in which team members are more receptive to identifying and addressing their own areas for improvement.

EXAMPLE IN PRACTICE: RESPONSIBILITY IN FEEDBACK

Consider a scenario in which a project didn't achieve the expected standards. Instead of immediately identifying areas where the team member fell short, a leader focused on blame might start by saying, 'You clearly misunderstood the direction. You need to figure out what went wrong here and make sure this doesn't happen again.'

Whereas another might say, 'On reflection, I could have been clearer about the project's objectives and given more timely feedback during the process. I'd like us to look at how we can improve on these points moving forward.'

This second approach starts with a tone of personal responsibility and is more likely to encourage the team member to reflect more openly on their contribution, thus cultivating an environment that regards feedback as a shared journey toward better results. By setting this tone, leaders encourage a culture in which their teams are more likely to engage constructively, approach feedback with openness, and view every conversation as an opportunity for collective growth and improvement. While this approach won't make negative feedback pleasant to receive, it will make the message far more likely to be heard and acted upon.

Ensuring lasting solutions: *Preventing issues recurring*

A common question around this skill set is 'What about when taking responsibility disempowers your team?' A skilled and balanced leader is committed not only to identifying areas they could take responsibility in but also to ensuring responsibility is shared effectively across the team. While taking ownership and refraining from blaming the team are critical aspects of responsible leadership, taking sole responsibility repeatedly can be problematic and ultimately does only half the job. Skilful leadership responsibility involves following through with meaningful action, which includes holding team members accountable for their roles in achieving outcomes. This balanced approach helps ensure similar issues don't recur and everyone understands their part in maintaining progress.

Proficient leaders recognise that identifying a problem is just the beginning. If leaders constantly shield the team from accountability, they risk creating a culture of dependency in which team members aren't encouraged to evaluate or improve their own performance. Effective leadership responsibility encompasses both resolving issues and empowering team members to own their contributions. By cultivating a shared sense of accountability, leaders foster an ethos of resilience and continuous improvement within their teams.

EXAMPLE IN PRACTICE: FINDING THE ROOT OF THE ISSUE

Imagine a scenario where a team is consistently struggling with last-minute changes to project requirements, which result in rushed and error-prone work. Rather than simply addressing each instance as it arises, a responsible leader takes action to prevent these issues becoming a recurring problem. They may implement a clear project-scoping process and make certain all requirements are thoroughly defined, documented, reviewed and approved at the start of each project phase. They then follow up to ensure these steps are being adhered to and are effective in preventing last-minute changes.

By taking this comprehensive approach, the leader isn't just addressing the issue – they're preventing it happening again. This example demonstrates how responsible leadership involves making a commitment to lasting solutions that enhance team stability, efficiency and morale.

How responsibility assists ambition

Ambitious people might ask, 'Why should I take responsibility for others? I'm here to drive results.' However, embracing responsibility is key to achieving those very goals. Leaders who model responsibility build credibility and respect, which are vital for career advancement. This approach boosts a leader's reputation for integrity, which consequently inspires trust and attracts more opportunities. Ultimately, responsibility is a strategic asset for ambitious leaders as it amplifies their influence, their team's success and their long-term impact.

Scenario comparison:
Blaming vs taking responsibility

Consider two scenarios where a project fails to meet its targets, and two team leaders are each reporting on the outcome to their respective line manager. Each leader's approach to the conversation demonstrates a different perspective on responsibility and accountability, which impacts not only their own leadership credibility but also their team's learning and development.

Scenario 1: Blame

Leader A says, 'I communicated the message, but my team just didn't listen. They aren't motivated, and I need a better team because this generation just isn't willing to put in the work.' The leader is clearly shifting the blame to their team, accusing them of being unmotivated and implying the team's failure is solely due to their lack of effort.

Leader A is deflecting responsibility by blaming external factors, such as generational stereotypes, rather than reflecting on what they themself could have done differently to achieve better results. As a result, the team is likely to feel alienated and demoralised. Leader A refusing to take responsibility fractures their relationship with the team, reduces trust and discourages open communication.

Scenario 2: Responsibility

Leader B says, 'I communicated the message, but it's my responsibility to ensure messages are clearly heard and understood. I'll follow up with face-to-face briefings and make certain the communication is reinforced with emails for reference. If motivation is the issue, then I'll take responsibility for finding ways to reignite it. I've scheduled one-to-one conversations with key team members to connect their personal goals to the team's objectives.'

In this scenario, the leader is taking ownership of the outcome and acknowledging it's their job to ensure clear communication and engender team motivation. They're committing to addressing the issues directly by following up with more personal communication and taking steps to engage team members through individual conversations. This approach will build trust and respect within the team, as the leader is both taking responsibility and implementing tangible solutions.

Let's now look at what might happen up the chain and how the line managers might describe each leader to their superiors.

Scenario 1: Blame

Line manager report: 'The project failed, and there don't seem to be any immediate solutions. Apparently, there's an issue with the team, but to be honest, there wasn't much detail given. There was no action plan and no effort to fix the root issues. From our conversation, it's hard to see anything improving under this leader. If we surround them with people who don't need leadership, they might be okay, but I don't see that as an option.'

Scenario 2: Responsibility

Line manager report: 'The project didn't hit its goals, but the leader has already stepped up in the situation. They've recognised where their communication fell short and are actively taking steps to fix it – they're exploring a range of options. They didn't shy away from the issues, but they were very forward focused. I need to keep an eye on whether they deliver, but I have a good feeling about it.'

Timeline comparison:
Blame vs responsibility

Let's now examine the longer-term impacts of repeated patterns of blame versus responsibility in leadership.

The habitual blame in Leader A's approach erodes trust and discourages ownership, which results in stagnation, lower performance and higher turnover as team members seek more empowering environments. In contrast, Leader B's consistent balance of accountability cultivates trust, adaptability and shared commitment, which builds a team culture that encourages reflection, skill development and sustained high performance.

These two approaches show how repeated patterns of blame or responsibility can shape team potential and long-term success.

Scenario 1: Blame
Immediate future

- » **Team morale drops:** Leader A continues to blame the team for missed targets and disengagement. The team members become demoralised as they feel unappreciated and unfairly criticised.

- » **Increased turnover risk:** Several team members start looking for new roles or disengage from their work. The lack of ownership from leadership leaves the team feeling unsupported, and high performers may begin to exit the company.

- » **No improvement:** Leader A focuses on excuses, possibly citing external reasons (such as generational attitudes or market conditions) without addressing internal processes or communication. Projects continue to underperform.

Mid-term future

- » **Worsening performance:** The team's overall productivity declines further. As high performers leave, the remaining staff become more disengaged, which causes more missed deadlines and failed objectives.

- » **Toxic environment:** Without any course correction, the work environment becomes increasingly toxic. Collaboration and trust break down entirely, and Leader A doubles down on blame, alienating the team further.

- » **Leader in danger:** Leader A's performance is now under scrutiny from their higher-ups. Without positive results or team engagement, their job security becomes precarious.

Long-term future

- » **Complete team breakdown:** Leader A's inability to take responsibility causes a high turnover rate, leaving only disengaged or underperforming staff on the team. The team's reputation within the organisation takes a hit.

- » **Leadership change imminent:** The line manager or higher leadership steps in to either reassign Leader A, implement a performance improvement plan or replace them entirely. Damage control is needed to rebuild the team's morale and performance.

Scenario 2: Responsibility

Immediate future

- » **Team morale stabilises:** After acknowledging the problem and taking responsibility, Leader B starts to meet with team members individually to address their concerns and connect their goals to the broader team/project objectives.

- » **Improved communication:** By reinforcing communication with follow-ups and personal interactions, the team feels more informed and engaged. Motivation begins to increase as team members appreciate Leader B's proactive approach.

- » **Initial signs of improvement:** The team's projects may not immediately hit full stride, but small wins start to emerge. Team members begin to take ownership of their roles again, supported by Leader B's focus on solutions rather than blame.

Mid-term future

- » **Positive momentum:** The team's performance improves steadily. Clear communication and a stronger sense of trust are allowing better collaboration and more consistent results. Individual one-to-ones and team meetings continue to nurture engagement.

- » **Increased accountability:** With Leader B setting the example, the team members start holding themselves and each other accountable for outcomes. The team feels more unified, and ownership of successes and failures is shared.

- » **Recognition of effort:** As the team hits more targets, Leader B publicly acknowledges their hard work, boosting morale further. As results improve, Leader B gains trust, not only from the team but also from upper management.

Long-term future

» **High performance and retention:** The team, now empowered by their leader's commitment to responsibility and trust, continues to perform at a high level. Turnover is low and engagement is strong, as team members feel supported and valued.

» **Leader development:** Within the organisation, Leader B gains visibility as a successful team builder and problem-solver. Their team's results position them for possible promotions or expanded responsibilities within the company.

» **Sustained success:** With a foundation of trust and accountability in place, the team can confidently take on bigger projects and challenges. Leader B's approach becomes a model for others in the organisation.

The challenges of responsibility: Holding people to account

Ultimately, responsibility in leadership isn't just about accepting blame; it's about safeguarding results and holding people accountable for their contributions. This is the most critical skill of effective leadership within the Kilter Leadership Taxonomy. As a leader, if you find targets are consistently missed or performance lags, it's your responsibility to adapt. This might seem like an impossible challenge, but true leadership emerges through recognising the issues, addressing them head-on, and ensuring that the team members are both supported and held accountable for their actions.

If problems persist, it's crucial to ask yourself this: 'What more can I do to guarantee success? How can I adapt my leadership style to meet the needs of this situation?' Leadership isn't static; it necessitates constant adjustments to the realities of your team's dynamics, capabilities and challenges. The ability to evolve your practices to meet the ever-changing demands of leadership is what sets skilful leaders apart from the rest.

In the end, it's not enough to simply say, 'I take responsibility.' A true leader must add, 'I take action to make certain we meet our targets, and I hold myself and my team accountable.' This approach raises a culture of accountability, continuous improvement and relentless pursuit of success, which ensures responsibility creates both ownership and achievement.

Responsibility at a cultural level: When everyone takes ownership, amazing things happen

Embedding responsibility in a team's culture can have a transformative impact. It fosters an environment in which blame is replaced with solutions and each individual feels empowered to contribute to the team's overall success. This cultural shift doesn't happen overnight; it's cultivated through leadership that models ownership and accountability at every level. But once it takes root, extraordinary things are possible.

Imagine a scenario where a sales target has been missed, but instead of pointing fingers, the entire organisation comes together to consider how they could have done better. In this case, marketing, sales, tech support and leadership all engage in an honest debrief in which they take responsibility for their roles in the outcome.

This debrief starts with the marketing team acknowledging its campaign failed to generate the expected leads: 'The message wasn't tailored enough for our target audience. Next time, we'll research the market more thoroughly and test different messages to improve engagement.'

The sales team is next to reflect: 'We missed following up on some key opportunities. We could have communicated more proactively, and we'll work on tightening up our processes to make certain no leads slip through the cracks. We must also improve our collaboration with marketing so we're both in sync on what messaging resonates with our customers.'

Tech support then steps forward: 'We've noticed a few customers complaining that the website had glitches at key points in their customer journey. We should have flagged this sooner. Next time, we'll work more closely with sales and marketing to ensure our digital infrastructure supports their efforts seamlessly.'

Leadership finishes the debrief by saying, 'We need to take responsibility for not supporting these departments sufficiently. We didn't generate enough cross-team communication, and the goals may not have been adequately clear. Moving forward, we'll focus on better coordination between all teams and set clearer expectations so we can hit our targets.'

In this scenario, no one person or department shoulders the entire blame. Instead, each team reflects on its own contribution and outlines the steps it will take to improve. This kind of collective ownership not only boosts morale but also strengthens every team's ability to meet future challenges with resilience and unity. Everyone is working together toward a common goal, and the responsibility culture ensures every failure turns into an opportunity for growth.

A school-trip debrief:
Collective ownership for future success

Now picture a different scenario: a school trip has descended into chaos due to last-minute planning. The activities were poorly organised, and the students were left confused and frustrated. At the debrief, the headteacher, a senior leader who helped oversee the trip, a junior teacher and a teaching assistant all step forward to offer their reflections and take responsibility for what happened.

The headteacher opens by saying, 'As the head of this school, it's my responsibility to make sure trips are planned well in advance and staff have the support they need. I should have checked in more often to ensure the plans were on track, and I'll make it a priority to put more structure in place for future trips.'

The senior leader follows up: 'I took on too much of the organisation at the last minute. If I'd delegated earlier and communicated better with the team, we'd have had clearer roles and more time to prepare. On subsequent trips, I'll make sure everyone understands their responsibilities well ahead of the trip.'

The junior teacher steps in. 'I didn't ask for help when I realised things weren't coming together. I thought I could handle it, but I should have raised my concerns earlier and suggested adjustments. Next time, I'll speak up sooner and collaborate more proactively with the rest of the team.'

Finally, the teaching assistant offers their perspective: 'I could have proactively helped with the logistics. I saw the pressure everyone was under, but I waited for instructions instead of taking the initiative. In future, I'll step up and take on more of the organisational tasks.'

In this debrief, no one person takes all the blame, nor does anyone deflect responsibility away from themself. Each member of the team acknowledges their role in the outcome and commits to specific improvements. This culture is one of shared ownership – everyone recognises they had a part to play, and they're all invested in preventing similar issues from arising again.

This collective responsibility creates a strong foundation for future success. When everyone feels accountable for the outcome and empowered to offer solutions, there's a better chance that the team will succeed next time. More importantly, this kind of responsibility culture makes certain that mistakes effect learning and growth, rather than defensiveness and blame.

Responsibility embedded in a team's culture largely reduces the need for negative feedback. By openly offering your own lessons learned, you not only take ownership of the outcome but you also diminish the defensiveness in the environment. Where people shift blame or refuse to accept responsibility, line managers are often forced to escalate their feedback's intensity to compel the team member to take ownership. This escalation can cause tension and strain the relationship between the leader and their team.

However, when you take responsibility voluntarily, you negate the need for such heightened feedback. Demonstrating that you recognise where things went wrong and offering a solution moving forward diffuses potential conflict and shows you're focused on improving, not dwelling on the past. The key, of course, is in the follow-through: taking responsibility only works if you deliver on the solutions you've promised. When team members consistently show they're learning from mistakes and adapting their approach, they build trust and reduce the need for corrective action.

No leader expects perfection, and even those who do are likely to accept an imperfect situation if they receive a responsible, proactive response. Offering responsibility, combined with a plan to move forward, signals you're committed to continuous improvement and you're taking steps to ensure better future outcomes. This balance of ownership and action drives progress, builds strong teams and fosters a culture in which everyone is empowered to take responsibility for their role in achieving success.

HEALTH WARNING: RESPONSIBILITY VS LEGAL ACCOUNTABILITY

While the skill of responsibility is essential to effective leadership, it's vital to distinguish between leadership responsibility and legal accountability. Leaders must understand that taking ownership of outcomes doesn't mean assuming legal liability for matters outside their jurisdiction. In the context of legislation and policy, responsibility should always be allocated where it belongs legally to guarantee accountability is clear and lawful boundaries are respected.

For instance, if you, as a leader, document or communicate that you take responsibility for an incident, you must be cautious if this implies you're accepting legal liability, such as breaching a policy or breaking a law. Such statements could unintentionally be interpreted as you assuming culpability, which might have serious legal implications. Therefore, while excelling in responsibility means striving to reflect and improve outcomes, you should always clarify your leadership role within legal constraints and then allocate formal responsibility appropriately. This awareness protects both you, as a leader, and the organisation, which ensures responsibility remains in line with legal requirements.

CONCLUSION

Responsibility is the most critical skill for effective leadership as it sets the tone for how leaders approach challenges, manage teams and drive progress. Responsibility goes far beyond assigning blame or taking credit; it's about embracing ownership in a way that fosters growth, continuous improvement and trust. Leaders who prioritise responsibility create a culture in which problems are met with solutions, accountability is shared and the entire team is empowered to succeed.

The key to this approach is shifting from a blame-focused mindset to one of proactivity and reflection. By focusing on what's within their control, leaders can identify opportunities for improvement and take meaningful action to achieve better outcomes. This proactive mindset both reduces stress and inspires trust and respect from teams as it demonstrates a commitment to accountability and progress, even in the face of setbacks.

Responsibility is the foundation upon which successful teams and organisations are built. When leaders consistently take ownership, set high standards and foster an accountability culture, they not only achieve results but also inspire trust, loyalty and long-term success.

Responsibility isn't a burden; it's a powerful tool for driving progress and shaping a high-performing, collaborative team culture.

3
Relationships

Relationships are at the heart of leadership. Strong and positive professional relationships form the foundation upon which successful teams, organisations and leaders are built. Effective leadership isn't just about setting vision and strategy or making critical decisions; it's equally about understanding people, building trust and cultivating collaboration. Relationships determine how leaders connect with their teams, how well teams function together, and how resilient the teams are in the face of challenges.

In *Unreasonable Hospitality*, Will Guidara – who helped lead Eleven Madison Park to become a three-Michelin-star restaurant and world number one – emphasises that when people (be they employees or customers) are treated with an extraordinary level of care and attention, exceptional results follow.[11] Leaders can apply this mindset by serving their teams with the same dedication and care that top-tier restaurants offer their guests. When a team is built on mutual respect, trust and the shared goal of serving each other as if they were customers in a three-Michelin-star establishment, extraordinary things are possible.

This chapter explores the importance of relationships in leadership, the central roles of trust and reliability in building those connections, and how leaders can nurture relationships through consistent action. We'll also look at conflict resolution; the importance of empathy; how competition, without clarity, can act as a silent poison within teams; and how considering who you would trust in critical situations reveals the core of what makes someone a valuable teammate.

The importance of relationships in leadership

Building and maintaining professional relationships is more than a desirable quality for a leader; it's a necessity. Leaders cannot be effective if they operate in isolation. Leadership is fundamentally about influencing others positively, and to influence people effectively, leaders must establish strong relationships grounded in trust, respect and mutual understanding.

When leaders build solid relationships with their team members, several positive outcomes follow:

- **Increased trust:** Trust is the foundation of any productive relationship. Team members who trust their leader are more likely to be open, share information and collaborate willingly. Trust facilitates open communication and a sense of safety within the team.

- **Higher engagement:** When leaders take the time to build relationships with their team, individuals feel valued and understood. This leads to higher levels of engagement as team members are more likely to invest energy and effort into the organisation's success.

- **Better performance:** Strong relationships create a positive and supportive environment, which directly impacts team performance. When people work in a culture of trust and respect, they're more likely to work well together, solve problems collaboratively and innovate.

- **Resilience in tough times:** Every team faces challenges, but robust relationships make teams more resilient. When leaders have established solid connections with their team members, they can better navigate crises or difficult periods, because team members have faith in the leader's intentions and capabilities.

- **Improved communication:** Strong relationships make communication more efficient and effective. Established trust and understanding means leaders spend less time proving their intentions are aligned with the team's best interests. This engenders clarity, reduces misunderstandings, and allows messages to be conveyed with higher impact and speed.

Leaders who treat their teams with exceptional care and attention – that is, looking out for their needs – cultivate an environment in which team members feel valued, supported and committed to success.

Reliability: Another word for 'relationship'

A relationship can be summarised by how much the other person can rely on you and what they can rely on you for. At the heart of any professional relationship lies reliability. Without reliability, trust can't form. In leadership, reliability means leaders consistently deliver on their promises, meet their responsibilities and maintain a level of predictability in their actions. When team members know they can count on their leader to follow through, they feel secure, and this security fosters deeper relationships.

Cultivating trust through reliability doesn't happen overnight; it's the result of consistent actions over time. Being reliable day in, day out means showing up for your team, being present in your leadership role and meeting expectations consistently.

Reliability isn't about grand gestures; it's about the everyday commitments and decisions that build a strong foundation for trust:

- » **Doing what you say you'll do:** Following through on commitments, whether big or small, signals to your team that you're dependable. Broken promises can erode trust quickly, even on minor issues.

- » **Being consistent in your behaviour and decisions:** Team members appreciate predictability. When you, as a leader, are consistent in your actions and decision-making, it removes uncertainty and helps build trust. In contrast, if you demonstrate erratic leadership behaviour, it can make your team members feel uneasy and unsure how to proceed.

- » **Owning up to mistakes:** Part of being reliable is taking responsibility when things don't go as planned. No leader is perfect, but as a reliable leader, you'll acknowledge mistakes, take accountability and work to rectify issues. This humility strengthens your relationships because it shows authenticity and integrity.

Delivering on your role and responsibilities

Reliability extends beyond showing up and following through; it also encompasses how well you, as a leader, deliver on your core responsibilities. Your leadership role is not only to set strategy or manage operations but also to support, guide and inspire your team.

Delivering on these responsibilities builds confidence and trust within your team:

- » **Providing guidance and support:** Team members rely on you, as their leader, to offer direction and resources. As a responsible leader, you'll make certain your team members have the tools, training and support they need to succeed. You'll make yourself available to provide feedback, direction and advice when needed.

- » **Ensuring accountability:** As a reliable leader, you'll hold both yourself and your team accountable. This means setting clear expectations, following up on progress and addressing issues when necessary. Reliability in leadership includes being the steady hand that ensures your team stays on course.

» **Being a consistent presence:** Leaders who are engaged and involved in their team's day-to-day activities build stronger relationships because they're present, accessible, and ready to offer support or feedback. Even if you, as a leader, aren't a natural people person, being consistently reliable cultivates respect and trust in those you work with. You don't need to be overly charismatic or outgoing to be dependable and trustworthy.

You don't need to be a people person to have strong relationships

One common misconception is that only those with a naturally outgoing or charismatic personality can build strong relationships in the workplace. However, reliability is an equal (if not more significant) predictor of long-term success than being socially outgoing. Being highly reliable means people know they can count on you, whether or not you're the type to engage in social chatter or team-building activities. A steady, reliable leader often engenders just as much trust – if not more – than one who's always charming but inconsistent in delivering results.

Robust relationships aren't built solely on charisma; rather, they arise from trust and dependability. These qualities enable leaders to create a solid relational foundation with their team, which makes certain that team members feel secure and valued. Reliability speaks louder than charm in the long run, and it's proven to be an indispensable asset for those striving to lead effectively.

Relationships as the best fuel for ambition

Short-sighted individuals often step on others to climb the ladder of success because they view relationships as disposable stepping stones. While this might offer some short-term gains, it creates a long trail of enemies waiting for that leader to slip up. A leader who burns bridges will swiftly find themselves without support, and any mistakes they make will be amplified by those eager to see them fail.

On the other hand, a leader who invests in strong, trusting relationships will reap the benefits over time. Instead of stepping over people, they build connections that bolster their teams' success. When you're reliable and treat people well, you create a network of allies who are there to catch any ball you drop. These relationships form the backbone of your professional support system, and those who trust and respect you will often go out of their way to help you succeed.

Imagine the difference: one leader walks into a room filled with individuals who are hoping for their downfall, while another walks into a room where their team members are actively clearing obstacles and preparing for their success. The leader who builds trusting relationships doesn't have to face challenges alone. Before they even show up, they have ranks of supporters ready to sing their praises, lend a hand and smooth the path. In a world where success often hinges on collaboration and collective effort, having a team that believes in you is the biggest advantage you can have.

Building reliable relationships to ensure long-term success
When leaders build relationships and demonstrate reliability day after day, they create a culture of trust and support that extends far beyond the individual. Reliable and trusted leaders cultivate environments in which team members feel confident and secure. In turn, this environmental security encourages innovation, collaboration and a sense of shared responsibility. It generates a ripple effect where each team member feels empowered to contribute their best efforts, knowing they have the backing of a dependable leader who has their best interests at heart.

Moreover, when you consistently deliver on your promises and support your team, you earn a good reputation that follows you. Others will want to work with you – not just because of your technical skills or knowledge but also because they know you can be counted on to get the job done. Your ambition, when driven by strong relationships, becomes more sustainable and far-reaching as it's supported by a network of trust and loyalty.

By developing these robust relationships, you'll uncover one of the professional world's fundamental truths: amazing people like working with amazing people. And when you have such amazing people on your team, your chances of success increase massively. This foundation – one built through delivering results, mutual respect and trust – sets the stage for extraordinary achievements and enduring success.

Ego is the enemy (yours and theirs)

There's a lot of press and a Hollywood theme of team members being smarter than their bosses – an entertaining and familiar trope in which the underdog employee consistently outwits their inept boss. While amusing on screen, this mindset is short-sighted and damaging in reality. No line manager has all the answers or is perfectly well-balanced. In *Chapter 1*, we explored the importance of recognising your own strengths and weaknesses, and *Chapter 2* highlighted how disempowering it can be to waste energy on blaming your manager for the challenges you face. Yes, your boss may have shortcomings, and yes, they might have gaps in their skill set, but it's your role to support them in those missing areas. This should be done subtly and respectfully, because stepping into a leadership role takes courage – and with that often comes ego. Egos are extremely sensitive to being made to look foolish.

Ryan Holiday, in *Ego is the Enemy*, reminds us that humility, collaboration and putting others first are key to success; he advises, 'Make other people look good, and you'll do well.'[12] Instead of trying to outshine your line manager or demonstrate you're smarter than them, it's much more effective to make them look good. By always having your line manager's back, you'll gain more influence and also provide your team with more protection and security. In fact, when you take the time to see the world through their eyes, you'll start to empathise with their position, understand the pressures they face and appreciate where their decisions are coming from. Holiday also reminds us that 'It's a temptation to think of ourselves as the exception, that we can afford to gloss over the rules, that we're different and special.'[13] However, leadership isn't about setting yourself apart; it's about building up others, including your line manager.

For example, imagine your boss is a disorganised leader who's full of creative ideas but struggles with the implementation details. Instead of calling them out when you're feeling frustrated, you could step in quietly to help organise their thoughts by offering a structured plan that allows their creativity to shine without things falling apart. In this way, you'll enable their strengths to come through while subtly filling in the gaps.

On the other hand, a results-oriented leader might be so focused on outcomes that they struggle to connect with their team on a personal level. In this case, you could act as a bridge between them and their team by creating opportunities for more meaningful engagement and translating your boss's high expectations into actionable tasks that motivate the team. Again, this won't undermine their focus on results, but this instead enhances it by effecting the necessary trust and connection with the team.

Your line manager might be a highly considerate leader who deeply values harmony but isn't achieving the results needed. In this scenario, you could step up by suggesting ways to balance their care for the team with a keener focus on accountability and targets, which will guide them to set clearer expectations without sacrificing their empathy. This approach protects the positive team dynamic while steering things toward greater success.

Additionally, you could take a more proactive role in driving your team to deliver results in all the areas they can control. Stepping into this space means you can help fill the gap between empathy and execution, which will make sure that, while the team continues to feel supported, it's also in harmony with achieving its key objectives. This could involve setting specific, measurable goals; creating a roadmap for delivery; and taking ownership of tracking progress to keep the team on course.

By leading actively in this way, you'll not only contribute to the team's success but also reinforce the importance of balancing empathy with performance. Your proactive leadership will ensure the team both maintains a positive culture and delivers on its potential, which creates a win-win outcome for both the team and the organisation.

Lastly, consider a detail-oriented leader who's stuck in their ways and resistant to change or innovation. Rather than challenging them directly, you could introduce new ideas in a way that respects their need for order – such as proposing small, manageable adjustments that show how efficiency can be improved without throwing everything into chaos. By 'finding canvases for other people to paint on,' as Holiday puts it,[14] you create a space for your leader to succeed without threatening their confidence or control.

In each of these examples, you aren't diminishing your own intelligence or capabilities; instead, you're demonstrating a different kind of leadership – one based on support, understanding, and the long-term success of both your manager and your team. When your fellow team members see you have your line manager's back, even though everyone else might be griping about them, this will indirectly build trust between you and your peers. This approach doesn't mean misrepresenting your opinion of your line manager; it simply means empathising with them, treating them with respect and focusing on solutions rather than complaints. You offering responsibility, solutions and support sidesteps the potential for conflict and creates a more positive working environment in which everyone can thrive. This approach, which is grounded in humility and service, allows you to build trust and influence, while still keeping ego in check.

If you think you can't be a successful leader simply because your line manager doesn't have a perfectly balanced skill set, then you're wrong. All leaders – and people – achieve success not because of what they're gifted at but because of what they overcome. Leadership isn't about waiting for the perfect environment or circumstances in which to excel; it's about finding ways to adapt, collaborate and grow, even in imperfect situations. By recognising challenges as opportunities to step up, support others and demonstrate resilience, you embody the very essence of leadership.

True success lies in how you navigate adversity and build success despite it – not in the absence of obstacles.

Conflict resolution and empathy in relationships

No matter how strong relationships are, conflicts are inevitable in any team setting. The key to maintaining positive relationships during conflict lies in how leaders handle disputes. Leaders must be prepared to address conflicts directly but with empathy, making certain all parties feel heard, respected and understood.

Addressing conflict directly

Avoiding conflict is one of the most common mistakes leaders make in managing relationships. However, ignoring conflict almost certainly only allows it to fester and worsen over time. A responsible leader understands that avoiding conflict isn't a solution; addressing it directly and constructively is essential for maintaining healthy team dynamics.

When conflicts arise, leaders should do the following:

- » **Engage with the issue early:** Don't wait for conflicts to escalate. Addressing issues as soon as they appear helps prevent misunderstandings spiralling into larger problems. By dealing with tensions promptly, leaders can mitigate damage and keep small issues from growing into major obstacles.

- » **Be transparent:** Transparency is vital to resolving conflicts. Leaders should approach conflicts with openness, sharing their own perspectives while also seeking to understand the viewpoints of others. This builds trust and reveals a willingness to engage in the problem-solving process, rather than shying away from it.

- » **Focus on finding solutions, not assigning blame:** Rather than concentrating on who's at fault, a good leader shifts the conversation toward solutions. The goal should be to resolve the conflict in a way that strengthens the team dynamic, instead of creating more division. Focusing on moving forward and finding resolutions that benefit everyone allows the team to emerge stronger from the conflict.

Empathy as a conflict-resolution tool

Empathy is a critical tool in resolving conflicts and maintaining strong relationships. Empathy means putting yourself in someone else's shoes, understanding their perspective and responding with compassion. Leaders who approach conflict with empathy are better able to de-escalate tensions, build mutual understanding and foster stronger relationships in the process.

Empathetic leaders do this:

- » **Listen actively:** Active listening means engaging fully with the person speaking. As well as hearing their words, this requires understanding their emotions and the underlying issues. This helps the leader get to the root of the conflict and address the real concerns. By listening without interrupting, the leader demonstrates respect and care for the person involved.

- » **Validate feelings:** Even if a leader disagrees with another's viewpoint, it's essential they validate that person's feelings. This means acknowledging that their perspective is valid and worthy of respect. By validating the other's feelings, leaders help engender trust and show they care about their team members' emotional well-being. When people feel heard and understood, they're more likely to open up and engage in productive dialogue.

- » **Encourage open communication:** Empathetic leaders cultivate an environment in which team members feel safe to express themselves openly. Promoting honest dialogue prevents misunderstandings from festering and allows the team to resolve issues before they escalate. When communication is open, team members are less likely to hold on to resentment, and leaders can address concerns before they become major problems.

Building trust through tough conversations

The opportunity conflict resolution provides to build deeper trust within the team is often overlooked. Many leaders avoid difficult conversations for fear of damaging relationships or making the situation worse. However, ducking these conversations can increase anxiety among team members as they may worry about how conflicts will be handled when they inevitably arise. Leaders who consistently avoid addressing issues leave their team uncertain and wondering how things will unfold when their leader finally loses patience.

True trust arises when tough conversations are approached with respect, fairness and dignity. When team members see their leader will sanction or correct behaviour without belittling or demeaning them, it strengthens the team bond. Leaders treating people with respect during moments of correction sends a clear message: *performance and accountability matter, but so do the individuals who make up the team.*

The result is a level of trust that stands the test of time. When team members experience first-hand that they can face a tough conversation and come out of it with their dignity intact, they become more resilient and secure in their relationship with their leader. They know future conflicts will be handled with care, not aggression. This reduces their fear of confrontation and encourages a culture of openness in which feedback and growth are welcomed rather than dreaded.

Competition without clarity: The silent poison within teams

Competition can naturally drive performance and motivation, but when it's approached without skilful leadership, it can become a silent poison that damages relationships and undermines team success. Competition for positions, recognition or resources within a team can cause a toxic environment in which team members view each other as opponents rather than collaborators.

Neuroscience research has shown that, when we see someone we perceive as a competitor or opponent fail, our brain releases dopamine – the reward chemical.[15] This natural reaction can be highly damaging in a team context. If team members take pleasure in their colleagues' failures, it creates an undercurrent of mistrust and disunity, which can sabotage the success of the team as a whole.

The dangers of internal competition

Unchecked competition within a team can have several negative consequences:

- **Erosion of trust:** If team members view each other as rivals rather than allies, trust is rapidly eroded. Collaboration suffers because people become reluctant to share information or resources, due to fearing it might give their 'competitor' an advantage.

- **Celebration of failure:** As mentioned previously, the brain's natural pleasure response to a competitor's failure can bring about a situation where team members silently root for each other to make mistakes. This seriously damages team morale and cohesion. In a high-performing team, one member's failure is everyone's failure because the team's success depends on each individual's success.

- **Reduced collaboration:** When competition takes over, people focus on personal success rather than the collective success of the team. This reduces collaboration and problem-solving, as individuals are more concerned with their own advancement than with supporting their peers.

Clarity: A skilled leader's role in mitigating the poison of competition

A skilled leader recognises the dangers of unhealthy competition and takes proactive steps to foster a culture in which collaboration, rather than competition, is the focus. While competition can drive performance, it must be managed carefully to ensure it doesn't create divisions within the team. One of the most effective ways to do this is by providing the team with clarity on how competition can coexist with collaboration, bringing both into line with the team's broader vision.

For example, if two team members are vying for the same position or opportunity, a skilled leader can offer clarity about how this situation can be a learning opportunity for both. They can highlight how each individual could learn from the other's strengths and contributions, which creates a sense that they're both making valuable contributions toward the team's goals – regardless of who ultimately gets the nod. This approach helps to maintain a positive, productive atmosphere in which competition becomes a means of growth rather than a source of division.

Being a successful team is by far the best security a group can experience, as the collective strength of the team protects each individual from failure. Skilled leaders build meaningful relationships even with the most challenging team members; this is because the leader understands the team's success depends on everyone working together, not against each other.

In managing competition, leaders should do the following:

» **Set collective goals:** Emphasise the importance of team success over individual success. When goals are in line with the team's collective performance, team members are more likely to support each other and collaborate toward a shared outcome.

» **Celebrate collective achievements:** Recognise and celebrate team achievements while making certain that everyone's contributions are acknowledged. This fosters a sense of unity and shared purpose, which reduces the emphasis on individual competition.

» **Clarify the shared learning opportunities arising from competition:** When two team members are competing for a similar opportunity, frame it as a chance for mutual growth. Help them see how their individual efforts not only elevate their own potential but also strengthen the team by pushing boundaries, sharing insights and raising overall performance.

» **Manage awkward or even people prone to malicious actions in their teams:** It's inevitable that leaders will encounter difficult, awkward or even malicious people within their teams. However, a leader demonstrates true leadership when they can build and maintain relationships with these individuals to help them integrate into the team dynamic. This not only improves the team's functioning but also highlights the leader's ability to handle complex interpersonal dynamics.

Ultimately, if one member of the team fails, the whole team fails. Skilled leaders create an environment in which each individual's success is intertwined with the success of the team as a whole. By fostering collaboration, providing clarity and managing competition carefully, leaders can make sure any competition becomes a healthy driver of performance rather than a source of division. This clarity strengthens the team dynamic, which demonstrates how competition can serve the shared vision when managed thoughtfully.

Balancing relationships with decision-making

Although strong relationships are critical for leadership, it's equally important to balance relationship-building with objective decision-making. Over-reliance on relationships, without boundaries, can lead to bias and cloud judgement. Leaders must maintain a balance between prioritising the needs and feelings of their team members and making decisions that align with the organisation's overall goals and mission.

Boundaries in leadership

A leader's role is both to build relationships and to ensure decisions are made based on what's best for the team and the organisation. That sometimes means making tough decisions, even when it may upset or disappoint individual team members. Strong relationships can occasionally create a sense of personal obligation that, if left unchecked, can lead to bias in decision-making. Leaders must make certain that, while they consider the well-being of their team, they do so in balance with the organisation's goals and long-term vision.

It's critical to create clear boundaries within these relationships, which will safeguard that decisions are made fairly, equitably and in the best interests of the team's objectives. Leaders who set and maintain appropriate boundaries will find their team members respect them more for being fair, consistent and objective in their leadership.

Serving the greater good of the team

Being a successful team is by far the best security any group can experience. When leaders can balance individual relationships with the team's purpose and goals, they fashion an environment in which the collective can flourish. Team members trust that decisions are made with integrity and not influenced by favouritism or personal bias. This balance strengthens relationships in the long term because team members know they're part of something larger in which their contributions are valued but the team's goals always come first.

Relationships are at the heart of effective leadership. Leaders who invest in building strong, trusting and supportive relationships create environments in which teams can thrive. By being reliable, addressing conflicts with empathy and being someone others can depend on, leaders lay the foundation for collective success. At the heart of leadership is the ability to balance the nurturing of relationships with making objective decisions that serve the greater good of the team and organisation. When strong relationships are paired with clear boundaries and fairness, they foster trust, long-term success and high performance.

A reliable leader is someone the team can consistently count on, who will follow through on commitments and offer steady guidance. They stay attuned to their team's needs and provide the necessary support, feedback and resources. These leaders prioritise professional relationships with everyone, regardless of personality differences or conflicts, and they build trust through transparency and care. Even difficult conversations strengthen – rather than weaken – these relationships because the leader has earned trust through consistent actions.

LEVEL 1: CHAPTER 3 – RELATIONSHIPS

A versatile leader works seamlessly with a diverse range of people, adapting to various personalities and team dynamics. These abilities to build trust, communicate effectively and create a positive, collaborative culture empower the entire team to succeed, no matter the challenge. True leadership lies in delivering consistently, being able to work with anyone and fostering an environment in which everyone feels valued.

THE FINAL CHALLENGE: THE 'BEYOND THE WALL' TASK

One of the best ways to assess the strength of your relationships and your ability to build a high-performing team is through the 'beyond the Wall' task. Imagine this: You're faced with a life-or-death challenge. You can only take six people from your organisation with you. The situation will be highly pressurised, thus requiring teamwork, trust and resilience. Everyone left inside the Wall is relying on you to make the right decision in selecting your team. If you fail, everyone dies.

Here's your challenge:

1. **Select your six**

    Who would you take with you? Remember, the stakes are high and your choice will determine the outcome.

2. **Reflect on your selections**
    - Why did you choose each person?
    - What traits or qualities do they share?
    - What traits do they lack? Why doesn't that matter in this context?
    - Did any of your selections surprise you?
    - Are there people you didn't choose who might have expected to be picked? Why did you exclude them?

3. **Ask the most important questions**

    Ask yourself the following:

- *Would you be in their six?*
  Reflect on whether the people you selected would choose you in turn for such a challenge. What does this say about the relationships and trust you've built with them?

- *Would you be in your line manager's six?*
  Think about whether your line manager would include you in their core team for such a critical mission. If not, why not? And what could you do to change that?

The lesson: To support your team with the highest probability of success, you need to ensure you're someone they would trust to bring along in the most challenging situations. This isn't just about technical competence; it's about trust, collaboration, reliability and the ability to inspire confidence under pressure.

This task is not only an exercise in reflection but a call to action. Build the relationships, trust and reputation required to be on anyone's 'six'. Make certain your contributions and presence make you indispensable in the eyes of both your peers and your leaders. Ultimately, leadership isn't about individual achievements; it's about creating an environment in which the team succeeds together – even in the most demanding circumstances.

CONCLUSION

Relationships are essential to effective leadership, as they influence how leaders inspire, connect with and guide their teams. Strong, trusting relationships create a foundation for collaboration, resilience and sustained performance. This chapter has emphasised the importance of building relationships as a core element of leadership success, not as a supplementary skill.

Trust is the centrepiece of strong professional relationships, and it's earned through reliability, consistent actions and authentic engagement. Leaders who follow through on their commitments, support their teams and communicate openly foster environments in which people feel valued and secure. Reliability is built over time through everyday actions: showing up, delivering on promises and being present for your team.

Balancing relationships with objective decision-making is another key skill, which makes sure fairness and organisational goals guide leadership decisions. Leaders who maintain professional boundaries while nurturing trust and collaboration achieve more long-term respect and success.

Relationships in leadership extend beyond individual connections; they shape team dynamics, enhance collective performance and build trust, which fuels sustainable growth. Leaders who prioritise relationships create environments in which teams thrive, trust is strengthened and challenges are met together.

4
Communication

Communication is one of the most critical skills in leadership, yet it's often misunderstood or oversimplified. Effective communication goes far beyond speaking; it involves ensuring your message is understood, resonates with your audience and aligns with your organisation's vision. Leaders must master the ability to communicate with clarity and purpose, and they must make certain their actions match with their words.

In this chapter, we'll examine the multiple dimensions of communication in leadership, including the importance of active listening, how leaders communicate through their actions, and how to approach difficult conversations with courage and compassion. We'll also discuss the role of timely and reliable communication in keeping teams aligned and building confidence, which ultimately generates a stronger overall performance.

Communication as a leadership foundation

Leadership is fundamentally about influence, and communication is the primary way leaders exert that influence. Whether you're leading a small team or an entire organisation, your ability to communicate effectively impacts everything – from setting clear goals and expectations to navigating conflicts and maintaining team cohesion. At the heart of leadership communication lies the need to connect with others on a deeper level, which drives not just action but also understanding and alignment.

Vision and clarity

Vision

Teams look to their leaders to articulate a clear vision, set goals and define expectations. However, simply stating a vision or goal isn't enough. Leaders must make sure their message is understood and embraced by those they're leading. This is where the 'Golden Circle' concept, popularised by Simon Sinek, becomes particularly relevant.

According to Sinek, successful leaders start by communicating the *why* behind their actions, before moving to the *what* and the *how*:[16]

- » **Why:** Leaders must begin with the purpose – the deeper reason behind the message or action. Why are we doing this? Why does this project matter? Communicating the *why* helps team members connect emotionally with the mission, which engenders a sense of shared purpose and motivation. A team that understands the underlying purpose of their work is far more likely to stay engaged and committed. Rather than blindly following instructions, they're also able to act on their own initiative; this is crucial if they find themselves in a situation they need to adapt to – which is highly likely.

- » **What:** Once the purpose is clear, leaders must explain what needs to be done. What specific goals or actions need to be achieved? This provides structure and ensures everyone understands the tangible objectives they're working toward. They'll also be able to communicate what it will look like when the goal has been achieved.

- » **How:** Finally, leaders must address the *how* – the steps or processes required to achieve the goals. Clear, actionable guidance makes sure the team knows the best way forward and what resources are available to support them.

Following this progression helps leaders ensure their communication resonates on all levels, which drives not only action but also a deeper connection to the purpose behind that action. Each leader may naturally feel more aligned with one of the three areas: *why* (purpose), *how* (process) or *what* (outcome). However, a skilled leader goes beyond their natural preference and is able to communicate across all three areas, so as to articulate the purpose behind the actions (*why*), the steps or strategies to achieve them (*how*), and the expected results (*what*). This comprehensive approach enables leaders to connect meaningfully with diverse audiences, which inspires clarity, understanding and commitment across the team.

Clarity

Effective communication begins with clarity. Leaders must take the time to think through their message and ensure it's simple, straightforward and free from ambiguity. A clear message is easier to understand and act upon. This clarity should extend beyond the message itself to include how and when it's delivered. Whether that's through written or verbal communication, making certain the message is clear helps reduce misunderstandings and keeps everyone in harmony.

Clear communication fosters trust. When a leader consistently communicates in a way that's transparent and easily understood, their team members are more likely to feel confident in their direction and less likely to experience confusion or misalignment. In contrast, poor communication can lead to frustration, since team members may feel they're being left in the dark or are lacking the information needed to do their jobs effectively.

In some cases, it may be preferable to delay communication altogether until a message can be delivered with clarity and accuracy. Skilled leaders understand that sharing partial or uncertain information can cause unnecessary anxiety and confusion. They'll hold off on delivering a message with parts that haven't yet been fully decided, as they recognise that incomplete information often disrupts focus and generates ambiguity within the team. By exercising this patience, leaders maintain a standard of communication that supports team cohesion and trust, rather than risking the disruption and misalignment unclear messages can cause.

Adapting communication styles

An effective leader knows that communication isn't one size fits all. Team members process information differently, which requires leaders to adapt their communication styles to meet diverse needs. By understanding the characteristics of Red, Yellow, Blue and Green team members, leaders can tailor their approach to gain maximum impact. For example, Red team members appreciate direct, results-oriented communication, while Yellow team members thrive when they're included in the process and encouraged to explore possibilities. Blue team members typically prefer clear, detailed information to build their confidence, and Green team members value collaborative, supportive communication that fosters team harmony.

Consider a scenario where a project deadline is approaching, and the leader needs to bring the entire team on board. One team member prefers long, written updates with clear steps, while another thrives on face-to-face conversations in which they can ask questions in real time. The leader tailors communication accordingly: for the team member who prefers written updates, a detailed email with bullet points, deadlines and resource links is provided; and for the team member who values real-time interaction, the leader schedules a brief 10-minute meeting to discuss the project's progress and explain expectations.

By adapting their communication style to meet each team member's preferences, the leader ensures all individuals receive the information they need to stay aligned and perform well. This adaptability is crucial to preventing confusion and disengagement, and it therefore reinforces trust and cohesion within the team.

A skilled leader takes responsibility for making certain their messages are understood by adapting their style as needed to match their audience's needs. They appreciate that effective communication is a two-way process, and they adjust their communication actively to ensure clarity and connection with each team member. In contrast, a leader who relies primarily on their natural communication style necessitates that their team adapts to them, which can lead to miscommunication and disengagement. Prioritising adaptability lets skilled leaders not only convey information more effectively but also foster an environment in which every team member feels valued and understood, thus strengthening the team's overall cohesion and trust.

Empathy in communication

Alongside clarity, empathy plays a vital role in leadership communication. Empathetic communication means recognising and considering the feelings, needs and perspectives of your audience. It's about understanding where your team members are coming from, both emotionally and professionally, and tailoring your message to meet them where they are. For example, in times of high stress or change, leaders must communicate the facts but also acknowledge the concerns and emotions of their team. When a leader shows empathy in their communication – whether by listening carefully, validating emotions or offering support – they build trust and nurture stronger relationships. Importantly, genuine empathy is paramount; without authenticity, any attempts at empathy can feel hollow and even erode trust rather than build it.

A key skill in empathetic communication, especially during conversations involving heightened emotions, is matching the urgency of the other person. If someone is expressing intense feelings or concerns, a leader should respond with similar levels of urgency and intensity, which demonstrates the issue is understood to be a priority and will be acted on promptly – if this is indeed the case. Conversely, if a team member raises something in a more indirect or reserved manner, responding with a measured, thoughtful approach shows the information is valued and will be considered carefully, without rushing or dismissing it.

Empathy is also especially important during difficult conversations. When delivering tough feedback or addressing mistakes, a leader who approaches the situation with empathy can mitigate defensiveness and help the team member feel supported rather than attacked. This strengthens their relationship and creates a culture that welcomes constructive feedback.

By matching the urgency and emotional tone of each team member, and by being genuine in their empathy, leaders build trust and show they're fully engaged and responsive – no matter the nature of the discussion. This responsiveness reinforces the value placed on each person's input and helps cultivate an environment in which everyone feels respected and heard.

Communication as a continuous process

Effective communication isn't a one-time event; it's an ongoing process that demands constant attention and refinement. Leaders must continually evaluate how their communication is received and whether it's driving the intended outcomes. This means seeking feedback from the team, being open to adjusting communication styles and making sure the lines of communication are always open.

Good communication also needs leaders to be present and engaged. Leaders who are approachable and accessible build stronger relationships and garner a sense of trust within the team. When communication is a two-way street – in which leaders listen as much as they speak – teams become more collaborative and solution-oriented.

Ensuring your message is understood

An effective leader knows successful communication not only conveys the message but also makes certain it's understood and engaged with thoughtfully. This requires a nuanced approach that takes into account the varied ways team members process information and contribute their insights.

For instance, some team members excel at spotting potential problems; however, if their concerns aren't channelled productively, they're often perceived as being negative. To harness their strengths constructively, a leader might consider speaking with these individuals ahead of meetings. This advance conversation allows these team members to voice their insights in a way that's helpful and allows the leader to prepare for any challenges raised, which ultimately creates a more balanced and solutions-focused discussion.

Similarly, introverted team members may benefit from receiving information before the meeting. Sending materials ahead of time lets them process the content independently, and they can then formulate ideas and questions at their own pace. This approach respects their preferred communication style and enriches the meeting with well-considered contributions that might otherwise remain unspoken.

It's also essential to build buffer time into the communication process to allow team members to follow up with thoughts or suggestions within 24 hours after the initial discussion. In meetings, some individuals – often those with a high Red or Yellow orientation – tend to contribute ideas readily and spontaneously. However, those with a high Blue or Green orientation might provide deeper or more reflective insights when given time to process. This follow-up period facilitates all voices being heard and valued, which generates more-comprehensive and innovative solutions.

By adapting their communication to the diverse strengths and styles within the team, a leader not only enhances engagement but also leverages each member's unique perspective, which encourages a more inclusive, thoughtful and effective collaboration environment.

The power of listening in leadership

Listening is often overlooked as being a critical component of effective communication. However, listening is just as important – if not more so – than speaking. Leaders who fail to listen to their team members miss out on valuable insights, feedback and opportunities to strengthen relationships. Listening isn't a passive activity; it necessitates active engagement and a genuine interest in what others have to say.

Building trust through listening

One of the most significant benefits of active listening is the trust it builds within teams. When leaders listen attentively, they demonstrate respect for their team members' opinions, ideas and concerns. This in turn develops a culture of open dialogue and transparency, in which team members feel safe to share their thoughts without fear of judgement or dismissal.

Effective listening also shows empathy, which is a critical trait for leaders who want to build strong, trusting relationships. Empathy allows leaders to understand their team members' perspectives, which helps in resolving conflicts, providing support and making more-informed decisions.

Active listening techniques

The skill of active listening can be developed with practice. Some key techniques you can use as a leader to become a better listener include these:

- » **Give your full attention:** When someone is speaking to you, eliminate distractions and focus entirely on the conversation. Put away your phone, close your laptop and make eye contact with the speaker.

- » **Ask open-ended questions:** Encourage deeper conversation by asking open-ended questions, which are those needing more than a yes or no response. For example, instead of asking, 'Did you have any problems with the project?' ask, 'What challenges did you face during the project?'

- » **Reflect and paraphrase:** Reflecting on what the speaker has said and paraphrasing it back to them shows you're actively listening and helps clarify any misunderstandings. For example, saying, 'What I'm hearing is that you felt the deadline was too tight. Is that correct?'

- » **Validate feelings and concerns:** Even if you don't agree with everything someone has said, it's important to acknowledge and validate their feelings. This builds rapport and trust.

Listening as a tool for feedback

Listening is a powerful tool for a leader to gather feedback. A leader seeking feedback from their team members – whether about their leadership style, a project or a company-wide initiative – shows humility and a willingness to improve. When leaders actively listen to feedback, they create an environment in which team members feel valued and heard, which boosts engagement and morale.

Communicating through actions

Although verbal communication is essential, leaders also communicate through their actions. Actions can speak louder than words, and what a leader does is often more impactful than what they say. Leaders must model the behaviours they expect from their team members, thus reinforcing their values without needing to say a word.

Aligning words and actions

One of the quickest ways for a leader to lose trust is to say one thing and do another. When leaders fail to line up their words with their actions, they appear inauthentic and unreliable. For example, if a leader emphasises the importance of punctuality but consistently arrives late to meetings, their message loses credibility.

To build and maintain trust as a leader, you must make sure your actions consistently align with your words. This includes the following:

- » **Leading by example:** If you expect your team to be collaborative, transparent and innovative, you must demonstrate these behaviours yourself. Leaders set the tone for the team, and your actions will shape the organisation's culture.

- » **Delivering on promises:** When you make promises or commitments as a leader, you must follow through. Failing to do so can erode trust and weaken your influence.

» **Acknowledging mistakes:** Leaders aren't infallible. When you make a mistake, acknowledging it and taking steps to rectify it communicates integrity and accountability. This sets a positive example for your team and fosters a culture in which it's okay to learn from mistakes.

Leaders communicate and reinforce their values through the decisions they make and the way they treat others.

Here are some examples:

» A leader who values diversity and inclusion might demonstrate this by actively seeking out diverse perspectives when making decisions and ensuring all voices are heard in meetings.

» A leader who values work-life balance might model this by setting boundaries around work hours, encouraging team members to take time off and respecting team members' personal time.

» A leader who values collaboration might show this by consistently working alongside their team members, seeking input from others and giving credit where it's due.

When leaders consistently model their values through their actions, they reinforce those values across the organisation, which shapes the culture and behaviours of their teams.

CASE STUDY: LEADING BY EXAMPLE

A leader who's focused on making certain their team prioritises process over outcomes takes deliberate, systemic and behavioural steps to reinforce this mindset in terms of both actions and communication. When the preliminary results come in, the leader gathers the team and shares a personal experience by explaining that, upon first seeing the results, they reacted immediately and began to manage their emotions. They recognised they have this tendency and made a conscious decision to shift their focus back to the process itself, and therefore they assessed whether they'd accurately followed the established steps and strategies.

To further solidify this process-oriented approach, the leader removes the outcome data from team meetings and correspondence; instead, they choose to highlight progress metrics and areas for refinement.

For example, rather than presenting the final results or comparing performance metrics, the leader focuses on celebrating the milestones achieved through adhering to the process consistently. In one meeting, the leader reviews the aspects of the process that the team has diligently followed, such as completing thorough planning, maintaining quality control and seeking feedback actively at each stage.

By doing so, the leader pinpoints specific process successes, such as a newly implemented project-tracking method that has enhanced efficiency, even though this change's final outcome may not yet be fully realised. They encourage the team to discuss areas where the process could be further improved, fostering a constructive dialogue that centres on progress and development.

Through these systemic and behavioural steps, the leader communicates clearly that success is measured by commitment to the process, not just by outcomes. By embedding this approach in everyday actions, feedback and communication, the leader ensures the team will internalise this process-focused mindset. Without these deliberate actions, the message could easily have been mixed, meaning team members would feel uncertain about whether the results or process was the true priority. Instead, the leader's consistent focus on process creates clarity, harmony and a strong foundation for continuous growth.

Matching courage with compassion in leadership communication

One of the most important aspects of leadership communication – particularly when navigating difficult conversations – is the ability to balance courage with compassion. Stephen Covey's leadership framework emphasises this delicate balance and highlights how successful leaders approach tough conversations or decisions with both honesty and empathy.[17] Leaders must confront uncomfortable truths (needing courage) while also understanding and considering the emotional and situational context of the person they're addressing (needing compassion).[18]

Courage and compassion in communication:

- **Courage** allows leaders to provide direct feedback, hold team members accountable and address issues without hesitation.

- **Compassion** safeguards that feedback is delivered with empathy, recognising the individual's feelings and unique circumstances.

Balancing these two elements is central to building trust and maintaining performance standards without demotivating or alienating team members. Here's how communication changes across the four quadrants of leadership – ranging from high to low levels of courage and compassion – and how a leader can address the same performance issue in different ways.

EXAMPLE IN PRACTICE: MISSED DEADLINES

High courage, low compassion: *The blunt approach*

In this scenario, the leader values honesty and directness but lacks sensitivity in delivering feedback. The message is clear, but it may come across as harsh or unfeeling, which will potentially damage the relationship.

Example: A leader notices a team member has consistently missed deadlines. They address the issue by saying, 'You're not meeting the standards expected of you. The deadlines were clear, and there's no excuse for falling behind. You need to get your act together if you want to stay on this team.'

Impact: Although the issue is addressed head-on with a clear sense of urgency, the lack of empathy could cause the team member to feel devalued or disrespected. This may create resentment and defensiveness, which could cause disengagement rather than improvement.

High compassion, low courage: *The avoidant approach*
Here, the leader wants to maintain harmony and avoid causing discomfort, but their reluctance to address the issue directly results in vagueness and ambiguity.

Example: The same team member who missed deadlines receives this feedback: 'I know things have been busy for you, and I understand how difficult it can be to manage everything. It's important that we keep up with the deadlines, but I know you're trying your best.'

Impact: Although the leader demonstrates understanding and empathy, the message lacks clarity and urgency. The team member may not fully grasp the importance of improving their performance, and the lack of directness could allow the problem to persist, which may result in both parties becoming frustrated over time – or worse!

Low courage, low compassion: *The avoidance approach*
When both courage and compassion are low, the leader may avoid addressing the issue altogether, either by ignoring the problem or providing passive-aggressive hints without offering constructive feedback.

Example: The leader might avoid discussing missed deadlines completely, instead making vague comments in meetings such as this: 'It's important that everyone stays on top of deadlines if we want to be successful.'

Impact: This approach doesn't address the problem at all, and the lack of feedback leaves the team member unaware of the severity of their underperformance. It may also confuse or frustrate the rest of the team, as the issue continues without any resolution. This creates an atmosphere of unaddressed problems and fosters a lack of accountability.

High courage, high compassion: *The balanced approach*
This is the ideal quadrant in which the leader strikes the right balance between directness and empathy. They address the performance issue clearly while showing understanding and offering support.

Example: In the same scenario of missed deadlines, the leader says, 'I've noticed you've missed a few deadlines recently, and that's affecting the team's progress. I understand you may be dealing with a heavy workload, so let's talk about what's happening. How can I support you in managing your tasks? And what steps can we take together to guarantee deadlines are met moving forward?'

Impact: This approach addresses the issue directly, making it clear that improvement is needed, but it also shows compassion and a willingness to work together to find a solution. The team member feels supported rather than attacked, which increases the likelihood of making a positive behavioural change and maintaining trust in the relationship.

Techniques for identifying the core issues in communication

When leaders address only the surface issues that team members raise, they're risking implementing incomplete or ineffective solutions. Effective leaders develop the ability to probe deeper using structured conversational techniques to identify the underlying causes of issues. This means they can tackle the real source of challenges and create more-sustainable, meaningful resolutions. Here's how leaders can develop the skill of uncovering core issues in communication.

Avoiding the trap of surface-level problem-solving

Leaders must be wary of focusing solely on surface-level concerns; this approach often means logistical issues are solved without addressing the emotional or relational components. For example, if a team member is distressed by a change in their routine, they may bring up travel or scheduling difficulties. An unskilled leader might focus on tackling these logistical issues, such as adjusting transportation times or offering a different schedule, but the core issue – perhaps the team member is afraid of feeling undervalued or is anxious about changes – remains unaddressed.

A skilled leader would instead recognise the potential emotional aspect underlying these surface concerns. They might acknowledge the logistical aspects, then say, 'I want to make sure this change works for you. Is there anything else about this adjustment that feels challenging or difficult?' This kind of response opens the door to deeper conversation, which will allow the leader to provide reassurance and address the root concern – such as the team member's need for stability or inclusion.

Strategic choices for the timing / setting method of communication

Choosing the right time, place and medium for communication maximises its impact and facilitates alignment. When leaders consider these factors thoughtfully, they enhance both their message's clarity and their audience's receptiveness. These strategic choices enable leaders to convey messages in ways that resonate, build trust and prevent misunderstandings. Here's a deeper look at each element.

Timing

A message's timing can greatly influence how it's received and the response it elicits. Urgent or sensitive messages benefit from a carefully considered approach to timing that balances immediacy and readiness, so as to guarantee constructive outcomes.

Here are some strategies to optimise timing:

» **Sensitive feedback and private conversations:** When providing important feedback – especially if it's critical or sensitive – deliver it when neither party is pressed for time rather than at the end of a busy day or week. If the recipient is preoccupied with high-priority tasks, wait until they can engage fully and thoughtfully. Timing feedback this way helps the individual to process it without feeling rushed or distracted.

» **Consider team energy levels:** People often have higher energy and focus earlier in the day or week, so these times are ideal for important discussions. For example, holding team meetings on Monday mornings or scheduling one-to-one conversations mid-morning can improve engagement and openness, which engenders more-productive exchanges.

» **Anticipate and prepare for processing needs:** For significant updates, such as a policy change or a new project direction, consider giving a heads-up or preliminary information ahead of the main discussion. A short email outlining the upcoming topic allows team members to prepare, process initial reactions and approach the conversation with clarity. This method respects individuals' need for time to adapt to new information and helps minimise resistance in team settings.

By timing communications strategically, leaders show respect for their team's mental bandwidth and create conditions that support positive, meaningful interactions.

Setting / method of communication

The setting in which communication occurs plays a vital role in how the message is perceived. Matching the setting to the communication's content and tone can amplify its impact, making sure the message is received as intended and without misinterpretation.

Here's how to choose the right setting or method of communication:

- **In-person meetings or video calls:** For complex discussions, performance reviews, or feedback that requires empathy and engagement, then in-person meetings or video calls are ideal. These settings allow for non-verbal cues to be read, issues to be clarified immediately and a sense of presence that enhances trust to be created. Leaders can gauge reactions, respond in real time and adapt their approach based on the individual's responses.

- **Emails or detailed written updates:** For informational or detailed updates that team members may need to reference later (such as policy changes or project specifications), a well-structured email or written document is more effective. Written communication is also beneficial for people who prefer to process information independently. This format ensures important details are accessible and can be revisited, which reduces the risk of miscommunication.

- **Phone calls or quick briefings:** For brief updates or clarifications that don't require an in-depth discussion, a phone call or quick team briefing can be effective. These settings are efficient and direct, and they provide a personal touch without requiring the time commitment of a formal meeting. They work particularly well for urgent matters or time-sensitive issues that need a rapid response.

Choosing the appropriate setting demonstrates consideration for both the recipient's needs and the nature of the message, helping the communication to be as effective as possible.

Communication:
Everyone's responsibility

Feedback is a two-way process that calls for both clarity and receptivity. Leaders must not only communicate their points effectively but also actively listen to how feedback is received. When approached responsibly, giving feedback builds trust, strengthens relationships and drives improvement. However, the success of these conversations often depends on the recipient's openness. Understanding the traits of those who resist feedback versus those who embrace it helps leaders to tailor their approach to ensure each conversation promotes growth and alignment with team goals.

The following framework is useful when contemplating this spectrum of the hardest and easiest people to deliver feedback to and the skills required to navigate these dynamics.

The hardest people to deliver feedback to:

1. **The delusional**

   Why it's challenging: These individuals have an inflated sense of their abilities and often fail to see their shortcomings. They may dismiss negative feedback as irrelevant or unjustified.

   Techniques to reach them:
   - Use specific, factual examples to illustrate your points.
   - Encourage self-assessment before offering feedback to help them see skills gaps independently.
   - Frame feedback as an opportunity for growth that's in line with their goals or aspirations.

   Time commitment: High. Breaking through their defensiveness often requires multiple conversations and a lot of patience.

2. **The emotional**

   Why it's challenging: They may take negative feedback personally and react with frustration, sadness or defensiveness. This makes it difficult to focus on the message without emotions escalating.

   Techniques to reach them:
   - Deliver feedback with empathy and reassurance.
   - Depersonalise the message by focusing on behaviours, not personality traits.
   - Provide solutions and support to ease their anxieties about change.

Time commitment: Moderate to high. Emotional responses can extend feedback conversations and require follow-up to make certain the message is absorbed.

3. **The cold**

   Why it's challenging: These individuals may seem indifferent, refusing to engage or take ownership of the feedback. Their lack of emotional response can stall progress.

   Techniques to reach them:

   - Clearly explain the consequences of their inaction and the importance of their contribution to team goals.
   - Use data or evidence to make the feedback compelling.
   - Build trust over time to encourage more openness and engagement.

   Time commitment: Moderate to high. Establishing a connection and nurturing accountability can be a long process.

The easiest people to deliver feedback to:

1. **The calm and stable**

   Why it's easy: They're solution-oriented and receptive to constructive criticism, which makes feedback conversations efficient and productive.

   Traits:

   - These individuals approach feedback rationally and see it as an opportunity to grow. They maintain an emotional balance and are open to discussion.

2. **The humble**

   Why it's easy: Their willingness to own their development creates a collaborative feedback process.

Traits:

- They exhibit self-awareness and recognise their areas for improvement. They're eager to learn and improve, and they often initiate conversations about feedback.

3. **The team-oriented**

    Why it's easy: They naturally amend their actions to align with feedback so as to achieve better team outcomes, which reduces the need for follow-up.

    Traits:

    - They prioritise collective success over personal emotions, and they view feedback as essential for the team's growth. Their focus on shared goals makes them open to suggestions.

REFLECTION EXERCISE FOR SELF-IMPROVEMENT

Consider, for your line manager, where you fall in this spectrum. Are you closer to their hardest or easiest feedback recipients?

Ask yourself these questions:

» Do I listen actively and seek clarification when receiving feedback?

» Do I demonstrate humility and a commitment to growth?

» Do I align my actions with feedback to show improvement?

Aspiration and action

Aim to position yourself among the easiest to deliver feedback to. This will strengthen your relationship with your manager and accelerate your own growth and impact within the organisation. Adopting traits such as self-awareness, emotional regulation and a focus on collective goals will guarantee you're seen as a reliable and growth-oriented professional.

CONCLUSION

Communication is a skill that defines leadership, and it shapes how leaders influence, inspire and align their teams. This chapter has shown that communication is far more than simply sharing information; it's about ensuring messages are clear, purposeful and tailored to the needs of the audience. Whether you're articulating a vision, navigating challenges or building alignment, effective communication fosters trust, drives engagement and strengthens team cohesion.

Leadership communication necessitates a balance between clarity and empathy. Clarity ensures the message is understood and actionable, while empathy recognises the team's emotions and perspectives. Leaders who adapt their communication styles to meet diverse preferences create an environment in which every team member feels valued and understood. At the same time, listening actively, validating concerns and following through on commitments demonstrate reliability and build credibility. Consistency between a leader's words and actions further solidifies trust and reinforces the values they want to instil in their teams.

The ability to deliver feedback effectively is another essential component of communication. This chapter has highlighted the importance of balancing courage with compassion when handling difficult conversations. Leaders who approach feedback with honesty and empathy not only address performance issues but also nurture trust and create a culture of continuous growth. Giving feedback isn't just about identifying problems; it's about effecting solutions and empowering team members to improve.

Good communication is an ongoing process that needs reflection, adaptability and refinement. By seeking feedback consistently and constantly, assessing the impact of their messages, and making adjustments, leaders can make certain their communication remains effective and impactful.

Strong communication builds a foundation for collaboration, resilience and mutual respect, which will equip teams to meet challenges and achieve shared goals.

As we move on to the next chapter, we'll explore how – by building on the skills established in this chapter – leaders can acquire the ability to develop others, which will enhance their leadership impact.

LEVEL 2

5
Developing Others

Developing others is one of the most vital skills in leadership, yet it's often overlooked. Many leaders excel at achieving their own goals, but they struggle when it comes to fostering the growth and success of their team members. This chapter explores why the ability to develop others is not just a valuable leadership trait but also is a key driver of long-term organisational success. It's easy for unskilled leaders to fall into the pattern of simply praising or punishing their team members, while hoping they'll learn through osmosis or by observing others. This approach, however, rarely develops the sustainable skills needed by individuals and teams for high performance over time. Notably, developing others and delegation are interdependent skills, with each reinforcing the other. This connection will be examined further in *Chapter 6: Delegation*, which highlights how these capabilities together empower leaders to build high-performing teams.

Skilled leadership entails providing more than just surface-level motivation or feedback. Developing others involves understanding each individual's strengths, areas for growth and personal drivers, combined with meaningful knowledge of the area the leader wants them to develop in. It requires continuous reflection and a deliberate approach to unlocking every team member's potential. Leaders who are capable of this understand that no two team members are the same; each requires a personalised approach that resonates with their unique skill set and motivators. Simply relying on general praise and/or punitive measures is insufficient and often engenders resentment and frustration – on both sides.

The foundational block of developing others is *trust*; without it, any efforts to facilitate growth and build skills within a team will be significantly less effective. Balanced leadership embraces the idea that successful teams are built through intentional skill development. This involves fostering a trust-filled environment in which individuals feel comfortable in stepping out of their comfort zones to grow. Leaders who are skilled in developing others know how to break down barriers to performance by identifying gaps in both motivation and skills, and then addressing them through consistent and constant feedback, mentoring, coaching, and learning opportunities. This type of leadership is about more than getting immediate results; it's about cultivating long-term growth that benefits both the individual and the team.

A leader taking ownership of both their own development and the development of their team can transform leadership into a force for sustained excellence that will drive success at every level of the organisation.

This approach requires leaders to break this challenge down into three primary areas: **motivation, skill set** and **opportunity**:

1. **Motivation:** Leaders will get the best results if they invest time in understanding what drives each team member personally. This can be done through regular, open conversations where the focus is on understanding the team member's personal goals, values and how they relate to the work at hand. By identifying these intrinsic motivators,

leaders can tailor their approach to each individual, using strategies that resonate with the individual. Avoiding a one-size-fits-all approach ensures that the leader is addressing what truly energises the team member. Motivation also covers what the individual is focusing on: they may be extremely motivated, but it could be by something detrimental to their development.

2. **Skill set:** If motivation isn't the issue, then the most likely reason for a team member not meeting standards is a skills gap. Leaders need to assess whether the individual has the necessary skills and confidence to perform at the expected standard for their role. In this case, filling the gap will involve offering additional training, resources or mentorship to build their competence and proficiency. Skills gaps, when left unaddressed, can lead to frustration and disengagement, even among otherwise motivated individuals.

3. **Opportunity:** Even if a team member has the right motivation and skill set, a lack of opportunity can significantly hinder their growth. 'Opportunity' refers to the right environment and pathways being available to enable individuals to apply their skills and stay motivated. When team members aren't given the chance to take on new challenges, grow into leadership roles or apply their skills, they can become disengaged – regardless of their initial enthusiasm. Leaders must focus on creating chances for development, whether through stretch assignments, career progression, or simply giving individuals the space to innovate and apply their talents.

The challenge for leaders is to determine whether an issue stems from a lack of motivation, skill set or opportunity. This requires a high level of emotional intelligence, the ability to evaluate team members on an individual basis, and the capacity to maintain high standards while facilitating development.

The three dimensions of development
Dimension 1: Developing motivation
The trap of self-motivation: An unskilled approach

If you, as a leader, don't invest in building a relationship with a team member, you're more likely to default to your own motivational triggers. For instance, if you're motivated by competition, you might assume that introducing competitive elements will drive your team. However, if the individual you're trying to motivate thrives on harmony rather than competition, this strategy may backfire. Rather than inspiring them, you might inadvertently increase their stress or disengagement, as the competition might feel toxic and have a very detrimental effect on their morale. Conversely, if you're put off by competition, but a member of your team thrives on it, if you fail to provide chances for healthy competition, you might be missing a chance to support and empower that team member. A competitive element might even inspire this team member to pay extra attention to tasks they aren't currently engaging with, thus enhancing their contribution and development.

Therefore, relying on your own motivational preferences not only risks alienating individual team members but also undermines your effectiveness as a leader. When your team members feel undervalued or misunderstood they can disengage, become resentful and their trust breaks down. Beyond the personal dynamics within your team, this approach can result in inefficiency due to time and effort being wasted on strategies that fail to resonate. This can leave your team at a disadvantage, allowing your competitors to gain ground while you struggle to align and energise your workforce. Motivation isn't a one-size-fits-all concept: people are driven by different values, goals and needs. This is why it's crucial to understand what matters to each team member before attempting to motivate them.

Relationships are the key to unlocking true motivation

To avoid the trap of projecting your own motivations onto others, it's imperative for you, as a leader, to build genuine relationships

LEVEL 2: CHAPTER 5 – DEVELOPING OTHERS

with your team members. That's why this fundamental block is needed before you start to support development in a sustained and meaningful way. When you know your team on a personal level, you can tailor your motivational strategies to align with each individual's personal goals and values. This approach goes beyond generic incentives and taps into what truly drives each person.

For example, some individuals may be motivated by having autonomy and the ability to make decisions; others might be driven by recognition or a sense of belonging within the team. Without taking the time to discover these individual drivers, you're likely to rely on broad, impersonal strategies that may not resonate with your whole team. Building strong relationships allows you, as a leader, to create meaningful connections between the tasks at hand and what matters most to each of your team members.

It's about connecting the work with something that feels personal and significant to them, not just to you.

Here are eight very broad areas to consider, based on the language used in *Chapter 1: Self-Awareness*; they're a starting point and not in any way intended to be a replacement for a relationship with your team members:

1. **Red-Blue team members**
    - These are motivated by clear goals, structure and tangible results.
    - Tailor your approach by providing measurable objectives, clear timelines and opportunities to demonstrate their efficiency and drive.

2. **Red-Yellow team members**
    - These are motivated by competition, recognition and social engagement.
    - Engage them with chances for friendly competition, public recognition for their achievements, and brainstorming sessions to channel their creativity.

3. **Blue–Red team members**
   - These are motivated by precision, organisation and the ability to see their efforts lead to action.
   - Provide well-structured plans and responsibilities, along with visible outcomes that reward their attention to detail and drive for results.

4. **Blue–Green team members**
   - These are motivated by structure, collaboration and harmony.
   - Appeal to their strengths by creating organised workflows that foster team cooperation and balance. Provide reassurance that their efforts are contributing to team stability.

5. **Green–Blue team members**
   - These are motivated by relationships, thoughtful planning and the desire to support others.
   - Nurture their engagement by highlighting how their work benefits the team and by offering opportunities to contribute to structured, people-focused initiatives.

6. **Green–Yellow team members**
   - These are motivated by relationships, creativity and cultivating harmony.
   - Encourage them by assigning tasks that involve collaboration, innovative problem-solving and maintaining a supportive team environment.

7. **Yellow–Green team members**
   - These are motivated by creativity, a sense of belonging and harmonious teamwork.
   - Provide opportunities for collaborative projects in which their ideas can flourish while fostering positive team dynamics and mutual respect.

8. **Yellow–Red team members**
   - These are motivated by innovation, fast-paced results and public recognition.
   - Inspire them through chances to lead dynamic projects, generate bold ideas and receive praise for their contributions in a high-energy environment.

HEALTH WARNING: AVOIDING MANIPULATION

The distinction between motivation and manipulation is critical. Manipulation uses tactics that persuade someone to act in a way that benefits you, but in a disingenuous manner. Although it may be tempting, it's a short-term fix that may yield initial results, but it erodes trust and ultimately causes long-term damage to relationships and team morale.

For instance, a leader might use *inaccurate* flattery to push someone into working harder, or they might dangle rewards in front of their team member that aren't genuinely meaningful. While this might get the job done at that moment, if the manipulation becomes common knowledge, it can leave the team member feeling used rather than valued. This type of behaviour doesn't inspire loyalty or trust. Once one team member feels manipulated, it can spread quickly throughout the entire team. Other members may begin to question their leader's integrity, wondering if their leader is manipulating them as well. *Manipulation can be a subtle yet corrosive force* – once it takes root, it can eat into the entire team's trust in their leader.

Integrity and motivation

To prevent manipulation and to cultivate genuine motivation, leaders must act with integrity. Integrity in leadership means being transparent about intentions and ensuring efforts to motivate come from a place of care and authenticity, rather than self-interest or coercion. When a leader's actions are grounded in a genuine desire to see their team grow and succeed, it shows, and this fosters a sense of trust and loyalty. This is why building relationships is so important:

it allows you to amend your leadership style to line up with the unique motivations of each person.

A leader who understands what motivates each of their team members can offer personalised support and guidance that feels authentic. For example, one team member might need obvious recognition for their achievements to feel motivated, while another might thrive when given more autonomy. *By aligning your leadership approach with your team members' unique drivers, you not only avoid manipulation but you also demonstrate you respect their individuality.* This builds a foundation of trust from which team members know they're being valued for who they are and not just treated as a means to an end.

CASE STUDY: MISGUIDED AND MANIPULATIVE MOTIVATION

Example 1: Misguided persistence

A leader who's motivated by career growth and personal achievements presents a team member with a proposal to take on a new responsibility. The leader frames it as a significant opportunity for the team member's career advancement and highlights how similar challenges propelled their own career. However, the team member – who values work-life balance and is satisfied with their current role –declines politely, citing their existing responsibilities and the desire to maintain focus on their current work as the reason for this.

Instead of considering what might actually motivate the team member, the leader persists, emphasising the long-term benefits and the potential for recognition and leadership roles. Despite the team member's continued hesitation and clear communication that they aren't seeking career advancement at this time, the leader remains convinced their own vision is what the team member needs. The more the leader pushes, the more disengaged and frustrated the team member becomes – and, ultimately, the more they feel unsuitable for the new responsibility.

Example 2: Flattery and manipulation

In another instance, a leader needs someone to take on a challenging new role and uses false flattery to persuade them. The leader tells the individual they're the only person trusted to handle the responsibility, implying that no one else is capable of this role. However, the individual becomes sceptical of this flattery and suspects the leader is simply trying to offload responsibility rather than genuinely recognising their unique talents.

Later, during informal conversations with colleagues, the individual shares their doubts, and others who have received similar praise begin to question whether they, too, were manipulated into taking on more work. As word spreads, the team members become increasingly wary of the leader's compliments and second-guess the sincerity behind them. This growing scepticism erodes trust within the team, as staff members start to feel undervalued and used for the leader's convenience, rather than appreciated for their genuine contributions. Over time, the leader's credibility suffers, and their previously motivating words lose their impact, causing the team to disengage.

Example 3: A skilled approach to motivation

In contrast, another leader has an open-minded approach to a conversation with a team member about new responsibilities. They begin by asking the team member what aspects of their work they find most fulfilling and what might make them comfortable with taking on something new. The team member explains that, although they're passionate about their core responsibilities, they're anxious about taking on additional administrative tasks, which would take considerable time and add significant stress. They also express that one of their key motivators is job security, which influences how they view changes in their responsibilities.

Instead of immediately pushing the team member into a role that doesn't fit with their strengths, the leader listens carefully and proposes a tailored solution. They suggest developing a project that will allow the team member to focus on what they enjoy – training and supporting team members – while another colleague takes on some of the operational responsibilities. Additionally, the leader addresses, with integrity, the team member's concern about job security by explaining that the new responsibility fulfils a long-term need for the organisation and stepping into this role will improve their position's stability.

This collaborative and transparent approach is more likely to leave the team member feeling valued and supported, as it encourages them to take on leadership responsibilities within their comfort zone while bringing their contributions in line with the organisation's future stability.

Something as simple as listening, to be able to communicate skilfully, should go without saying, but this step is often overlooked – especially under the pressures of deadlines, scrutiny and competition. However, this fundamental skill consistently pays dividends. An authentic and balanced strategy both motivates the team member in the short term and builds a foundation of trust and respect for future opportunities. Other team members observe this personalised approach and feel confident their own needs and strengths will also be respected, which will lead to improved morale and a more positive culture throughout the organisation.

As a leader, you must recognise that, in many cases, it's not always feasible to accommodate a team member's apprehensions fully. However, by listening first and connecting on a genuine level, you're much more likely to foster mutual respect and open the team member's path to higher performance. This empathetic and adaptable approach creates a sense of partnership in which the team member feels heard and understood, even if not all requests can be met.

Long-term benefits of this approach

Open and supportive conversations between leaders and team members establish a trust-based approach that nurtures psychological safety and mutual respect. By taking the time to understand team members' motivations and address their concerns, the leader creates an environment in which individuals feel comfortable sharing their thoughts, anxieties and aspirations. This transparent and empathetic approach empowers the team member to grow at their own pace by aligning their responsibilities with their strengths, which helps them build confidence without feeling overwhelmed. As they complete tasks successfully and see the positive impact of their contributions, they're more prepared to embrace larger roles in the future, fostering sustainable growth.

This approach sets a precedent for the entire team beyond individual interactions, which promotes a culture of trust, collaboration and personalised support. When team members observe a leadership style that respects their unique strengths and goals, they feel valued and engaged, which enhances morale and boosts retention. This thoughtful strategy exemplifies a strength-based leadership model, which leverages individuals' talents to create a more effective and cohesive team. Over time, this approach not only develops the individual but also reinforces a workplace culture that prioritises personal development, satisfaction and meaningful contribution, thus ensuring both individual and organisational success.

Dimension 2: Skill set development
Being told you have a skill deficiency in a certain area isn't an insult, and a professional who constantly develops new skills is an invaluable asset. If you've established that your team member is motivated and focused on the right things, but they're still not meeting the required standard, the issue almost certainly lies with their skill set. In such cases, praise, recognition or sanctions are unlikely to make a meaningful difference; instead, providing targeted development opportunities and tailored skill development becomes essential to unlocking their potential.

Consider this: *if someone is physically unable to lift 100kg, no amount of financial incentive or threat of job loss would suddenly enable them to achieve it.* The only way to reach that goal is through incremental progress; that is, gradually pushing beyond their comfort zones and building strength over time.

Performance in a team is far more complex than strength exercises, which is why developing skills requires a leader who's adept at guiding that growth. This isn't easy to achieve, and many leaders fall short, so those who do extremely well in this area gain a significant advantage. One effective framework for this is Blanchard's Situational Leadership model, which provides a structured approach to tailoring leadership styles based on an individual's development stage.

SITUATIONAL LEADERSHIP: BLANCHARD'S MODEL

Blanchard's Situational Leadership model, from *Leadership and the One Minute Manager: Increasing Effectiveness Through Situational Leadership*,[19] offers a framework for understanding how to adapt leadership styles according to an individual's levels of competence and commitment. Regarding developing someone's skill set, leaders must first assess where that person currently stands in terms of ability and mindset. Blanchard outlines four leadership styles: **directing**, coaching (which we'll refer to as **mentoring**), supporting (which we'll refer to as **coaching**) and **delegating**. The style names have been changed as I've found this offers a clearer distinction. Each corresponds to a different developmental stage, as follows.

Stage 1: Directing

At this stage, the individual is typically new to a task and lacks the necessary skills, although they may be highly enthusiastic. The leader's role is to provide clear instructions, set expectations and offer close supervision to make certain the person gains a foundational understanding of the task. The leader should break the tasks down into smaller, manageable steps and give frequent and constructive feedback. Blanchard's model stresses the importance of being directive while motivating through encouragement.

For example, if a team member has just been assigned a new and unfamiliar role or responsibility, the leader must step in with specific guidance to demonstrate how to perform the task, plus outlining key performance indicators (KPIs). This phase focuses on skill acquisition through repetition and clarity, and it's the leader's responsibility to help the individual gain confidence as well as technical abilities.

Stage 2: Mentoring

Once a team member begins to develop competence, although they may still lack confidence or motivation, the leader must transition into a mentoring role. This phase involves less micromanagement and more dialogue. The leader continues to guide them but now seeks input from the individual, encouraging questions and critical thinking. This dual focus on performance and development elicits growth by making the employee feel supported while also promoting autonomy.

At this stage, the leader helps the individual connect their developing skills with broader organisational goals, which reinforces the value of their contribution. Mentoring also involves motivational discussions in which the leader seeks to understand any dips in commitment, which are potentially caused by the increased complexity of the tasks the individual now faces. Feedback, through regular check-ins, becomes more about guiding the team member toward better decision-making than dictating their every move.

Stage 3: Coaching

As a team member moves into this phase, they are more competent, but they might still encounter occasional dips in implementation or confidence, which is often due to their lack of experience in navigating the full range of external factors. A skilled coach can play a transformative role at this stage by asking thought-provoking questions that help the team member broaden their perspective. Through these questions, a coach can enable their team member to connect seemingly unrelated skills into a cohesive skill set, which turns isolated strengths into a comprehensive and adaptive approach. This not only enhances their problem-solving capabilities but also builds their confidence in tackling complex scenarios. By nurturing this integrative thinking, the coach helps the individual refine their leadership agility and prepares them to excel in diverse and challenging environments.

Stage 4: Delegating

In the final stage, the individual is both competent and committed, meaning they require little to no supervision. At this point, the leader fully delegates tasks, trusting the employee to take ownership and make decisions independently. The leader's role is to monitor overall progress, offer support only when requested, and continue to foster the employee's leadership potential by encouraging them to take on higher responsibilities or mentor others.

Delegating is about empowering individuals to leverage their skills and confidence to make decisions that are in harmony with organisational objectives. Leaders should use this stage to encourage continuous professional development by providing stretch goals that challenge the individual's current skill set, thereby maintaining their engagement and enthusiasm.

EXAMPLE: DRIVING INSTRUCTION

To illustrate these stages, consider how a driving instructor might support four different learner drivers who are at varying levels of competence and commitment:

Stage 1: Directing

For a beginner, the instructor might need to direct every aspect of a specific manoeuvre, such as changing gears going up a hill:

» 'Clutch in, change gear down to second, clutch out and press back on the accelerator as you release the clutch.'

Stage 2: Mentoring

As the learner gains some familiarity but lacks confidence, the instructor might transition to a mentoring role, offering less direct guidance:

» 'You're going up a hill, so you need to change down to second gear.'

Stage 3: Coaching

For a more experienced learner who occasionally needs help connecting concepts, the instructor might ask open-ended questions to prompt critical thinking:

» 'You're going up a hill; what do you need to do with the gears?'

Stage 4: Delegating

Once the learner becomes both competent and confident, the instructor can delegate tasks fully, trusting them to make decisions independently:

» 'Drive up that hill.'

This progression demonstrates how a leader's role evolves from being highly directive to empowering the individual to act independently by tailoring their approach to meet the learner's development needs at each stage.

The difference between mentoring and coaching

Although the terms 'mentoring' and 'coaching' are often used interchangeably, they each serve a distinct purpose in the context of development and leadership. These two approaches represent different levels of guidance and involvement, depending on the needs of the individual.

Mentoring

Mentoring still retains a *teaching element*, particularly when individuals have begun to develop some competence, but they lack confidence or commitment. In this phase, the mentor guides them by breaking down tasks into manageable chunks while grouping foundational steps together. Although the individual is gaining some independence, the mentor provides *key information* or *reminders* to make sure the individual stays on track.

For example, in a restaurant kitchen, a head chef mentoring a junior cook might say, 'When making the sauce, sauté the onions and garlic first – these provide the aromatics, which form the flavour foundation of the dish. Then add the tomatoes, as they contribute an element of acidity that enhances the overall flavour profile.' Here, the head chef is not only instructing them on the steps to follow but is also sharing the reasoning behind them, thus helping the junior cook understand the role each ingredient plays in the dish. This balance of instruction and explanation builds the cook's technical skills and culinary knowledge.

Coaching

In contrast, coaching involves *little to no teaching*. Instead of providing direct instructions, the coach's role is to ask *probing questions* to help individuals:

» **Organise their options** and decide on the best course of action.

» **Consider the wider implications** and how their choices might affect the outcome.

» **Remember lessons learned** from previous experiences and apply them to current or new challenges.

» **Adapt learned skills** to unfamiliar or complex situations so as to build their problem-solving and critical-thinking abilities.

For example, a head chef coaching a more experienced cook might ask, 'What ingredients do we need to build the aromatics for this dish?' or 'This needs some acidity to balance the flavour; what could we add?' This approach encourages the cook to think critically and independently, drawing on their understanding of culinary principles to troubleshoot and refine the dish. The head chef is facilitating the cook's thought process rather than providing answers, which enables the cook to take ownership of their decisions and develop greater confidence in their skills.

Key distinctions between the two

The fundamental difference between mentoring and coaching lies in the degree of teaching and the balance of responsibility:

- **Mentoring** still involves *imparting knowledge* and guiding individuals by providing key information when necessary.

- **Coaching** shifts the responsibility to the individual and focuses on *encouraging self-discovery* and *problem-solving through reflective questioning*.

Understanding these differences allows leaders to tailor their approach to meet their team members' unique needs. Mentoring is ideal when someone is still growing their competence, but coaching is more appropriate for those who already possess the necessary skills but need help refining their approach or applying their abilities to new and broader contexts.

Understanding the drama and empowerment triangles in leadership

Leadership is a balance of providing support while empowering others to take ownership of their growth and performance. How leaders choose to act and behave shapes team dynamics significantly. Two contrasting models – the **Drama Triangle** and the **Empowerment Triangle** – provide a powerful lens through which these dynamics can be understood.

The Drama Triangle:
Toxic roles that hinder growth

Conceptualised by Stephen Karpman, the Drama Triangle highlights three destructive roles often found in dysfunctional team dynamics:

1. **The Persecutor:** A leader in this role exerts excessive control or criticism, which causes team members to feel demoralised or helpless. The Persecutor creates an environment of fear instead of accountability.

2. **The Rescuer:** This role is marked by over-involvement, where the leader 'saves' team members from challenges instead of enabling them to solve problems independently. Despite being well-intentioned, rescuing cultivates dependency and stagnation. Additionally, the Rescuer can inadvertently exacerbate the Victim mindset by siding with the Victim and blaming external factors or others for their issues. By doing so, the Rescuer reinforces the Victim's sense of powerlessness, creating a cycle in which neither party addresses the problem's root cause.

3. **The Victim:** In this role, the team member feels powerless and blames others or circumstances for their lack of progress. The Victim relinquishes accountability, which furthers the cycle of blame and inaction.

These roles perpetuate a culture of dependency, blame and stagnation, which obstructs personal and team growth. Additionally, these roles are often fluid, with individuals shifting between them depending on the dynamics of the situation. For example, if a Victim isn't 'rescued', they may adopt the role of Persecutor and lash out at those they perceive to be neglecting them. Similarly, a Rescuer who becomes frustrated with a victim's refusal to accept help may transition into the Persecutor role by criticising or controlling the Victim out of exasperation. This fluidity reinforces the toxic cycle, making it even harder for teams to break free from these destructive patterns.

The Empowerment Triangle:
A blueprint for resilience and accountability

In contrast, the Empowerment Triangle (created by business consultant and author David Emerald, and officially known as The Empowerment Dynamic) flips these toxic roles into constructive ones, thus fostering a culture of accountability and growth.

The dynamics are shifted toward collaboration and empowerment:

1. **The Driver:** In this role, the team member takes ownership of their progress and actively seeks solutions and accountability for their outcomes.
2. **The Supporter:** In this role, the leader provides structure and encouragement to ensure team members have the resources and confidence needed to succeed.
3. **The Coach:** In this role, the leader offers guidance through questions, feedback and support, which allows team members to develop skills and solve challenges independently.

By a leader positioning themself as a Supporter and Coach to their team members' Drivers, the Empowerment Triangle creates an environment in which team members excel as accountable and resilient professionals.

Linking the Empowerment Triangle to leadership stages

Leaders play a critical role in making certain their team members remain in the Driver position, by the leader progressing through *three stages of support*: **directing**, **mentoring** and **coaching**.

» **Supporter role: Stage 1 (directing) and stage 2 (mentoring)**

In the early stages, leaders act as Supporters, who offer clear guidance and structure. This approach builds team members' confidence and provides a foundation for independent problem-solving. However, leaders must avoid slipping into the Drama Triangle roles:

- Acting as a Rescuer leads to dependency, which stifles team members' growth.
- Acting as a Persecutor creates fear and disengagement among team members.

» **Coach role: Stage 3 (coaching)**

As team members gain competence, the leader shifts to a Coaching role, which facilitates independence by asking thoughtful questions and providing actionable feedback. The focus here is on empowerment, but vigilance is essential:

- Reverting to Rescuer mode undermines autonomy.
- Adopting a Persecutor stance diminishes both openness and confidence in being vulnerable.

» **Sustaining the Driver role: Compassionate leadership**

At this stage, team members fully embody the Driver role by taking responsibility for their tasks, decisions and development. Leaders now act as occasional guides who offer support when challenges arise. Compassionate leadership ensures balance:

- High levels of *compassion* alone can lead to rescuing behaviours.
- High levels of *courage* alone risks critical or overly direct feedback, which pushes team members into disengagement.

Intentional leadership makes certain that team members remain empowered, which fosters a culture of resilience and autonomy.

The pull of the Drama Triangle

The roles within the Drama Triangle – the Persecutor, Rescuer and Victim – are natural because they offer immediate emotional rewards. The Rescuer feels validated and indispensable, the Persecutor feels in control, and the Victim avoids responsibility.

However, these roles are toxic for both individual and team performance:

- **They reinforce dependency**: Rescuers prevent team members developing independence, which traps them in a cycle of reliance.

- **They erode confidence**: Persecutors garner fear and insecurity, which pushes team members to retreat into victimhood.
- **They block accountability**: Victims disengage, avoid ownership and place the blame elsewhere.

Balancing development and maintaining standards

One of the most crucial challenges for leaders is facilitating team members' development at the same time as ensuring standards remain consistently high. This balance requires skill, patience and strategy. A common pitfall in this area is leaders' tendency to swing between extremes: moving directly from stage 1 (directing) to stage 4 (delegating). In other words, they shift from micromanaging to granting complete freedom, thus bypassing the important intermediate stages of mentoring and coaching.

When delivery standards inevitably drop under such circumstances, the leader often reacts by reverting from stage 4 (delegating) to stage 1 (directing). This understandable response demonstrates a lack of the finesse required to truly empower team members. It creates a cycle of frustration in which the leader feels overwhelmed by constant firefighting, and their team members struggle to build their confidence and autonomy.

The appeal of high levels of control

Maintaining high levels of control and directing every member of the team may seem appealing at first glance. It can give the leader a sense of security through knowing every decision and action is being closely monitored. However, this approach is *highly inefficient*, particularly when it comes to time management. Stage 1 (directing) requires the most significant time commitment as it involves constant oversight and input.

By contrast:

» **Mentoring** requires slightly less time because it involves chunking foundational steps together while still delivering key information.

- » **Coaching** takes even less time as it focuses on asking questions to guide independent problem-solving.
- » **Delegating** demands the least time as the leader only needs to monitor outcomes and provide occasional support.

Leaders must acknowledge that directing every member of the team at all times is not only *impractical* but also *unsustainable*. It's essential to use time efficiently and strategically by focusing direct involvement where it's most needed, but fostering independence in areas where team members are ready to take the lead.

The cost of poor balance

Although it's challenging to master this balance, it's well worth the effort. Leaders who invest time in mentoring and coaching their team members reap long-term rewards, both in performance and relationships.

On the other hand, failing to strike this balance comes with significant risks:

- **Broken relationships:** Constant micromanagement or abrupt shifts between extremes can erode trust and damage relationships between leaders and their team members.
- **Reputation damage:** A team that fails to deliver high-quality work consistently risks losing credibility with stakeholders, customers and other departments.
- **Time loss:** Nothing is more time-consuming than repairing damaged relationships or trying to rebuild a team's reputation after repeated failures.

A strategic approach to balance

To excel in this area, leaders must do the following:

- » **Diagnose needs accurately:** Invest time in understanding each team member's competence and commitment.

- » **Apply the right approach:** Use the most appropriate leadership style (directing, mentoring, coaching or delegating) based on the individual's developmental needs.
- » **Monitor and adjust:** Regularly assess team performance and adjust the level of support accordingly, without overreacting to temporary dips in delivery.
- » **Be patient:** Empowering team members to develop autonomy takes time, but it ultimately leads to higher efficiency and stronger results.

Leaders must also remember that their time is finite. While it can feel tempting to maintain control over every detail, stepping back to mentor and coach enables the team to grow stronger and more capable. This balance requires skill and effort, but the payoff is immense: a team that not only performs consistently but also thrives independently, which frees up the leader to focus on higher-level priorities.

Dimension 3: Creating opportunities for development

Once a leader has identified their team members' individual motivations and developed skill sets, they must make sure their team members have the opportunities to apply their emerging skills in real-world scenarios. This involves creating an environment in which employees can take on new challenges.

Leaders can create these openings by doing the following:

- » **Allocating reach assignments:** This is assigning tasks that go beyond the individual's current role and allows them to apply and refine their new skills. These assignments should be challenging but not overwhelming, which will help to push the individual out of their comfort zone in a supportive way. The perfect scenario is finding projects and responsibilities that are a burden for one person and a reach for another. By handing these on, a leader will lighten the load on their more senior leadership and create exciting opportunities for their up-and-coming leaders.

» **Deputising:** This is pairing developing individuals with more experienced team members to foster a culture of learning and collaboration. Mentorship not only provides a safety net for those taking on new challenges but also offers a pathway for developing skills through observation and guidance.

» **Providing cross-training:** When a leader encourages their team members to learn different roles within the team or organisation, it broadens their skill set and prepares them for future leadership openings. Cross-training is particularly useful in organisations where flexibility is key, as it creates a more resilient and adaptable workforce.

» **Permitting autonomy with accountability:** Allowing employees the freedom to take ownership of projects while ensuring they're accountable for the outcomes cultivates both competence and responsibility. A leader giving their team members the autonomy to make decisions and manage their work encourages personal ownership and initiative. At the same time, the accountability aspect safeguards that individuals remain focused on achieving high standards and delivering on their commitments.

Maintaining engagement through feedback and reflection

Feedback plays a crucial role in the skill development process. Constructive, timely feedback allows individuals to understand where they're doing extremely well and where there's room for improvement. Leaders should encourage reflective practice, which prompts employees to consider what they've learned from both their successes and challenges. Reflection helps to solidify learning and inspires individuals to take ownership of their development.

As team members grow, the nature of feedback should evolve. Early on in their development, feedback should be more directive and focused on specific tasks. As their competence increases, feedback should shift toward strategic guidance, which will help individuals to see the broader impact their actions have on the organisation.

By nurturing a culture of continuous feedback and reflection, leaders can create a learning environment that both develops skills and builds confidence and a sense of purpose.

Developing others is one of the most rewarding aspects of leadership, but it requires patience, empathy, and a deep understanding of individuals' motivations and needs. Blanchard's Situational Leadership model offers a robust framework for tailoring leadership approaches to the developmental stage of each team member. Focusing on personalised growth, creating opportunities and offering the right level of support at the right time allows leaders to cultivate a highly skilled, highly motivated and highly engaged team that's capable of driving organisational success.

CONCLUSION

Developing others is a vital yet often underestimated leadership responsibility. To support the growth and success of each individual, it necessitates intentionality, patience and a personalised approach. Leaders who focus on fostering their teams' development create a culture of growth and empowerment that will drive long-term organisational success.

Motivation, skill set and opportunity are the three pillars that enable leaders to unlock potential. Motivation isn't a one-size-fits-all concept; leaders must understand what genuinely drives each team member, which they do by building trust through meaningful relationships and tailoring strategies to individuals' needs, thus ensuring an authentic and effective approach.

Handling motivation with integrity furthers loyalty, engagement and a sense of belonging.

Skill development requires a similarly deliberate approach in which leaders identify competence gaps and provide targeted support through training, mentorship or coaching. By using frameworks such as Blanchard's Situational Leadership model, leaders can adapt their style to guide team members from learning to autonomy, while turning skill deficits into opportunities for sustainable growth.

Finally, even the most motivated and skilled individuals need the right challenges to which they can apply their abilities and thus advance. Creating stretch assignments, cultivating collaboration through cross-training, and balancing autonomy with accountability lets leaders provide opportunities to keep team members engaged and developing continuously.

By investing in their team members' motivation, skills and opportunities, leaders create a culture of trust, growth and resilience. Such leaders enable individuals to reach their potential, while also driving collective success. Developing others isn't just a leadership skill; it's a commitment to creating a lasting impact across the whole organisation.

6
Delegation

Delegation is a vital part of effective leadership. It's more than assigning tasks; it's empowering others, creating space for creativity, and building an environment of trust and accountability. A skilled leader who's built a strong foundation within their team understands how to guide them to exceed expectations through ownership and development. By establishing trust and clear communication, a leader creates a motivated team that's ready for new challenges. The skill of delegation goes hand in hand with developing others, which highlights an obvious overlap between this chapter and the last one. Together, they form a cohesive approach to facilitating team growth and increased leadership capacity.

When the team understands the leader's high standards and knows they'll be supported while being given the autonomy to succeed, this allows the leader to focus on elevating the team's skills, thus making them more capable of taking on greater responsibility and contributing meaningfully. A skilled leader uses delegation to give their team room to solve problems, make decisions and grow in confidence. This fosters creativity and builds a culture of accountability and ownership in which team members actively contribute to achieving excellence. Empowered teams shift from waiting for instructions to proactively seeking solutions. By trusting the team with responsibility, the leader nurtures innovation, engagement and independence, which leads to a stronger, more capable group that delivers results consistently. Effective delegation isn't about lowering standards; rather, it's finding the right balance between autonomy and accountability. An accomplished leader will make sure the team continues to meet expectations of high quality while gaining confidence and competence.

Through thoughtful delegation, a leader boosts performance and the organisation's overall capacity to excel. This approach builds an efficient, adaptable team that's ready to face future challenges.

The role of delegation in leadership

Delegation is a leadership tool that lets leaders utilise the collective and individual strengths of their team. Effective leaders understand they can't do everything themselves and distributing tasks appropriately is part of their team taking responsibility. By doing so, leaders are empowering their team members to own the delegated tasks, thus cultivating senses of responsibility and accountability within the team.

Self-awareness plays a crucial role in effective delegation. Leaders must understand their strengths, weaknesses and limitations in order to delegate well. If they lack this understanding, they may either delegate too much without providing proper guidance or may fail to trust their team and resort to micromanagement.

Multiple benefits are effected by good delegation. The first major impact of high-quality delegation is on the individual leader themself. Passing on tasks and projects frees leaders to focus on other areas – whether they be personal frustrations, projects that don't align with their own skill set or tasks that drain their energy. Delegating allows leaders to reclaim time and energy, which enables them to focus on higher-priority areas or tasks with potential for a larger impact. When leaders delegate effectively, they shift their energy toward strategic thinking and long-term planning, thus making certain they're concentrating their efforts where they can make the most-significant differences.

The second benefit is the impact on the team. Delegation provides chances for team members to take ownership of responsibilities, apply their skills and develop their critical-thinking abilities. A lack of such opportunities weakens each team member's ability to think independently and make decisions. These opportunities offer each team member space to grow and to develop their confidence and ability to contribute meaningfully to the organisation.

Moreover, delegation is essential for maintaining critical-thinking skills within the team. Leaders must make certain they're giving their teams (collectively and individually) enough freedom and responsibility to solve problems independently, rather than leaders holding control too tightly. A skilled leader knows that delegation isn't merely about reducing their own workload but is also about creating an environment in which team members can develop and sharpen their problem-solving skills.

Effective delegation benefits both the leader and the team (collectively and individually). For the leader, it creates space to focus on more-strategic and more-impactful areas. For the team, it fosters a culture of trust, accountability and continuous development, in which individuals grow through taking opportunities that challenge them. Delegation isn't just about efficiency; this practice is vital for cultivating a resilient, adaptable and capable team.

Situational Leadership and delegation

Delegation isn't a one-size-fits-all approach. The Situational Leadership model, which we covered in *Chapter 5*, provides a framework for adapting delegation based on team members' levels of development. To recap, according to this model, there are four developmental leadership approaches – **directing**, **mentoring**, **coaching** and **delegating** – and each corresponds to a team member's levels of competence and commitment. This flexible approach enables leaders to provide the right balance of guidance, support and autonomy, which ensures team members have what they need to succeed while maintaining high standards.

EXAMPLE IN PRACTICE: REORGANISING THE SHOP FLOOR

Let's look at a specific example involving four team members, with each at a different level of development (stage 1, stage 2, stage 3 and stage 4), who have collectively been given the task of reorganising a shop floor:

- **Stage 1:** This team member is enthusiastic but inexperienced in shop floor organisation. As their leader, you would adopt a *directing* style. This provides them with clear, step-by-step instructions on how to approach the task; explains why certain decisions are made; and offers close supervision. This makes certain they understand the process while they're building their foundational skills.

- **Stage 2:** This team member has some experience but either lacks confidence or may have lost some motivation due to past challenges. They're also likely to come across issues that may frustrate or demoralise them. Here, the *mentoring* style works best. You would still supply guidance as they tackle the project, but you'd allow for more input from them – such as asking questions, encouraging them to problem-solve and offering constructive feedback. This boosts their confidence while making sure they stay on the right track.

- **Stage 3:** This team member is already competent and able to achieve the task independently, but they may learn from their mistakes along the way. While they're capable of completing the task, they might make decisions that – although well-intentioned – could lead to suboptimal outcomes. As their leader, you'd use the *coaching* style to provide emotional support while allowing them to take ownership of the project. Instead of giving explicit directions, you'd steer them away from potential mistakes by asking well-placed, big-picture questions, such as 'What do you want the outcome to be?' and 'What do you want to avoid?' These questions help the team member to reflect more deeply on their approach, which allows them to navigate any potential challenges without you, as their leader, stepping in to dictate their actions. This approach not only prevents errors but also enables the team member to gain a lasting understanding through self-discovery – which is something they might miss if you simply give direct instructions. This results in a more confident, more independent team member who's grown through the process without feeling micromanaged.

- **Stage 4:** This team member is fully capable and motivated. They can handle their elements of the task independently, so you would adopt a *delegating* style to give them complete ownership of the task while you focus on other priorities. At this stage, your role is to share the desired outcome, monitor their progress from a distance and be available for guidance only if needed. You trust them to make the right decisions and execute their tasks effectively.

The benefits of delegation

For the leader

Delegating tasks frees you, as the leader, to focus on higher-level strategic priorities or areas where your skills can make the most impact. Delegation also helps you manage stress, avoid burnout and ensure you aren't overwhelmed with tasks that can be handled by others. Your skilled delegation can drive long-term growth in your team while maintaining high standards across the board.

For the team members

Delegation gives your team members the chance to step up, develop new skills and gain confidence in their abilities. It cultivates a sense of ownership and responsibility that encourages critical thinking and problem-solving. Over time, as well as helping them to become more independent and capable, it also prepares them for more-advanced roles and responsibilities.

For the culture

Delegation creates a culture of accountability and growth. When team members are consistently given opportunities to take on challenges and develop their skills, the team becomes stronger and more resilient. This fosters innovation, improves overall performance and helps the organisation grow. A team empowered through effective delegation is better equipped to adapt to new challenges and take on more-complex tasks in the future.

Delegation through Situational Leadership allows you, as a leader, to balance high standards with giving your team the chance to grow. By adapting your delegation style to each individual's levels of competence and commitment, you create a supportive and challenging environment that drives both personal and organisational success.

Fear of letting go – 'Yes, Chef!'

As a leader, your fear of being unprepared or uninformed can be reframed as a driver for building a structured, empowered team. The key is acknowledging you don't need to have all the answers; you simply need to have a process and team dynamic that guarantees solutions are found and standards are upheld.

Prioritisation and delegation

You can approach all team delegations like a head chef who oversees a kitchen: you focus on setting clear priorities and delegating tasks based on team members' roles and strengths. A head chef doesn't cook every dish, but they make certain every plate reflects their vision and standard.

Final accountability

By reviewing the 'final plate' – be it a project, report or decision – you maintain oversight. If a task doesn't meet your standards, as appropriate to the member of your team and their level of confidence or competence, you can do the following:

- » Send the 'final plate' back with constructive feedback for improvement while trusting it will come back adjusted.
- » Offer guidance (*directing, mentoring* or *coaching*) and collaborate with the individual to refine their work, thus fostering both accountability and growth.

Balancing feedback with leadership growth

It's important to balance how feedback is given with leadership growth:

- » **Feedback for growth:** When sending a 'final plate' back, you should focus on constructive and empowering feedback. Frame corrections as being part of a shared commitment to excellence rather than as criticism.
- » **Guidance with accountability:** If repeated issues arise, work alongside the team member initially to show them how to meet the standard. Then gradually transition responsibility back to them, while ensuring they feel equipped and confident. Tailoring your approach, as suggested in the Situational Leadership model, makes sure the feedback matches the individual's readiness – offering more direction for those who are new and encouraging autonomy for experienced team members.

Developing others while retaining standards

The head-chef analogy also falls into line with the Kilter Leadership Taxonomy's focus on developing others. This involves creating an environment in which team members do the following:

- » Feel trusted with tasks appropriate to their skills.
- » Understand the standard of excellence expected of them.
- » Receive coaching and mentorship that builds their competence and confidence.

Avoiding micromanagement

To avoid the risk of you becoming overly controlling as a leader, you could do this:

- » Set clear expectations at the outset.
- » Provide the tools and guidance your team needs.
- » Step back and allow autonomy while making it clear you're available for support.

EXAMPLE IN PRACTICE: HEAD-CHEF MODE

Rather than being driven by fear, you can channel this energy into structured processes:

- » Hold regular briefings to ensure there's alignment on priorities within the team.
- » Implement a feedback loop, such as 'tasting the dish' midway through the process, to prevent last-minute surprises.
- » Lead by example – that is, modelling the standards you expect and showing vulnerability when you don't know something – as it advances a learning culture.

Delegation as a tool for stability and success

Delegation is a powerful tool for fostering team growth as well as ensuring the long-term success and sustainability of an organisation. It goes beyond task distribution since it serves as a means to build competence, confidence and capacity within the team. In sectors such as education, in which recruitment challenges are common and external incentives may not attract top talent, developing homegrown talent through delegation becomes essential for success. By nurturing internal talent, leaders create a self-sustaining cycle of growth that benefits the entire organisation.

Effective delegation provides team members with chances to learn new skills, take on greater responsibility and build their confidence.

LEVEL 2: CHAPTER 6 – DELEGATION

Leaders who delegate with development in mind help their team to stretch beyond their current capabilities. Assigning challenging tasks allows individuals to step out of their comfort zones and develop resilience. Consistent feedback throughout this process not only supports growth but also cultivates an environment in which delegation is a tool for continuous learning and improvement.

This approach shapes future leaders by empowering team members to tackle new challenges. In environments where external recruitment is difficult, it's even more critical to develop internal talent. Building the skills and confidence of existing team members safeguards that the organisation has the internal strength to meet future challenges, thus reducing its reliance on external hires and supporting long-term sustainability.

Delegation also builds resilience within teams. By giving team members responsibility and trusting them with important tasks, leaders encourage problem-solving, innovation and learning from mistakes. These experiences develop technical skills as well as nurturing essential foundational skills such as adaptability, leadership and perseverance. Over time, a team that's been empowered through thoughtful delegation becomes more self-sufficient and confident in handling complex challenges independently.

Additionally, delegation stimulates ownership and accountability, which are key drivers of personal and professional growth. When individuals are trusted to make decisions, they're more likely to invest in their work fully and take pride in the outcomes they achieve. This sense of ownership they develop deepens their commitment to the team's success and effects a more engaged and motivated workforce. It also reduces how dependent they are on their leader for every decision, which allows team members to develop leadership qualities by taking on significant responsibilities.

Finally, delegation promotes a culture of continuous learning and development. As team members take on new challenges regularly, it creates a group attitude of embracing learning from both successes and setbacks. This culture encourages innovation, adaptability and long-term sustainability – which are vital traits in today's fast-paced environments.

The power of delegation in managing rebellious behaviour

Delegation is often viewed as a tool for distributing tasks, but one of its more subtle powers lies in the creative ways it can be applied to resolve complex leadership challenges. A skilful leader can use delegation not only to manage team members' workload but also to address authority and disciplinary issues within a team. One such example comes from the world of cricket when former England captain Nasser Hussain demonstrated the power of delegation to manage a rebellious force within his team.

As captain of the England cricket team, Hussain faced a delicate problem with one of his top players: Graham Thorpe. Hussain shared the story that Thorpe, who's known for his talent on the field, repeatedly broke the dress code during team functions. Hussain, as captain, was caught between two competing priorities: he didn't want to reprimand one of his best players too harshly, thus risking a disruption in team morale, but he also couldn't afford to let this disregard for rules undermine his authority – especially in front of the junior players.

Rather than resorting to punishment or allowing the behaviour to continue unchecked, Hussain skilfully found a solution through delegation. He handed responsibility for setting the dress code to Thorpe himself. In doing so, Hussain gave Thorpe ownership of the problem, subtly reinforcing accountability without damaging their relationship. Naturally, once Thorpe was in charge of setting the dress code, he adhered to it.

This creative use of delegation not only solved the immediate issue but also preserved Hussain's authority as captain. By placing Thorpe in a position of responsibility, Hussain ensured Thorpe's compliance while allowing his star player to maintain his dignity and autonomy. This approach also sent a message to the rest of the team about accountability and leadership, and without the need for a heavy-handed reprimand.

The story illustrates how delegation can be a powerful tool for handling a range of challenges beyond simple task distribution.

LEVEL 2: CHAPTER 6 – DELEGATION

Leaders who understand the dynamics of their team can use delegation to empower individuals, resolve conflicts and maintain authority in subtle but effective ways. In Hussain's case, delegating the dress code decision to Thorpe transformed a potentially disruptive situation into an opportunity for growth, which reinforced team cohesion and their respect for leadership.

Delegation, when applied thoughtfully, can solve far more than just workload issues. It can be a strategic leadership tool for managing personalities, fostering accountability and maintaining harmony within a team – all while safeguarding that a leader's authority remains intact.

Avoiding the pitfalls of unskilled delegation

While delegation is a powerful tool, it can backfire if not done thoughtfully. Poor delegation can lead to confusion, frustration and inefficiency within the team. As discussed in *Chapter 1: Self-Awareness*, leaders must be mindful of their own tendencies toward over-delegation or under-delegation, both of which can stifle growth and performance.

Over-delegation occurs when leaders offload too many tasks without providing sufficient guidance or support (usually when they jump directly from stage 1, directing, to stage 4, delegating). This can leave team members feeling overwhelmed and unsupported, which can potentially cause burnout or errors. On the other hand, under-delegation happens when leaders fail to trust their team, which results in micromanagement, stifled creativity and missed opportunities for development. Both approaches undermine the team's ability to grow, and it can prevent the kind of self-reliance that's necessary for long-term success – particularly when external recruitment is limited and internal development is essential.

In organisations where talent development is vital for maintaining competitiveness, it's even more important to avoid these pitfalls. Poor delegation can create bottlenecks in the workflow and erode the sense of autonomy and trust that's essential for high-functioning teams. To avoid these issues, leaders must strike a balance by providing clear instructions, setting realistic expectations and offering the resources necessary for success.

Techniques for effective delegation

Effective delegation requires a thoughtful, structured approach. Here are several techniques that can help leaders delegate more effectively:

- » **Define the task clearly:** Leaders must make certain the task is well understood by the team member, with specific goals and outcomes defined. This is crucial for avoiding misunderstandings and guaranteeing everyone is on the same page.

- » **Match tasks to a team member's strengths and stage:** Effective delegation necessitates understanding the unique strengths and weaknesses of each team member and assigning tasks accordingly. Delegating tasks that line up with both an individual's strengths and their stage of development ensures they're more likely to succeed.

- » **Provide support and resources:** Delegation doesn't mean abandoning the task. Leaders must make sure their team member has the tools, resources and support they need to complete the task successfully. This includes guiding them when needed but avoiding micromanagement.

- » **Follow up regularly:** Delegation isn't a 'set it and forget it' approach. Leaders must regularly check in on progress, offer feedback and adjust the course if necessary. This engenders accountability and keeps the team member on track.

- » **Allow autonomy:** Trust is essential in delegation. Leaders must give the team member the autonomy to complete tasks in their own way, while still being available to offer guidance if needed. This empowers the team member and fosters a sense of ownership.

Using delegation experiences to become a better team member

The act of delegating tasks as a leader teaches valuable lessons, not just about managing others but also about how to handle tasks delegated to you. By reflecting on what you've appreciated – or not appreciated – when delegating, you'll gain insights that can improve your own approach as a team member. Understanding how delegation works from both perspectives allows you to contribute more effectively and cultivate better collaboration when tasks are assigned to you.

One key element is *communication of changes*. Clear communication is essential when delegating tasks, particularly if there are any significant shifts in direction or expectations. When a task is delegated to you as a team member, it's equally important to ensure you stay in close communication with those doing the delegating, especially when the project scope changes. Keeping everyone informed builds trust and safeguards alignment.

The need to be *ruthless with deadlines* is another important takeaway. As the delegator, you know the importance of meeting deadlines and how it affects a project's overall progress. When you're assigned tasks, make sure you're equally committed to hitting their deadlines. If you foresee any issues in meeting them, communicate this early so adjustments can be made without disrupting the workflow.

Regular updates – even brief ones – are a habit worth cultivating. You may have experienced how helpful it is to receive consistent updates on a project's progress when you delegate, so be sure to do the same when you're handling delegated tasks. Brief but regular check-ins keep everyone heading in the same direction and prevent misunderstandings.

Another lesson learned from delegating is the importance of *seeking clarity before a project goes too far*. If you've ever delegated a task, only to find it was completed incorrectly due to miscommunication, you understand how costly that can be. As a team member, make sure you return for clarification when necessary, especially before making significant decisions that could impact the outcome. This avoids wasting time and makes certain that the work meets expectations.

An often overlooked but critical aspect of delegation is *removing ego from the situation*. As a leader, you'll have learned that success isn't about personal recognition but about the team achieving its goals. Applying this lesson when tasks are delegated to you means you're open to feedback, not precious about your role in the project and focusing on delivering the best result rather than protecting your own ideas.

You must also *understand your delegation preferences*. If you appreciate autonomy when you're given tasks, you should recognise that others may expect the same when they delegate to you. Conversely, if you prefer to receive guidance and have regular check-ins, don't hesitate to ask for it when needed.

As a leader, you need to *respect other people's priorities*. Sometimes, delegated tasks aren't the only things on your plate, and you need to keep this in mind when tasks are assigned to you and therefore communicate if competing priorities may affect your ability to meet deadlines.

Just as you expect *flexibility* when delegating tasks under changing conditions, you must apply the same mindset when you're delegated tasks. Team members being *adaptable* helps the team stay cohesive and productive in dynamic situations.

Your experiences as a delegator can provide valuable insight into how to handle tasks more effectively when tasks are assigned to you. By being proactive in your communication, respecting deadlines, seeking clarity and staying flexible, you contribute to a smoother, more-collaborative working environment. Ultimately, these practices help you become a more reliable and effective team member.

CONCLUSION

Delegation is an indispensable leadership skill that transcends the act of assigning tasks. It serves as a catalyst for growth, accountability and sustained success within an organisation. When approached with care and strategy, delegation empowers team members to develop their skills, take ownership, and foster a culture of trust and resilience. For leaders, it creates the space for them to focus on higher-level priorities while enabling team members to expand their potential and confidence.

Effective delegation requires a thoughtful approach that's tailored to the competence and commitment of each individual team member. Frameworks such as Situational Leadership demonstrate how leaders can adjust their delegation style to provide the right balance of guidance and autonomy. By recognising the unique strengths and developmental needs of each team member, leaders can foster a sense of ownership that drives both individual and collective success.

This practice isn't solely about task distribution; it builds a stronger, more-capable team that's prepared to tackle future challenges. Leaders nurture innovation and accountability by allowing individuals to make decisions, solve problems and learn from their experiences. Over time, this process transforms team members into confident contributors and prepares them for greater responsibilities.

In organisations facing challenges such as limited recruitment pipelines, delegation becomes a strategic tool for cultivating internal talent. Providing opportunities for growth and development helps leaders to ensure their teams are adaptable and self-sustaining. This not only strengthens the team's capacity but also reinforces a culture of continuous learning and improvement.

Delegation is as much about leadership as it is about trust and empowerment. It positions leaders to achieve more focus and impact at the same time as equipping teams with the tools to thrive. Through skilful delegation, leaders can create an environment in which everyone contributes to success, which drives long-term progress for individuals, teams and the organisation as a whole.

7
Creating Advantages

In leadership, every situation presents both problems and opportunities. Both are real, but the key to effective leadership is choosing to focus on the truth that's most helpful to your team at any given moment. This chapter explores how leaders can develop the ability to see both sides of a situation, and then choose to focus on chances to inspire progress, motivate teams and turn challenges into opportunities.

Skilled leaders aren't those who avoid or dismiss problems; they're the ones who acknowledge the difficulties but choose to focus on the potential within them. This ability to reframe challenges separates good leaders from great ones. It's not about ignoring reality; instead, it's making the conscious decision to focus on solutions rather than being disempowered by obstacles. By seeing opportunities where others see setbacks, leaders can gain an advantage where others struggle and falter.

Finding the advantage in challenges is a skill that can be developed, just like any other leadership skill. It involves acknowledging both the problem and the opportunity within every challenge, and then focusing on the actions that drive growth, resilience and innovation. By building on foundational leadership skills – self-awareness, responsibility, communication and team development – leaders can create an environment in which challenges inspire curiosity and creativity, which transforms problems into catalysts for progress.

By the end of this chapter, you'll have discovered ways to lead your team through difficult situations by recognising the opportunities for growth hidden within every challenge. You'll learn how to focus your team on solutions, which empowers them to see adversity as a chance for innovation and progress, and this will ultimately enhance your ability to lead with resilience, adaptability and vision.

The dual reality: Problems and opportunities in every situation

In every leadership scenario, both problems and opportunities coexist. The reality of a situation is rarely all positive or all negative, and balanced leaders recognise both. Acknowledging problems is essential for addressing weaknesses or risks, but dwelling on the problem too much can paralyse or demotivate the team. On the other hand, focusing solely on opportunities without addressing the problems can engender failure due to a lack of preparedness. A skilled and balanced leader can step back from their initial reactions – whether that's fear, frustration or excitement – and see the bigger picture. They acknowledge both the difficulties and the potential solutions, which enables them to have a balanced mindset as they guide their team through uncertainty.

For example, a team might be handed a challenging (even unreasonable) last-minute deadline, which is obviously a problem. But within that problem lies an opportunity: the chance to improve processes, discover new efficiencies or prove the team's ability to work under pressure. Both realities exist simultaneously, but the most helpful truth is the one that focuses on what can be learned or gained from the situation.

LEVEL 2: CHAPTER 7 – CREATING ADVANTAGES

In this scenario, a skilful leader might also communicate to their team the long-term benefits of rising to the occasion. Meeting deadlines repeatedly – no matter the challenges – builds the team's reputation for reliability and excellence. This reputation often leads to the team being entrusted with high-priority tasks and more high-profile assignments, which in turn opens doors for individual promotions and enhances job security. The leader's ability to frame the situation as both an immediate challenge and a pathway to better opportunities can inspire the team to approach the task with energy, purpose and a shared sense of ambition.

In addition, it's important to appreciate that – in many leadership contexts, particularly when working with line managers or senior leadership – it's rarely necessary to draw attention to the fact there are obstacles or difficulties in a project. This is typically assumed to be the case. No project or plan is without its share of hurdles, and it's human nature to identify the problems rapidly. For this reason, leaders who immediately point out the barriers they're facing, but without proposing solutions, are unlikely to stand out from the crowd.

A professional leader understands that identifying problems* is simply step 1 – everyone sees the difficulties. What sets a good leader apart is the ability to move quickly through the process from problem identification to solution-seeking. When a team is facing challenges, it's far more helpful to shift the focus on to solving those problems. Leaders who can maintain momentum by proposing actionable solutions demonstrate not only their capability but also their resilience and readiness to lead in tough situations.

It's worth noting that some individuals possess an exceptional and vital skill set for identifying potential problems before they arise. This ability is highly valuable to a team's success and shouldn't be mistakenly labelled as 'negativity'. (We'll explore this further in Chapter 11: Team Dynamics). There's a distinct difference between identifying problems – so as to move on to solutions – and dwelling on them.

Golden opportunities (problems)

What truly separates a great leader from a good leader is their ability to go one step further: not only identifying solutions but seeing the potential advantages hidden within the challenge. This critical skill will set you apart from your peers. Rather than merely overcoming a problem, skilful leaders find ways to leverage said problem for the benefit of the team or organisation. They understand how challenges can align with the deeper *why* of the team or organisation; that is, its core purpose and driving motivation. Whether it's a learning experience, a chance to develop an individual's skill set, or an opportunity to galvanise a team and strengthen cohesion, great leaders tie their actions to this fundamental purpose. (We'll explore the importance of a team's *why* further in *Chapters 11: Team Dynamics* and *13: Culture Creation*.)

For example, imagine a band that's facing a last-minute issue with their equipment not working. This is an undeniable problem as it prevents them performing their usual polished set. However, their *why* for performing live is to give their fans unique and memorable experiences. Bearing this in mind, the band moves quickly to a creative solution: delivering a stripped-back acoustic version of their set, including some rare songs that haven't been played for a long time or have never been heard before. While the problem itself hasn't been erased, the band has transformed what could have been a disaster into an opportunity to meet their purpose in an innovative and meaningful way. In doing so, they create a truly special moment for their fans – and one that both reinforces their commitment to their mission and showcases their adaptability under pressure.

Choosing to focus on the most helpful truth

In leadership, choosing which truth to focus on is a powerful decision. While it's vital not to ignore the reality of problems, it's far more helpful to ask, 'What opportunities are here, and how can we use them?' This choice empowers leaders and their teams to take control of the situation, thus shifting from a mindset of limitation to one of possibility. Rather than becoming immobilised by obstacles, leaders who choose to focus on opportunities will inspire action and creative problem-solving. By deliberately shifting focus to the opportunities present in any given situation, leaders open the door to inventive solutions and empower their teams to take action. Moreover, a leader who's relentlessly positive and consistently seeks advantages where others see problems or find reasons to complain will stand out and have a significant advantage. Developing this mindset requires resilience, flexibility and a proactive commitment to uncovering opportunities in every situation.

For example, consider a scenario in which budget cuts are on the horizon. The problem is immediately obvious, but a leader who focuses solely on the constraints might stifle any chance for positive outcomes. Instead, asking, 'What can we do within these new limits?' might help a leader to discover opportunities to streamline processes, rethink spending priorities and even foster innovation under pressure. This shift in focus doesn't lessen the challenges, but it does transform the situation from one of limitation to one of possibility.

A compelling illustration of this principle can be found in *The Power of Full Engagement* by Jim Loehr and Tony Schwartz.[20] They present the example of someone on their way to a job interview who gets a flat tyre. In one version of the story, the interviewee blames the world for their terrible luck. Flustered and angry, they struggle to change the tyre, get covered in oil and arrive at the interview discouraged, already believing the opportunity is lost. They focus on what could have been and let the situation dictate their mindset.

In the second scenario, the interviewee takes a different approach. While recognising the inconvenience of the flat tyre, they focus on the opportunity within the problem: the chance to stand out. They change the tyre with minimal fuss, arrive at the interview composed and use the story of overcoming this challenge to differentiate themselves from the other candidates. The situation hasn't changed – the flat tyre is still a reality – but the mindset shift transforms the outcome. Instead of dwelling on their misfortune, they focus on what they can control and use the situation to their advantage.

This example illustrates an important reflection that applies to leadership as well. The interviewee who stood out didn't just overcome a challenge; they tied their actions to their *why*. Their purpose wasn't merely to attend an interview; it was to demonstrate their ability to stay calm under pressure, maintain a great attitude and show they could deliver in difficult circumstances. In this way, leaders who consistently align their actions with their *why* – their team's purpose or values – can turn obstacles into opportunities for growth and progress. The reality is that both truths exist, but focusing on the opportunity is what enables forward momentum and growth.

This mindset of choosing opportunity over limitation separates amazing leaders from those who simply manage. It's not about denying that the obstacles exist, but is about using those obstacles as stepping stones toward progress. By consistently making the choice to seek out and act on opportunities, leaders not only overcome challenges but also create new pathways for success.

Reframing problems as opportunities for growth and security

While problems can seem overwhelming, they often contain the seeds of opportunity. Leaders who excel at turning problems into opportunities understand that each setback is an invitation to rethink, redesign or rebuild in a better way. The act of reframing – which is looking at the same situation from a different, more constructive perspective – allows leaders to direct their teams through challenges with resilience and creativity.

A key barrier to this mindset is the natural human desire for perfection and quick success. Our ego and emotions innately crave situations in which everything goes smoothly and we meet our goals swiftly and without any setbacks. As leaders, when things are going well and there are no challenges, we usually feel successful and secure. Our team seems to be functioning perfectly, and we believe we're in control, our leadership is strong and everything is safe.

However, this sense of security is an illusion. In reality, there's no true success without struggle. If everything feels too easy, it likely indicates we aren't growing, and without growth, we won't be achieving anything of meaningful value. Growth comes from overcoming obstacles, and without facing and embracing challenges, our sense of success is fragile. Problems and struggles build resilience, creativity and strength in teams and leaders alike. If we find ourselves in a seemingly problem-free environment, it's a sign we're in our comfort zone, which means we're probably stagnating.

Additionally, even when things are running smoothly, it's inevitable problems will arise. It's a natural part of any process – whether that's in leadership, business or life. Our mindset often leaps to 'If only I were better,' 'If only my team were stronger' or 'If only circumstances were fairer, then this wouldn't be so hard.' But deep down, we know this isn't true. Every leader, every team and every organisation faces struggles, and no matter how skilled you are or how prepared your team is, challenges will come. The idea that success can be achieved without difficulties is an illusion our minds create to avoid discomfort. However, real progress isn't made when things are easy; it occurs when we rise to the occasion, time and again, and use the challenge to drive improvement.

True freedom, success and security come not from avoiding problems but from developing the mindset that aids you in facing challenges head-on with a positive attitude. The most successful leaders don't just walk toward difficulties – they do so with a smile, knowing each obstacle presents a chance to grow, strengthen their team and refine their strategy. This approach builds confidence and resilience, not only in the leader but within the team and the organisation as well.

For example, imagine a situation where several of your team's key support staff are promoted to assist another team that's struggling. This change creates an immediate problem: your team is now under-staffed, so it's more difficult to meet the high standards you've consistently achieved. Many leaders in this situation would be tempted to push back, due to feeling the strain of fewer resources and higher pressure. However, within this problem lies a powerful opportunity: the chance to adapt your leadership, find new efficiencies and help solve a widespread issue your line manager is likely facing across the organisation.

When your line manager delivers the news, they probably expect resistance or frustration from you, as they've most likely faced this reaction elsewhere. It would be easy for you to respond by focusing on the downsides – the challenges of losing key staff members, the impact on your team's ability to hit targets and the potential for morale to drop – but you could choose a different path instead. You could focus on the opportunity hidden in the challenge and respond with gratitude and a positive outlook. For example, saying, 'Thank you for giving these members of my team this opportunity. They're absolute professionals and thoroughly deserve the promotion. Having fewer people on the team will certainly add a degree of challenge, but we're a strong team, and I'm confident we'll come up with a solution for maintaining the high standards we've set. We're all grateful to have the chance to step up for the wider organisation. We pride ourselves on being a team that solves problems and can be relied upon.'

This response not only reflects your ability to handle the immediate challenge with grace and composure, but it also demonstrates your commitment to the greater good of the organisation. You've reframed the problem – understaffing – as a chance to adapt, support the larger team and build resilience within your own team. You've also positioned yourself as a leader who can face difficult circumstances and find ways to thrive.

Contrast this with another team leader who reacts differently when faced with the same situation. They might respond to their line manager with frustration: 'Without those staff members, we'll likely miss all our targets. This will make it harder to retain the rest of my team, and I'll need to change every rota, which will only create more problems. I'm sure even more issues will come up, and I'll struggle to keep the team functioning effectively.' While this leader's reaction to the problems caused by losing key staff is understandable, their focus on the negative aspects of the situation does little to inspire confidence or offer solutions. They've highlighted what will go wrong, but they haven't demonstrated an ability or willingness to find a path forward.

Now, ask yourself this: *Which leader is more likely to receive additional resources if they ever request them moving forward? Who's more likely to gain influence in decision-making? Who'll probably enjoy better job security and be considered for the next promotion?*

The leader who embraces the opportunity and focuses on the organisation's problems – rather than just their own – is far more likely to be considered a valuable asset to the company. They'll be trusted to lead through adversity, make tough decisions and maintain high standards, even when faced with challenges.

Your response in moments of pressure defines your leadership. Leaders who can face these challenges head-on, with positivity and creativity, are the ones who both secure the resources they need and position themselves for future opportunities and promotions.

Ultimately, a leader who embraces this mindset not only grows personally but also elevates those around them. Their team learns to face challenges with courage, knowing they have a leader who sees every problem as a pathway to further success. This shift in perspective – from fear of failure to the excitement of possibility – sets outstanding leaders apart from the rest. Such leaders – who can smile as they walk toward the fire, and who turn every challenge into an opportunity – are the ones who create lasting success for themselves, their teams and their organisations.

HEALTH WARNING: BALANCING PROBLEM RECOGNITION WITH OPPORTUNITY FOCUS

One of the biggest challenges in leadership is balancing the need to identify problems while focusing on opportunities. Problems must be addressed; ignoring them can cause bigger issues down the line. However, too much focus on the problem can stifle progress and demoralise the team. The key to effective leadership is striking the right balance by acknowledging the realities of the situation while steering the team toward what can be achieved.

This balance is directly tied to *Chapter 3: Relationships*, in which strong leaders build trust by being transparent about challenges while maintaining an optimistic vision for the future. Teams respect leaders who are open and honest about the difficulties they're facing but they're equally inspired by those who focus on what's possible and motivate them to keep moving forward.

As a leader, maintaining this balance is also crucial for preserving your integrity and your team's respect. If you're blindly or disingenuously positive, pretend challenges don't exist, or downplay the seriousness of problems, you risk losing your team's trust. Over time, this erosion of trust can make it nearly impossible to communicate effectively or gain your team's commitment in a meaningful way. Team members will begin to feel disconnected from reality and may perceive you as out of touch or untrustworthy. Without trust, it becomes difficult to lead, inspire or get your team to buy into your vision.

Instead, as a skilled leader, you clearly and honestly acknowledge the challenges you're facing, presenting an accurate picture of the difficulties at hand. This transparency is essential for maintaining the trust and respect of your team. However, the vital next step is to pivot the conversation quickly toward 'Where's the opportunity here?' By providing a path forward, you help the team see that while the challenges are real, so are the opportunities. The focus is shifted from what's going wrong to what can still be achieved.

This approach keeps the team solution-focused and engaged, which turns potential stagnation into forward momentum. Leaders who can strike this balance – acknowledging the difficulty while providing a vision for what's possible if the opportunity is seized – are the ones who inspire commitment, foster trust and maintain the respect necessary for long-term success. By offering your team both honesty and hope, you create an environment in which challenges are seen not as roadblocks but as opportunities to grow, innovate and excel.

The Kilter Problem-to-Opportunity Framework

This framework is a practical and helpful guide for leaders looking to turn challenges into opportunities. By following these steps, you can shift your mindset, inspire your team, and transform obstacles into pathways for growth, innovation and success. The **Kilter Problem-to-Opportunity Framework** provides a structured approach to navigating difficult situations while keeping focused on your team's purpose – their *why*:

1. **Acknowledge the reality of the problem**
   - Recognise that every situation has both challenges and opportunities.
   - Avoid dismissing or ignoring the problem; instead, definitively identify the difficulties involved.

2. **Reframe the challenge against your team's purpose**
   - Shift your mindset from 'this is a setback' to 'this is an opportunity'.
   - Ask yourself how this challenge relates to your team's purpose or *why*.
   - Determine the potential advantages or lessons this challenge could generate that reinforce or move your team closer to fulfilling their purpose.
   - Identify the motivators linked to your team's purpose – whether it's delivering exceptional value, creating meaningful impact or achieving a shared goal.
   - Link the challenge to your team's purpose and then determine how the opportunity within this challenge can strengthen the team's alignment with that purpose.
   - Use the problem as a chance to innovate, strengthen processes or build team resilience, all while making certain that meeting the challenge becomes a meaningful step toward achieving your collective *why*.

3. **Balance problem identification with being solution-focused**
   - Don't dwell on the problem excessively, as it can demotivate the team.
   - After acknowledging the issue, quickly pivot to discussing actionable solutions.
   - Maintain a transparent approach that builds trust while steering the focus toward positive outcomes.

4. **Communicate constructively**
   - Be honest with your team about the challenges, but frame the conversation around the possibilities and how addressing the issue is in line with their purpose.
   - Inspire confidence by presenting a well-defined vision of how the team can overcome the issue and emerge stronger.

5. **Involve the team in finding solutions**
   - Foster a collaborative approach by encouraging team members to brainstorm and contribute ideas.
   - Highlight the team's strengths and past successes to boost morale and engagement, tying these back to their purpose so as to reinforce their sense of ownership and motivation.

In leadership, challenges often appear to be setbacks, but a skilful leader knows how to reframe them as opportunities for growth and innovation. Here's an example in which a sales team faces disappointment from losing a high-profile contract, only to be reassigned to a low-profile job with limited immediate rewards.

EXAMPLE IN PRACTICE: BIG OPPORTUNITIES IN LOW-PROFILE JOBS

1. **Acknowledge the reality of the problem**
   The team leader gathers the team to openly acknowledge they've lost the high-profile contract and been assigned

a low-profile job. The leader validates the team's disappointment by recognising the situation's emotional impact and financial implications.

Leader's message:
'I know losing this contract hurts, and I share your frustration. The job we've been given doesn't seem exciting at first glance and doesn't have the immediate financial rewards we were aiming for. But let's look at this together and see what we can build from here.'

2. **Reframe the challenge against the team's purpose**
   The leader shifts the conversation by reframing the challenge in a way that aligns with the team's *why*.

   Leader's actions:
   - Reinforces the team's purpose: becoming the most innovative and impactful sales team in the company.
   - Connects the situation to the team's deeper motivators: gaining recognition and raising the standard for how work is done.
   - Frames the low-profile job as an opportunity to demonstrate how the team's innovation and dedication can elevate even the most routine tasks, thus creating something remarkable that lines up with their purpose.

   Leader's question:
   'Let's remind ourselves why we're here: to illustrate this team can set a new standard for excellence. How can we take this low-profile job and make it a showcase for our purpose? If we turn this into something extraordinary, we're not just proving ourselves but we're also building the kind of reputation that aligns with who we are and what we stand for.'

3. **Balance problem identification with being solution-focused**
   Rather than dwelling on the lost opportunity, the leader encourages a solution-focused mindset.

Leader's approach:
- Acknowledges the immediate challenge: the job has less financial incentive and lower visibility.
- Pivots to actionable solutions: redesigning how low-profile jobs are approached to create greater efficiency, profitability and client satisfaction.
- Frames the work as a way to demonstrate how the team's values and purpose can drive excellence, regardless of the assignment.

Leader's message:
'This is our chance to evidence that our purpose – which is to excel and lead the way – applies to every task we tackle. If we succeed here, we can reshape how the company approaches these jobs, gain recognition and create opportunities for everyone on the team.'

4. **Communicate constructively**

The leader frames the situation positively, thus inspiring the team with a clear vision of success.

Leader's communication:
'I believe in this team and our ability to turn any challenge into an opportunity. This isn't just about completing a job; it's about reinforcing who we are, what we stand for and how we exceed expectations. Let's take this challenge and make it something the company will remember and aspire to replicate.'

5. **Involve the team in finding solutions**

The leader encourages collaboration by inviting the team to contribute ideas on how to do the job innovatively and effectively.

Team collaboration:
- Brainstorm ways to improve the client experience and streamline processes, all of which are in line with the team's purpose.

- Identify creative ways to measure success metrics and showcase them for this job.
- Leverage the team's past strengths and accomplishments to inspire confidence in their approach.

Team's input:

'Why don't we treat this like a flagship project? We can document what works, create a playbook and present it as a case study that shows how our team's purpose drives success, even in routine tasks.'

6. **Leverage the opportunity for growth**

    The team executes the job with a focus on excellence, innovation and setting a benchmark. They document their successes and challenges, thus creating a model for handling similar jobs in the future.

    Potential outcome:
    - The job becomes a success story within the company.
    - The team's innovative methods gain attention from senior leadership.
    - Their work influences how low-profile jobs are approached company-wide, elevating the team's reputation and providing new opportunities for recognition and reward.

    Leader's reflection:

    'By aligning this job with our purpose and tackling it with creativity and excellence, we've proved what our team can achieve. This success positions us as innovators and leaders who are ready to take on bigger challenges and make a lasting impact on the organisation.'

Despite the team's initial frustration, their leader applies the Kilter Problem-to-Opportunity Framework to turn the situation around. By reframing the challenge in line with the team's purpose and leveraging the task's potential, the leader transforms the low-profile job into a showcase of excellence, which sets a new benchmark for the organisation. This example illustrates how a proactive and purpose-driven leadership approach can turn obstacles into pathways for more success.

CONCLUSION

Successful leadership is defined not by the absence of challenges but by how leaders respond to them. The ability to transform problems into opportunities is one of the most valuable skills a leader can develop. This mindset doesn't deny difficulties exist; instead, it acknowledges them while focusing on the possibilities they present. Leaders who embrace this perspective inspire their teams to rise above obstacles and create solutions that drive innovation and growth.

Focusing on the opportunities within challenges requires both self-awareness and strategic vision. Effective leaders recognise setbacks are inevitable, but the way they frame those setbacks shapes their team's response. By balancing being transparent about challenges with a forward-looking attitude, leaders can foster trust while keeping their teams motivated. This balance allows for a solution-driven environment in which every obstacle becomes a stepping stone for progress.

The key lies in developing the skill of reframing. Leaders who shift their focus from limitations to possibilities will unlock the potential within their teams and organisations. For example, when resources are constrained or goals seem out of reach, reframing the situation as an opportunity to innovate or streamline processes can energise a team to discover new ways of working. This approach builds resilience, which is a highly important trait for achieving long-term success.

Additionally, through involving their teams in the problem-solving process, leaders cultivate a culture of collaboration, ownership and accountability. When individuals feel empowered to contribute, they become more engaged and motivated, which turns adversity into a shared journey of growth.

8
Turning Work into Results

Success in leadership is measured by how effectively your efforts translate into two distinct aspects: **results** and **reputation** (or leadership '**currency**'). Results are the tangible outcomes of the work of you and your team – sales, project milestones or key achievements – while reputation reflects the trust, integrity and influence you cultivate. While these aspects develop naturally over time, they require deliberate attention to ensure opportunities are maximised and potential isn't wasted.

Results and reputation are interconnected but not interchangeable. Strong results usually enhance reputation, but a strong reputation doesn't always guarantee better results. Leaders who aren't intentional in aligning these dimensions risk undermining their own efforts by achieving results without building trust or influence, or by cultivating reputation without delivering the tangible outcomes that matter to stakeholders.

This chapter focuses on the craft of transforming effort into meaningful results while building and sustaining reputation. It will also address the common pitfalls, such as inadvertently eroding the currency gained through hard work. With the right skills, leaders can avoid these traps, and balancing both aspects creates a lasting impact and safeguards that their leadership efforts will drive meaningful and sustainable success.

Success aspects
Aspect 1: Results

Results are the tangible evidence of a leader's effectiveness. They validate your efforts and provide clarity on whether your goals are being met. In organisational contexts, results are often the primary indicators of performance, whether that's hitting sales targets, delivering projects or achieving KPIs.

At its core, generating better results as a leader is simple: it hinges on your ability to identify and focus on the actions that deliver the biggest impact. Although leadership involves navigating complexities, the foundation of success often lies in one straightforward principle: *selecting the right actions and doing them well.*

This is where the **80/20 rule** – or the Pareto Principle – comes into play. This rule suggests that 80% of your results will come from just 20% of your actions. For leaders, this means the majority of your team's success hinges on a small number of highly impactful efforts. Identifying and prioritising these key actions is the critical skill for turning effort into results.

The process begins by analysing your goals and asking, 'Which one or two actions will drive the most-significant tangible outcomes?' Once identified, these actions must receive the most emphasis, resources and focus from you and your team. Channelling energy into these high-impact areas will help you deliver meaningful outcomes with greater efficiency and clarity.

This section will explore how to consistently identify those essential actions, bring them into line with your objectives and ensure they're done effectively. It's not about doing more; it's about excelling at what matters most. Through this deliberate focus, leaders can transform effort into consistent, measurable successes.

LEVEL 2: CHAPTER 8 – TURNING WORK INTO RESULTS

The most crucial skill for generating results lies in selecting high-impact actions: the efforts that deliver the best outcomes with the least wasted energy. Being able to focus on what truly matters sets the foundation for success. However, achieving results isn't solely about making the right choice; it also necessitates a range of supporting skills and practices. From learning from excellence to setting clear objectives, optimising processes and measuring progress, each step plays a vital role in turning effort into measurable achievements. Together, these skills make certain that teams not only meet their organisational expectations but also demonstrate their capabilities and leadership effectiveness. The following actions comprise a structured approach to delivering meaningful results consistently.

Example 1: Leader A – A leader who selects the most effective action

Leader A takes the time to analyse the situation and identifies the single most impactful action to address their team's challenges. Instead of defaulting to traditional methods or spreading their resources too thin, they focus all their team's efforts on the one area that will yield the best results. For example, when facing low customer engagement, Leader A prioritises improving the customer onboarding experience – a high-leverage point that quickly boosts customer retention and satisfaction. As a result, their targeted approach leads to significant, measurable improvements, which reinforces both the team's effectiveness and Leader A's reputation as an impactful leader.

Example 2: Leader B – A leader who works hard but chooses the wrong focus

Leader B invests just as much effort as Leader A, but they fail to evaluate which actions will truly make an impact. Instead, they default to traditional areas of focus – such as launching a new marketing campaign – without assessing the impact they've had in the past. Despite their hard work, the campaign generates little return as it fails to address the core issue of customer retention. Leader B's results fall flat, frustrating the stakeholders and highlighting the risks of prioritising the wrong actions, even when devoting significant effort to them.

Selecting the action that will have the most impact – rather than defaulting to what has been done before or what *should* work – may sound simple, but it's a critical leadership skill that takes time and deliberate effort to master. This skill requires being able to assess situations objectively and think strategically, as well as having the courage to focus on what will truly drive meaningful results. That said, it isn't the only factor needed to turn your team's efforts into tangible achievements. A range of other leadership skills, from setting clear objectives to optimising processes, all play their part in ensuring your team's hard work translates into measurable success.

Here's a list of the supporting skills a leader can develop to drive results:

- **Learn from excellence:** Study teams, organisations or individuals who are excelling in the areas where you want to improve. Analyse their methods, identify transferable strategies, and adapt their best practices to your unique challenges and context.

- **Select high-impact actions:** Identify and prioritise the actions most likely to deliver the results you aim to achieve. Approach this with humility and creativity, recognising that, while imitation provides a foundation, true innovation often requires breaking new ground and tailoring solutions to your specific circumstances.

- **Set clear objectives:** Ensure your team understands what success looks like and what metrics will measure it.

- **Optimise and monitor processes:** Streamline workflows and eliminate inefficiencies that can impede progress. Monitor the processes that will drive the selected high-impact action.

- **Measure progress:** Use data to track alignment with goals and identify areas for improvement.

- **Celebrate achievements:** Recognise and reward successes so as to sustain motivation and reinforce positive behaviours.

Each of these steps makes sure the team's efforts turn into measurable achievements. The results will not only meet organisational expectations but also serve as evidence of your team's capability and your leadership effectiveness.

> **EXAMPLE IN PRACTICE: USING NUDGES TO INCREASE PARKING TICKET COMPLIANCE**

Parking ticket compliance has long been a challenge for municipal authorities, with many individuals delaying or neglecting payments despite repeated reminders and the risk of escalating penalties. Historically, the default approach to addressing this issue relied on punitive measures, such as threatening fines, court actions or additional fees for late payment. However, these methods often yielded limited success, which causes persistent non-compliance and mounting administrative costs.

Learn from behavioural science. Researchers in behavioural science, including insights shared in *Nudge* by Richard Thaler and Cass Sunstein,[21] observe that encouraging people to pay their overdue parking tickets requires more than just threats of penalties or escalating fines. Instead, they recognise that tapping into *social norms* – the idea that people are heavily influenced by what others are doing – could drive better compliance:

» **Select high-impact actions:** To address low compliance rates, the focus shifted from punitive measures to strategies that leveraged subtle psychological cues:

- *Social norm messaging*: Letters were redesigned to include statements such as 'The vast majority of people in your city pay their parking tickets on time.' This framed timely payment as the social norm.

- *Highlighting positive behaviour*: The message concentrated on what others were doing right, rather than reprimanding non-compliance.

» **Key leadership takeaway:** By understanding and leveraging human behaviour, the team behind the parking ticket compliance nudge demonstrated the importance of prioritising *high-impact, low-friction actions*. This approach underscores how leaders can align processes with behavioural insights to achieve extraordinary results efficiently and sustainably.

HEALTH WARNING: THE CRITICAL SKILL OF BALANCE

Leadership success depends on a delicate balance between process and outcome. Leaders who focus too little on results risk failing to deliver in competitive environments, while those who fixate solely on outcomes often undermine their ability to achieve them with integrity. The ability to generate results isn't a by-product of luck but a deliberate skill that demands effort, creativity and balance.

Achieving results effectively comes from identifying the most impactful actions that lead to your target and converting those actions into processes that can be executed consistently at both the team and individual levels. Without this balance, outcomes are either left to chance or pursued at the cost of ethical compromises, burnout or unsustainable practices.

As you read on, consider how bringing processes and outcomes in line can both drive success and foster a culture of integrity, focus and long-term impact. This section will guide you in mastering the art of turning impactful actions into repeatable systems that deliver consistent results with purpose and accountability.

Process vs outcome:
The leadership balancing act

Leaders often face a dilemma: should they concentrate on the steps that drive success (**process**) or the final measures of success (**outcomes**)? This balance is not only foundational to turning work into results but also essential across the Kilter Leadership Taxonomy.

The ability to bring process and outcome focus into line is particularly crucial at the higher levels of leadership, where strategic decisions require foresight, adaptability and a nuanced understanding of priorities.

Understanding process and outcome

To navigate this balance effectively, leaders must first understand the difference between the two:

- **Process** refers to the controllable actions, steps and systems that build consistency and momentum. For example, a sales team may have a process that involves researching their client, rehearsing the pitch and then delivering it with authenticity.

- **Outcome** refers to the measurable results that validate success, such as quarterly revenue targets, which demonstrate the sales team's effectiveness.

Paying too much attention to one at the expense of the other creates risks. Over-focusing on outcomes can lead to short-term thinking, burnout and ethical compromises. Conversely, over-focusing on processes may result in a lack of either urgency or alignment with organisational goals.

EXAMPLE IN PRACTICE: MASTERING PROCESS AND OUTCOME

The balance between process and outcome becomes clearer when considered through relatable scenarios:

The golfer

A process-focused golfer concentrates on a few key elements – remembering their hand position as a physical anchor, practising controlled breathing to relax their muscles, and visualising a smooth, full swing of the club. This mastery of controllable elements makes it more probable they'll achieve a specific score (outcome).

The teacher
A process-focused teacher designs clear and well-thought-out lessons, engages pupils effectively, and communicates new learning through modelling and questioning. This mastery of these controllable elements makes it more probable their pupils will achieve high scores (outcome).

These examples highlight the importance of managing both the journey and the destination. Leaders who prioritise process ensure their teams build habits and systems for long-term success, while a focus on outcomes keeps everyone consistent with the overarching goals.

If this approach seems soft or lacks the edge needed to gain results, it's been misunderstood. Consider the outcomes for both the golfer and the teacher if they spent their time fixating solely on the score at the end of the day or the test results their pupils might achieve, respectively. Every success and misstep – whether real or perceived – could have a massively destabilising effect, which causes erratic performance and unnecessary stress.

Now contrast that with the results of 100 holes or 100 lessons in which, regardless of external pressures or context, these two consistently focused on excelling at their processes. Over time, it's far more probable that their outcomes would not only improve but also remain higher and more stable. Mastering the process creates resilience, which allows individuals to navigate challenges without losing sight of the actions that ultimately drive success. This balance of process and outcome is the foundation for sustained excellence.

Aspect 2: Reputation or currency – building trust and influence
Although getting results may secure your role in the short term, *currency* is what sustains and amplifies your leadership impact over time. Currency reflects the trust, respect and credibility you develop as a leader who consistently delivers and acts with integrity.

Building currency requires paying attention to three key components:

1. **Integrity:** Acting in a way that's consistent with your values and organisational principles, even under pressure.
2. **Consistency:** Delivering reliable results over time and fulfilling promises.
3. **Empathy:** Building trust through meaningful relationships and understanding your stakeholders' needs.

Leaders who build currency gain influence in their organisations and teams. They can leverage this trust to advocate for resources, to secure autonomy, and to inspire loyalty and commitment. For example, a leader who's consistently exceeding targets while fostering trust is more likely to gain decision-making authority and navigate organisational challenges effectively.

Results and currency: Interdependence in leadership

Results and currency often intersect, thus reinforcing each other in effective leadership. Tangible achievements validate your efforts and establish credibility, while having strong currency allows you to secure resources and opportunities for future success. However, any currency achieved without integrity is unsustainable. Leaders must ensure the currency they build is in line with their values and serves their team and organisation authentically. Cutting corners or pursuing short-term wins at the expense of trust undermines leadership in the long term.

Instead of relying on *false* currency – including charm, charisma, shared interests or playing on valued traits such as delivering difficult messages or being a loyal sounding board – leaders should focus on producing real results. Although these traits can help foster rapport and respectful relationships, using them solely to gain promotions or responsibilities beyond your skill set risks failure and erodes trust. When performance falters, the superficial currency that led to the advancement disappears rapidly, often leaving behind damaged credibility and strained team dynamics.

As a leader, aim to deliver *real* currency by prioritising competence, integrity and results over appearances. Promotions should come from genuine contributions, not superficial influence. This approach ensures lasting trust, sustainable success, and meaningful growth for both you and your organisation.

Finding real currency

While leadership currency is essential, it must be grounded in purpose to create lasting impact. Currency – your trust, reputation and influence – should align with your team's mission and values. Simon Sinek's Golden Circle framework offers a useful perspective, which emphasises the importance of focusing not just on the *what* (your results or reputation) but also the *why* (your larger mission or purpose).[22] For example, Apple's *what* may be creating innovative products such as iPhones, but their *why* is rooted in challenging the status quo and driving innovation.

Similarly, as a leader, your actions to build currency with your line manager – such as supporting initiatives, delivering consistent results or offering valuable insights – should go beyond serving immediate needs. Instead, these behaviours should contribute to shared goals and be in harmony with the broader organisational purpose. When currency is used manipulatively – such as leveraging trust or influence solely for personal advantage – it undermines both the relationship and the team's cohesion. While such tactics might yield short-term gains, they wear away trust over time and create the perception of self-interest, which ultimately damages your reputation and limits growth opportunities.

Real leadership currency isn't about quick wins or self-serving moves. It's about consistently demonstrating integrity, aligning your efforts with shared objectives and fostering trust that benefits the entire team. By keeping your actions tied to a clear sense of purpose, you make certain that your currency builds sustainable success rather than fleeting influence.

Two schools:
A tale of purpose and currency

The balance between *what* and *why* can significantly impact outcomes, as illustrated by the contrasting approaches of two schools with the same overarching purpose: 'To grow hearts and minds.'

School 1: Lost in the currency

In this scenario, the school becomes overly focused on *immediate* currency: test scores and academic metrics.

The pressure to achieve higher standardised test results leads to this:

» Narrowly focusing the curriculum on exam preparation.

» Teachers drilling students for scores, often at the expense of creativity and engagement.

» Students achieving high marks but lacking emotional intelligence, resilience and/or curiosity.

This relentless focus on the *what* causes the school's broader purpose to be overshadowed. Over time, both teachers and students experience burnout and disengagement, which undermines the very foundation of learning.

School 2: Using currency to serve the *why*

In contrast, the second school integrates its currency into its wider mission of holistic education. While test scores remain important, they're framed as part of a larger goal.

The school does the following:

» Teaches students stress management and emotional resilience alongside academic skills.

» Encourages teachers to develop their pupils' lifelong learning skills and habits.

» Views tests as opportunities for growth and for practice under pressure, rather than as final judgements.

This balance makes sure both academic success (the *what*) and the development of well-rounded individuals (the *why*) are achieved. The students do extremely well not just in exams but also in life skills, while the teachers remain engaged and motivated.

Monitoring and messaging: Shaping team culture

Leadership is as much about *what you monitor* as about *what you say*. What you choose to measure signals to your team what matters most, which shapes their behaviours and priorities. Monitoring the correct process is very often a high-impact action, as discussed in the results dimension, because it places focus on controllable elements that drive success. Most team members will respond to what's being monitored, regardless of their individual nature, which means skilfully selecting what to track is a critical area to develop as part of your leadership craft. Leaders choosing wisely can reinforce habits and systems that effect consistent, sustainable outcomes.

For instance:

- » **Monitoring only sales figures** may bring about the neglect of client relationships or long-term client retention.
- » **Monitoring time spent in the office** may prioritise visibility over productivity.

Leaders must strike a balance that guarantees their monitoring practices nurture sustainable and impactful performance at the same time as reinforcing organisational goals. What you monitor and reward will, brick by brick, become your team's currency and develop the culture of your organisation.

Selecting and building the right currency

Choosing the right currency is one of the most strategic decisions a leader can make. Results are often seen as the ultimate currency; however, focusing on the processes – the actions and behaviours under your control – can create a more sustainable pathway to success. Leaders can elicit and reward process-driven behaviours to foster long-term performance and trust.

LEVEL 2: CHAPTER 8 – TURNING WORK INTO RESULTS

The power of process as currency

Returning to processes – which are controllable and repeatable actions that maximise the probability of successful outcomes – then by focusing on process, leaders can do the following:

» Shift emphasis from unpredictable outcomes to controllable behaviours.
» Ingrain habits that lead to consistent success.
» Foster a culture of accountability and diligence.

Examples of process-driven currency:

» **Retail leadership**: A manager may emphasise behaviours such as greeting customers warmly and maintaining a positive attitude. By rewarding these actions, they create a culture of service excellence, which eventually effects stronger sales and customer loyalty.

» **Sales leadership**: A leader might prioritise consistent follow-ups, empathetic listening and personalised pitches. By celebrating these behaviours, they embed a commitment to customer care within the team.

The Walsh–McCullum approach: Let the scoreboard look after itself

Bill Walsh and Brendon McCullum revolutionised leadership in their respective sports by shifting their teams' focus from results to implementation. Walsh, a legendary coach of the San Francisco 49ers, and McCullum, a transformative leader in international cricket, both fostered cultures in which players valued staying present and delivering their best effort moment by moment, regardless of whether they were winning or losing. This approach alleviated pressure, built resilience and produced consistent success.

Walsh believed the most critical currency his players could generate was the flawless execution of their roles. Practices were meticulously designed to prepare players so thoroughly that they would perform instinctively under pressure. By breaking the game into controllable tasks – such as perfecting a quarterback's timing or a lineman's stance – Walsh redefined success as the mastery of process. He created trust by valuing discipline and preparation over short-term outcomes, which reinforced his mantra: 'The score takes care of itself.'[23]

McCullum applied similar principles in cricket, which empowered his players to back their strengths, even when the wider world labelled their style as risky. This approach enabled the players to bring a strong performance to high-pressure and seemingly hopeless situations on a regular basis. It also fostered an environment in which young or inexperienced players quickly and routinely came to excel on the world stage, showcasing their abilities with confidence and composure. By reframing high-pressure situations as opportunities to display their skills, rather than being threats, McCullum encouraged his team to value execution above all else, thus creating a culture that consistently delivered show-stopping results.

Together, Walsh and McCullum demonstrate that success stems from remaining present, trusting preparation and focusing on implementation. Celebrating disciplined effort rather than outcomes meant they fostered environments in which players could thrive, which proved in due course that results are the natural by-product of mastery in the moment.

Notably, neither Walsh nor McCullum were fully appreciated at the beginning of their respective tenures because their approaches challenged conventional wisdom and were often met with scepticism. Their personal fortitude to stay the course despite criticism was instrumental in transforming their teams and validating their methods over time, which highlights the resilience required to lead transformational change.

Key currency in Walsh and McCullum's leadership
Walsh's and McCullum's leadership philosophies revolve around identifying and developing key forms of currency within their teams.

This currency represents the values and behaviours they prioritised to drive success:

- » **Presence and focus:** Both leaders made it clear that the most valuable currency their players could generate was staying present and fully focused on their roles, regardless of the game situation.
- » **Mastery of execution:** Walsh and McCullum emphasised excellence in decision-making and executing skills, which shows that delivering consistently in the moment is the ultimate measure of success.
- » **Freedom to take risks:** McCullum fostered a culture in which players could take calculated risks and express their natural abilities, which made fearlessness a key currency in his teams.
- » **Resilience under pressure:** Both leaders reframed pressure as an opportunity to showcase skills, in which composure and adaptability were valued as essential team assets.
- » **Commitment to preparation:** Thorough, disciplined preparation was a non-negotiable currency for both Walsh and McCullum, which made certain their players were ready to act under any circumstance.
- » **Trust and accountability:** Both leaders built trust by valuing discipline, consistency and individual responsibility, which made these attributes integral to their teams' respective cultures.
- » **Process-oriented success:** Celebrating progress and process in preference to immediate outcomes instilled a deep understanding that success was a by-product of effort and discipline.

Selection as a reflection of currency

Within their teams, the selection of players who would participate in a game/match soon required the currency outlined previously. Their players understood that earning and keeping their place demanded both technical skills and their commitment to presence, execution, preparation and adaptability. This transformed their daily approach and embedded these values in their practices, preparation and games/matches. The resulting culture emphasised growth, discipline and accountability, which motivated players to excel and align themselves with team standards. This connection between selection and values fostered a shared purpose, which elevated their performance and enabled the teams to thrive under pressure.

HEALTH WARNING: AVOIDING THE PITFALL OF HUMILIATION

Building leadership currency takes time, effort and consistency, but it can be eroded in an instant through a moment of humiliation. Such moments – whether public or private, intentional or accidental – undermine trust, credibility and relationships. Leaders must remain vigilant against behaviours that would humiliate their team members, line managers or even themselves. Avoiding humiliation is not only about protecting reputations but also about maintaining a culture of mutual respect and accountability.

Here are some examples of actions that can humiliate others and erode leadership currency:

- » **Public chastisement or open disagreement:** Criticising someone harshly in front of others – whether it's during a team meeting, in front of clients or at a public event – damages their confidence and undermines their standing with others.
- » **Talking behind their backs:** Gossiping, criticising or questioning someone's abilities in conversations with others creates a toxic environment and shatters trust.
- » **Failing to meet deadlines:** Missing deadlines without prior communication or with leaving others to bear the brunt of the consequences signals a lack of professionalism and accountability, which can embarrass those reliant on you.

LEVEL 2: CHAPTER 8 – TURNING WORK INTO RESULTS

- » **Turning up late to meetings:** Habitual lateness, especially without explanation, demonstrates a disrespect for others' time and can publicly undermine the importance of the meeting or those leading it.

- » **Delivering on responsibilities poorly:** Producing subpar work reflects poorly not only on you but also on your team or manager, effectively publicly questioning their judgement in delegating tasks to you.

- » **Failing publicly:** Whether it's a major presentation, a key project or any visible responsibility, if you fail to deliver due to lack of preparation or effort, it embarrasses those associated with the task as well as you yourself.

- » **Engaging in scandals or questionable behaviour:** Behaviours that bring public disgrace – such as ethical violations, legal troubles or inappropriate conduct – reflect poorly on the entire organisation and humiliate those connected to you.

- » **Ignoring your team's or manager's input in decisions:** Overriding or dismissing their contributions without proper discussion can belittle their expertise and leave them feeling devalued.

- » **Displaying favouritism:** Showing undue preference for certain individuals or groups can alienate and humiliate others as it implies their contributions are less valuable.

- » **Deflecting blame on to others:** Shifting responsibility for mistakes on to team members or managers in front of others damages relationships and creates a culture of fear and mistrust.

As a leader, you must guard against these aforementioned behaviours by fostering respect, accountability and professionalism. Simple actions – such as providing discreet feedback, addressing disagreements diplomatically and taking responsibility for your own actions – go a long way toward preserving trust and leadership credibility. By avoiding the pitfall of humiliation, you ensure your leadership currency remains intact and the relationships within your organisation thrive.

Building leadership currency:
Demonstrating respect and accountability

The exact opposite of humiliating behaviours are deliberate actions that foster trust, strengthen relationships and enhance your reputation as a leader. To maintain and grow leadership currency, focus on creating an environment of respect, accountability and professionalism.

Here are some examples of behaviours that build and preserve trust and credibility:

» **Provide private and constructive feedback:** Offer feedback one-on-one in a supportive and solution-focused way. Ensure it's aimed at growth – not punishment – to maintain dignity and trust.

» **Speak positively about others behind their backs:** Praise and support your team members or line managers when they're not present, thus reinforcing their value and building their reputation.

» **Meet deadlines consistently:** Honour deadlines to demonstrate reliability and respect for others' work schedules, which ensures smooth collaboration and shared success.

» **Arrive at meetings on time or early:** Respect others' time by being punctual and prepared, which signals your professionalism and commitment.

» **Deliver high-quality work:** Exceed expectations by consistently delivering excellent results. This reflects positively on you, your team and your line manager, and therefore enhances everyone's credibility.

- » **Prepare and perform publicly:** Make certain any public-facing responsibilities, such as presentations or deliverables, are performed with due preparation and effort, which projects confidence and reliability.

- » **Model ethical and professional behaviour:** Conduct yourself with integrity and avoid situations that could bring shame or scandal to you or your organisation. Transparency and fairness engender trust.

- » **Acknowledge others' input and involve others in decisions:** Highlight and appreciate the contributions of your team members and manager in decisions, which shows you value their expertise and collaboration.

- » **Treat everyone equitably:** Demonstrate fairness and impartiality by giving all team members equal opportunities to contribute and succeed. This reinforces a culture of respect and inclusion.

- » **Take responsibility for mistakes:** Own your errors openly and use them as learning opportunities, thus showing humility and accountability. This fosters a culture of shared responsibility and continuous improvement.

These actions not only help maintain your reputation and leadership currency but also contribute to a positive, high-trust organisational culture. By treating others with respect and leading with integrity, you create a foundation for long-term success, collaboration and loyalty.

CONCLUSION

Leadership success is a dynamic interplay between tangible results and the intangible currency of trust, influence and credibility. Both are vital to sustaining long-term impact, but achieving a balance between them requires intention, focus and adaptability. The results demonstrate your effectiveness as a leader, while leadership currency determines your ability to motivate others, secure resources and maintain trust under pressure. Together, they create the foundation for impactful and sustainable leadership.

At the heart of turning effort into results lies the ability to identify and prioritise high-impact actions. The 80/20 rule reminds us that most results come from a small portion of our actions, which makes selecting and executing these efforts crucial. However, getting results isn't simply about focusing on the *what*. It also involves building the systems, processes and team culture that support long-term success. Leaders must monitor progress, celebrate achievements and adapt continuously to shifting priorities and challenges.

Equally important is the cultivation of leadership currency. This currency is developed through integrity, consistency and empathy – all qualities that inspire trust and foster collaboration. Leaders must safeguard their currency by avoiding actions that humiliate or erode trust, while also actively demonstrating respect, accountability and professionalism. Simple but deliberate actions – such as timely communication, fair decision-making and recognising others' contributions – can strengthen relationships and enhance influence.

Leadership is about balancing process and outcomes, aligning short-term goals with long-term purpose, and building an environment in which both results and relationships thrive. By focusing on the right actions and fostering trust through integrity, leaders can navigate complexity, drive performance, and leave a lasting impact on their teams and organisations. In doing so, they transform not just results but the very culture and potential of their leadership.

LEVEL 3

9
Managing Emotions

This chapter will concentrate on providing actionable information for you to develop emotional management skills in leadership. These strategies are built around three primary steps:

1. **Separation:** The ability to identify which part of your brain is in the driving seat. This involves recognising whether the **emotional system (E-system), rational system (R-system)** or **program system (P-system)** is influencing your response. Leaders who understand this can pause and assess whether their current reaction is in line with their values and objectives.

2. **Work through:** The skill of taking your emotional message and processing it in a constructive way. This step involves engaging with the reaction from the E-system, understanding its purpose, and working through it to ensure the actions taken are helpful rather than impulsive or counterproductive. By validating their emotional reaction without letting it dominate, leaders can maintain clarity and control.

3. **Plan and action:** The ability to develop a balanced plan that works for both your emotional and rational needs. This involves creating strategies that honour the input from the E-system while being guided by the R-system. The result is an action plan that's consistent with your values and long-term goals, which makes certain your decisions are sustainable, well-rounded and effective.

This chapter is designed to offer actionable advice on how to manage your emotions – and to support your team in doing the same. It provides a starting point for building emotional resilience and improving your leadership skills, but it isn't intended to offer comprehensive psychological guidance. Concepts such as simplifying the complexity of the brain's components into three primary systems are drawn from the work of Professor Steve Peters – including strategies such as separating your true self from yourself when influenced by your instinctive emotional system and using normalising and acceptance. This chapter features interpretations of that work; for a deeper and more detailed understanding, Professor Steve Peters' books *The Chimp Paradox*[24] and *A Path Through the Jungle*[25] are highly recommended. His frameworks provide valuable insights into managing emotions and making decisions effectively.

If you're experiencing issues with your mental health, it's crucial to seek professional medical advice. This chapter isn't intended as medical advice or a substitute for professional care. Emotional resilience and leadership skills are important areas for personal development, but they must be approached with the appropriate support when mental health challenges arise.

Stage 1: Separation
Understanding the three key systems of the brain

The human brain is one of the most complex and extraordinary systems in existence, and even the world's foremost neuroscientists are continuing to uncover new insights about its intricate workings. However, although we may not yet understand everything, we can focus on what's known and immediately applicable: how our brains influence our emotions, behaviours and decisions. By understanding the interplay of its three primary systems – the emotional (E), rational (R) and programmable (P) systems – we can better manage our emotions. In turn, this becomes one of our most powerful tools as leaders for supporting ourselves and our teams.

The three systems of the brain:

1. **The emotional system (E-system)**

   The E-system is our brain's first reactor, which rapidly evaluates situations to determine if they're a threat or an opportunity. Largely operating in our limbic system, it governs our immediate, instinctive reactions; these are driven by parts of the brain such as the amygdala, which processes fear, reward and other primal emotions. This system is extremely simplistic with a binary focus: to move us away from pain and toward pleasure. It triggers emotional reactions almost instantaneously, which often override more-nuanced thought processes, to prioritise immediate survival or comfort. None of the brain's systems can stop these emotional reactions, but they can be managed through effort and deliberate action.

   While this simplicity can be incredibly powerful – it triggers a range of emotional alarm reactions in milliseconds to protect us – it can also be limiting. The E-system's reactionary nature often takes over our thinking, which leads to impulsive decisions or overreactions. These emotions may feel like commands, but they aren't. No matter how urgent they seem, they're merely suggestions; that is, signals or alarms for us to notice, evaluate and consciously decide how to respond to them.

   Recognising when the E-system is in control is a vital first step in managing our emotions. Having this awareness allows us to pause, step back and engage other cognitive systems to make more considered decisions. Although the E-system plays a fundamental role in shaping our emotional nature (a concept that's explored further in *Chapter 1: Self-Awareness*), it's essential to understand its limitations and to develop strategies with reflective and intentional responses to balance its influence.

2. **The rational system (R-system)**

   The R-system resides in the dorsolateral prefrontal cortex and governs our logical, analytical and deliberate thinking. This part of the brain allows us to plan, reason and regulate our emotions. Unlike the E-system, the R-system operates more slowly, and it requires focus and effort to evaluate information and weigh outcomes.

   This system is crucial for responding thoughtfully to emotional triggers and making balanced decisions. Deliberately engaging the R-System during challenging situations helps us override impulsive reactions from the E-system, thus providing a sense of control and clarity.

3. **The programmable system (P-system)**

   The P-system is the brain's ability to remember information and to automate tasks and routines through repetition and habit formation. This enables us to function efficiently without consciously thinking about every action – for example, driving a familiar route or responding to daily challenges in habitual ways. Importantly, the P-system can be deliberately shaped by the R-system; this allows us to develop habits and behaviours intentionally that align with our goals and values. It's where we store our emotional and factual memory, but this may be inaccurate or limiting. This system interplay is foundational to how our character evolves around our nature (another topic studied further in *Chapter 1: Self-Awareness*). While this system helps conserve mental energy, it can also reinforce unhelpful patterns, such as reacting to stress with avoidance or frustration.

Consciously developing positive habits and emotional responses programs the P-system to serve us better, and this makes healthy behaviours automatic over time. Moreover, if we have responses planned or drilled for when our E-system is activated, we're far more likely to run those programmed routines. In contrast, if no plan or drilled response exists, our reaction can become chaotic and uncoordinated. Through deliberate practice and preparation, we can shape our P-system to respond effectively, even under pressure, which makes sure our habits and responses are in harmony with our goals, rather than defaulting to unhelpful or counterproductive patterns.

Why these systems matter in managing emotions

Understanding these three systems allows you to harness their strengths and address their limitations. The E-system offers rapid, instinctive reactions, but it needs oversight from the R-system to ensure those reactions are appropriate. However, the R-system sometimes acts slowly when its analytical functionality overcomplicates decisions or stifles skill execution. Meanwhile, the P-system facilitates automating emotional resilience and other behaviours through consistent practice, but it isn't infallible; it can be programmed with inaccurate, faulty or limiting information. When this happens, the P-system's outputs can negatively influence both the E-system's instinctive reactions and the R-system's analytical processes. By balancing these systems and recognising their vulnerabilities, you not only manage your emotions effectively but also model emotional intelligence for your teams.

Applying this understanding to leadership

When you manage your emotions with awareness of the E-, R- and P-systems, you cultivate a more composed and authentic presence that can inspire confidence and trust in your team.

For example, during high-pressure moments, you can do the following:

» **Recognise** when your E-system is in overdrive, pause and, where possible, engage your R-system to respond thoughtfully.

» **Reprogram your limiting beliefs and habits** through the P-system by developing patterns such as seeking feedback or practising mindfulness to reinforce calm responses.

» **Teach and support** your team in recognising their own emotional systems, and thus empower them to respond with improved self-awareness and resilience.

Mastering the separation of these three systems may take time, but even incremental improvements can transform how you lead, communicate and inspire others. Managing emotions isn't just a personal skill; it strengthens relationships, enhances decision-making and fosters an environment in which teams can thrive.

It's also important to recognise that no two natures or E-systems are the same. One person's E-system may be domineering and aggressive, which drives impulsive reactions; however, another's may be highly prone to control and organisation, which creates rigid patterns. The techniques or truths that work well for one person might hinder another. Although we can discuss the fundamental principles for managing our emotions, it ultimately requires personal practice and discovery to develop this skill set. It's through experimentation, reflection and adaptation that each leader can learn what works best for their unique E-system, which facilitates them leading with balance, authenticity and effectiveness.

Identifying who you want to be

This might sound woolly or soft, but this strategy is firmly rooted in neuroscience. One of the most crucial steps in managing emotions and making effective choices is knowing how you ideally want to be as a leader and as a person. This clarity is best guided by the R-system, which aligns your decisions with your long-term goals and core values. However, it's equally vital to deliberately program this ideal self-image into the P-system. If you neglect this intentional programming, your self-image is likely to be shaped unconsciously by your E-system, which often causes unhelpful or reactive patterns based on fear, insecurity or impulsive emotions.

Start by asking yourself, 'What kind of traits do I want to present to the world? Or what do I want my peers and competitors to say about me?' Perhaps you want to be patient, resilient, kind, assertive or reliable. These traits represent the ideal version of yourself – the *you* who reflects your values and inspires pride. Consciously engaging the R-system to clarify these traits and repeatedly practising behaviours that embody them will program your P-system to make these responses more automatic. This deliberate process ensures that, even in stressful situations, your actions are more likely to match with the person you aspire to be, rather than being shaped by the fleeting, instinctive reactions of your E-system.

The next step is programming ways to deliberately present yourself in line with your ideal traits, even when the pressure is on. This involves developing the ability to act consistently with your values, no matter what emotional or external challenges you face. As mentioned earlier, this task isn't easy; it requires you to overcome millions of years of evolution that means your E-system often takes control in high-pressure moments to guarantee your immediate survival, rather than long-term consistency with your values.

This deliberate programming is a skill, and like all skills, it improves with practice. By repeatedly engaging your R-system to choose responses that reflect your best self and then reinforcing those behaviours through your P-system, you can build habits that allow you to stay composed, deliberate and value-driven even in the most stressful situations. Over time, this practice transforms your reactive impulses into deliberate responses, which helps you lead with authenticity and emotional resilience, even under pressure.

Recognising traits you don't want to present

Something that's just as important as identifying the traits you want to embody is recognising the traits you sometimes exhibit that you don't want to show to the world. These are often behaviours that are driven by the emotional, impulsive side of the brain. Under stress, frustration or fear, this part of your brain can take over, which can cause you to act in ways you regret later. You might become impatient, defensive, overly competitive or even dismissive.

These emotional reactions aren't inherently bad; they're survival mechanisms designed to protect you. However, when left unchecked, this can cause you to react with traits you aren't proud of – such as anger, anxiety or impulsivity. The goal isn't to eliminate these emotional reactions; it's to manage them, so you can consciously choose to present the best version of yourself rather than reacting out of fear or frustration.

Ask yourself, 'What traits do I sometimes display that I don't want to?' For instance, do you come across as aggressive when stressed? Do you become overly critical when things don't go your way? Identifying these traits is the first step in managing them, which ensures they don't define your interactions with others or how you view yourself. By consciously projecting who you want to be – and recognising those traits you don't want to embody – you can harness the speed and energy of the E-system to reinforce positive behaviours. This deliberate focus not only prevents unhelpful patterns but also helps you find an authentic mindset that aligns with your values and long-term goals.

The power of choice:
Aligning with the you you're proud of

Before we delve into strategies for emotional management, it's vital to understand why emotions often take over. Our E-system, which is deeply embedded in our evolution, acts as an immediate warning system to protect us from danger. This system is much faster than the rational brain because, for millions of years, quick reactions were key to our survival. When our ancestors faced threats such as predators, their brains needed to respond immediately – whether by running, hiding or fighting. Pausing to rationalise, such as considering whether a tiger was hungry or aggressive, would reduce the person's chances of survival.

LEVEL 3: CHAPTER 9 – MANAGING EMOTIONS

In these situations, the brain instinctively shuts down the slower R-system and triggers immediate action by drawing on past experiences and memory to guide rapid responses. This explains why, even in modern times, our emotional reactions can override rational thinking when we feel stressed or threatened. Although this survival mechanism once protected us, it often leads to impulsive reactions today that conflict with our long-term goals and values.

A challenge for leaders is to recognise this process and learn how to re-engage the rational brain, even when emotions are trying to take control. Understanding this will allow you to begin to manage your responses and make choices in line with the best version of yourself.

More power of choice:
Aligning with the ideal situation you want to create

While it's critical to identify the traits you want to embody as a leader, it's equally important to define the ideal situation you want to create for yourself. For instance, your ideal situation might be to live a purposeful life in which you contribute meaningfully at work and come home to a family you love. By first identifying this overarching goal, you give yourself a clear destination to align your daily actions and decisions with. This clarity gives you a powerful reference point when navigating challenges or emotional reactions in the present moment.

Let's consider a common workplace scenario. You, as a leader, feel frustrated because you perceive your leader peers are receiving more praise than they deserve. This emotional reaction could easily derail your focus and create feelings of resentment or disengagement. However, by programming your P-system with a clear understanding of your ideal situation – living a purposeful life and contributing meaningfully at work – you can establish a response that's consistent with this vision.

For example, the program you create for your P-system might remind you that 'Others getting praise doesn't either diminish my ability to contribute meaningfully or move me further from my ideal situation. My ultimate goal is to contribute with meaning, and I can still take pride in my work, build positive relationships and focus on what I value most.' This mindset enables you to pause, remember your ultimate goal and reframe the situation constructively, which allows you to act in a way that supports your long-term objectives, rather than reacting out of frustration or insecurity.

A critical function of the P-system is its ability to activate your R-system when emotional triggers arise to make certain it takes the driver's seat. Unlike the E-system – which is limited to suggesting emotions and then fight, flight or freeze reactions – your R-system can create actionable plans to work toward your long-term goals. For instance, in this situation, your R-system might suggest that 'Even though they're getting more praise, I can still deliver on my key responsibilities and take pride in my work. I'll also make sure to praise my peers when they do well, because I want to be a good team player and contribute to a supportive environment. Furthermore, I'll take a moment to congratulate the one who's receiving the praise, as building lasting, meaningful relationships is far more valuable than trying to win petty competitions at every opportunity.'

Additionally, utilising the separation skill helps you identify not only the behaviours and actions that align with your ideal situation but also those that direct you away from it. Your E-system, if left unchecked, will often react instinctively, thus prioritising immediate gratification or defensiveness. However, deliberately programming your P-system empowers your R-system to guide your decisions and behaviour consistently toward your desired outcomes.

By repeatedly engaging your R-system to return to your ideal situation, you reinforce the behaviours and thoughts that move you closer to your aspirations. Over time, this practice transforms your emotional triggers – such as feeling undervalued – into opportunities to focus on what truly matters. This approach both helps you manage your emotions and strengthens your alignment with your long-term vision, which fosters resilience, focus and satisfaction in both work and life.

Stage 2: Work through
Key skills for managing emotional reactions

We'll examine four key skills that are essential for working through emotional signals and making deliberate, value-driven choices – particularly in high-pressure situations. These skills are often discussed in leadership and self-development circles, but they're rarely broken down into actionable, connected practices. By both focusing on them individually and understanding their interconnectedness, we can aim to provide practical strategies for building emotional resilience and self-control.

The skills we'll address include these:

» **Normalising the current situation:** The ability to normalise what's happening in the moment is vital for reducing emotional overwhelm. This skill involves acknowledging the reality of the situation without judgement, which allows you to approach challenges with a calm, composed mindset.

» **Personal acceptance:** Recognising and accepting what's within your control and what isn't. It involves letting go of the need to control every outcome and focusing instead on how you can respond in a way that matches your values and goals.

» **Gaining perspective:** Gaining perspective helps you to step back and see the bigger picture, rather than getting caught up in the intensity of the moment. This skill helps you prioritise what truly matters, which makes sure your decisions are thoughtful and in line with your long-term objectives.

» **Planning and selecting the most helpful action:** This involves identifying the most constructive way forward and taking deliberate, purposeful steps toward it. Having the ability to choose the best action under pressure ensures your responses are intentional and support your goals.

» **Translation – understanding and interpreting the E-system:** This skill involves breaking down and interpreting the E-system's signals or warning messages, which present as emotions. Without the ability to translate these emotions effectively, individuals often misunderstand their meaning. The resulting actions may fail to address the E-system's concerns, leaving the emotional warnings unresolved and perpetuating stress or frustration. Developing the ability to decode these emotional messages enables you to respond in a way that calms your E-system and supports a more effective and aligned course of action.

These skills may sound straightforward, but they're incredibly challenging to develop and even more difficult to execute effectively under pressure. We'll now discover how these skills can be practised, strengthened and applied in real-world scenarios, which will help you respond with clarity and purpose when it matters most.

Reframing normalising as a skill

The E-system is designed to react quickly, and it often perceives challenges, such as complaints or missed deadlines, as immediate threats. While this instinct was essential for survival in our evolutionary past, it can elicit overreactions in modern leadership situations. For example, a customer complaint or a missed deadline might trigger feelings of frustration or anger as the E-system interprets these events as personal failures or looming disasters. This is partly because the E-system starts with an idealised, 'perfect' image of how any given situation should unfold, and then it fires to bring our attention to any of the situation's aspects that deviate from this perfection.

Underlying this process is the role of the brain's error-prediction neurons. These neurons work by continuously comparing incoming information with our expectations. When the actual outcome doesn't match up with what we anticipated, these neurons generate an error signal to alert the E-system to potential issues. While this mechanism is invaluable for learning and adapting, it can also amplify minor discrepancies, which causes the E-system to overreact to deviations that are inconsequential in the bigger picture. By normalising the situation – reassuring ourselves that certain imperfections are routine and not threats – we can switch off these error-prediction neurons, which effectively calms the E-system and reduces its reactive responses.

Experience plays a vital role in helping us establish what's normal in any given context. Over time, we learn certain imperfections – such as occasional delays or critical feedback – are routine aspects of leadership and don't indicate failure. Developing the skill to pause, question and recalibrate expectations is both impactful and essential. By deliberately asking, 'Is this normal?' we can interrupt our E-system's reactive cycle, shift to the R-system, and establish a more realistic and productive perspective. This ability to step back, adjust expectations and focus on what truly matters enables leaders to respond with clarity and composure, rather than being driven by instinctive overreactions.

Consider the following scenarios:

- **Is it normal for customers to complain?** Yes, every business receives complaints; it's a part of serving people with diverse expectations and needs.

- **Is it normal for suppliers to miss deadlines?** Yes, external pressures, resource constraints and miscommunications make this a common occurrence.

- **Is it normal for leaders to feel nervous when faced with customer complaints?** Yes, it's natural to feel nervous because leaders care about the outcome and reputation of their organisation.

- **Is it normal to feel frustrated or angry when deadlines are missed?** Yes, unmet expectations naturally evoke emotional reactions.

Recognising the normality of these situations allows the perceived severity of them to be defused. Instead of viewing them as extraordinary problems, we can treat them as challenges to manage – which is something every leader faces and can handle. A crucial part of the normalising skill set is identifying your natural emotional reactions to situations. As discussed in *Chapter 1: Self-Awareness*, this depends on your nature: high-Red leaders will likely have strong, action-oriented emotional reactions; while high-Blue leaders may experience unsettled emotional signals whenever procedures or compliances are broken.

The key is accepting what your initial reaction from the E-system will naturally be, rather than resisting or judging it. This acceptance allows you to shift responsibility quickly to your P- and R-systems, which enables you to work logically through the emotional reaction and develop a constructive plan of action. By recognising and managing these initial impulses, leaders can avoid making unfiltered decisions driven by unchecked emotions and instead move toward effective, rational outcomes.

EXAMPLE IN PRACTICE: THE NORMALISING SKILL

Managing emotions rather than being controlled by them is often misclassified as a 'soft skill'. However, nothing could be further from the truth. The ability to manage your emotions effectively is one of the most powerful tools for achieving results and performing at the highest level. Good emotional management allows you to act with clarity, authority and intention, rather than reacting impulsively in ways that undermine respect and trust. We'll now look at an example where a leader demonstrates this skill by first establishing what's normal about the situation, then defining the desired outcome, and finally taking the most helpful action.

Imagine a scenario where a team member becomes dismissive and rude during a conversation. Their line manager initially feels anger rising, triggered by the tone and disrespect of the team member. Instead of reacting impulsively, the leader pauses and reflects on the situation. First, they ask themself, 'Is this normal?' They recognise that, although rude behaviour isn't acceptable, team members occasionally act out due to stress or frustration. Understanding this helps the leader normalise the situation, switch off their error-prediction neurons and reduce the emotional intensity, which allows them to approach it with composure.

Next, the leader considers the desired outcome of the interaction. They ask themself, 'What do I want to achieve here?' They realise their goal is to resolve the issue respectfully, remind the team member of their value to the team and, most importantly, address the behaviour constructively to avoid it recurring.

With this clarity, the leader chooses the most helpful action. Using a preprogrammed response, they say calmly and authentically, 'I understand you're upset, and I want to hear your concerns because your perspective matters. However, the tone of this conversation isn't constructive. Let's address the issue respectfully so we can work toward a solution. If this tone continues, there will need to be consequences.'

By approaching the situation this way, the leader focuses on de-escalating the conflict, reinforcing boundaries and addressing the behaviour in a productive manner. Importantly, the leader doesn't take the situation personally, as they recognise the team member's behaviour may stem from external frustrations rather than being a direct attack. This perspective helps the leader remain calm and intentional.

Had the leader followed their E-system and reacted with anger or defensiveness, the conversation could have escalated. This may have alienated the team member, eroded trust and damaged morale. Worse still, the rest of the team might have perceived the leader to be lacking emotional control, which would weaken their authority and the team's cohesion.

By normalising the situation, focusing on the desired outcome and taking thoughtful action, the leader ensures the conversation remains constructive. The team member – who's been reminded of their value while also being called out for their behaviour – is more likely to re-engage respectfully. As well as this approach resolving the immediate issue, it also strengthens the leader–team-member relationship and reinforces a culture of accountability and mutual respect within the team. Over time, this consistent approach is more likely to foster trust, clarity and a healthier team dynamic.

Shifting from reaction to acceptance and helpful action

Accepting events as normal helps reduce the intensity of the E-system's emotional reactions. This creates space for the R-system to assess the situation rationally and move toward constructive solutions. Additionally, being able to accept a situation is the first step in mastering a highly underrated yet invaluable skill: the ability to set an ambitious but realistic outcome, devise a rational plan and implement helpful actions consistently to achieve that outcome. Although this process may sound straightforward, it's an exceptionally challenging discipline to master. Being able to gain understanding and operate under pressure with such clarity and purpose is often overlooked in leadership development, but the advantage it provides can't be understated. Those who can consistently balance acceptance with proactive execution often excel as leaders who are capable of navigating complexity and achieving sustained success.

Here are some examples:

» **Customer complaints:** Instead of reacting defensively to a customer complaint, a leader can focus on empathising with their perspective, identifying the root cause and finding ways to improve future interactions.

   A leader might respond to their team like this: 'Customer complaints are part of the job; they're opportunities for us to improve. Let's focus on how we can address this respectfully and learn from it.'

» **Missed deadlines:** Rather than lashing out at a supplier or team member when a deadline is missed, a leader can calmly assess the factors that contributed to the delay and collaborate on a recovery plan.

For instance, saying, 'Missed deadlines are frustrating, but they happen. Let's understand what caused the delay and how we can adjust things to stay on track, so we can find a way to make this less likely to happen again.'

» **Nervousness in leadership:** Instead of seeing nervousness as a weakness, a leader can acknowledge it as a natural reaction to high-stakes situations. They can use it as a signal to prepare and focus their energy on leading effectively.

A leader might reflect on it like this: 'Feeling nervous shows I care about this situation. I'll channel this energy into staying calm and resolving the issue. All leaders feel nervous, but the successful ones work with it.'

The long-term impact of normalising and acceptance

The ability to accept and normalise challenges must be practised for it to become second nature. Like any skill, this takes time and deliberate effort. However, once it's ingrained in the P-system, this perspective gives leaders – and their teams – a significant advantage. It reduces emotional hijacks, enhances decision-making, and elicits a calm, bold, solution-focused approach to problems.

When leaders consistently model this mindset, it also shapes team culture. Teams learn to view challenges not as catastrophes but as manageable parts of their work. This builds resilience, trust and a shared focus on constructive action.

Expectation and acceptance: The role of perspective – fairy tale vs reality

A vital aspect of managing emotions is understanding how unrealistic expectations shape our reactions. Emotions often arise from expectations that are based on an idealised version of reality, or 'fairy-tale scenarios'. These expectations can set us up for disappointment, frustration or even anxiety when reality doesn't match our imagined outcomes. This disconnect occurs because the brain's error-prediction neurons – which are responsible for comparing expectations with actual results – generate a 'prediction error' when there's a mismatch. This prediction error is what triggers emotional reactions, such as frustration or disappointment.

For example, common fairy-tale scenarios might include these:
- All bosses should be gifted in every single area of leadership and have the time to get to know you personally.
- Every new team member should have a strong work ethic and a high level of intelligence.
- People will always treat you with respect and fairness.
- No one will be malicious or petty.

These expectations reflect an ideal world, but life is far more nuanced. Expecting perfection in leadership, colleagues or interactions often results in frequent prediction errors, which amplifies emotional distress when reality falls short. By recognising that people have strengths and weaknesses, and that not everyone will behave ideally, we can reduce these prediction errors and foster a more balanced response.

To manage your emotions effectively, it's essential to pause and ask yourself, 'Is my expectation realistic, or is it a fairy tale?' This reflective question helps recalibrate your expectations, which grounds them in reality and reduces the likelihood of disruptive emotional reactions arising. Adjusting your expectations to align them more closely with reality can decrease a situation's emotional charge and effect greater acceptance, minimising your brain's prediction errors.

There are steps and helpful actions you can take to integrate this perspective into your daily practice:
- » **Understand the value of struggles:** If your team didn't struggle with challenges, they wouldn't need a leader, and so your role wouldn't exist. Challenges aren't evidence of failure; they're opportunities for you to guide and add value. Reminding yourself of this reframes obstacles as a core part of leadership, rather than being an undue burden, which reduces the emotional reaction caused by unmet expectations.

» **Success is built on responses to mistakes:** Every successful project faces difficulties and missteps. Projects become successful not because they're flawless but because of how effectively teams respond to and learn from errors. Accepting this reality can help you manage your frustration when mistakes occur, and you can come to view them as a natural part of progress rather than a personal or team failing. This mindset recalibrates your expectations, which leads to fewer prediction errors.

» **Recognise the imperfection of people:** Everyone, including you is flawed and learning continuously. Team members will make mistakes, show occasional lapses in judgement, or require support in areas where they lack confidence. Recognising these human traits allows you to respond with empathy and patience, which engenders a collaborative environment and reduces the amount of emotional reactions triggered by unrealistic expectations.

» **Accept external uncontrollables:** Sometimes, factors outside your control will derail plans, such as unexpected market shifts, organisational changes or personal conflicts. Accepting that these situations are part of life enables you to focus on what you can control: your responses, adaptability and ability to influence outcomes positively. This acceptance mitigates the emotional impact of external unpredictability.

By regularly reminding yourself of these truths, you bring your expectations in line with reality, which minimises the emotional distress from the prediction errors caused by fairy-tale thinking. This perspective allows you to focus your energy on what truly matters: guiding your team through challenges, learning from difficulties and maintaining composure in the face of imperfection. Over time, these reflective practices foster resilience, emotional balance and better leadership effectiveness.

Embracing imperfection and flexibility

Jane McGonigal, in her book *SuperBetter*,[26] provides a practical tool for managing emotional states: a scale of 1–10 to assess how you're feeling, with 10 being good and 1 being bad. You're invited to rate your emotional state and then ask yourself this: What would make this feeling two points better? And what would make it two points worse? This exercise helps you to think practically about how to improve the situation and what might exacerbate it. It brings perspective and encourages you to identify actionable steps to either calm or improve your emotional state. An additional benefit of this exercise is that it helps you move from your E-system to your R-system. Shifting from the emotional to the rational system allows you to step back, process your feelings more objectively and think practically about the next steps. This deliberate transition aids you in channelling your emotional insights into clear, actionable strategies for managing the situation effectively.

Reality – expectations = happiness (and results)

Managing emotional disappointment and finding the advantages in reality needs you to be fully present in the situation as it is and to make the most of the opportunities available for you and your team. When you operate under a fairy-tale mindset, you risk facing emotional disappointment when reality doesn't meet those idealised expectations. Although aiming high is important, being overly optimistic or unrealistically negative can hinder you seeing both the best in a situation and the best path forward. Instead, by adjusting your expectations and being present, you reduce the unrealistic goals' emotional impact and open yourself up to more constructive opportunities.

Shifting to a reality-based mindset allows for personal and professional growth as it reframes challenges and setbacks as learning opportunities rather than failures. This fosters resilience and adaptability, which are key traits in leadership roles. In the end, managing these expectations comes down to asking, 'Is this helping?' If your expectations help you and your team approach challenges with positivity and enjoyment, then it's beneficial to continue pursuing them. However, if you have unrealistic expectations of yourself or others – which causes frustration, disappointment and lowered performance – then adopting a more realistic perspective will likely help you find balance, clarity and more-effective ways to move forward.

High expectations and ambitious targets are essential for achieving exceptional standards and ambitious goals. However, challenges arise when there's an unrealistic expectation – for example, that these goals will be straightforward to achieve or that accomplishing such ambitions won't involve significant effort and obstacles. Excellence is achieved by maintaining high aspirations while recognising and embracing the challenges involved in reaching them. We must couple our high expectations of what we're capable of with realistic expectations of the commitment, skill and persistence it will take to achieve them.

SCENARIO: MANAGING UNREALISTIC EXPECTATIONS IN THE WORKPLACE

When we're given an unexpected deadline, it's natural to feel frustration, anger or anxiety – which are all perfectly reasonable emotional reactions. However, without emotional regulation, these feelings could overwhelm us and cloud our judgement. Taking a moment to gain perspective can help recalibrate our rational response and clarify the actual level of challenge.

For instance, using a scale of 1–10, you might initially rate the situation as a 6 in terms of difficulty. You recognise that a lower rating, such as a 4, would apply if any team members were unexpectedly off sick or if there were technical issues that could disrupt the work. Conversely, an 8 might represent a situation in which you had designated, distraction-free time to focus on the task, or if you had additional support from a team member. This simple exercise serves two purposes: it not only helps to recalibrate your response but also identifies potential solutions. For example, if you realise that having time dedicated to the task would improve the situation, you could request that from your manager or carve out that time yourself.

This process highlights the dynamic interplay between your E-system and R-system. By recognising the emotion, grounding your perspective and considering practical solutions, you allow both systems to work together as intended. This creates a balanced response that keeps your emotions in check while also facilitating constructive action, which helps you to address the situation more effectively.

Accepting that obstacles are a normal part of any process allows you to focus on solutions rather than becoming emotionally overwhelmed by setbacks. Leveraging your skill of perspective enhances your emotional stability, which makes you far more effective as a leader and enables you to maintain morale within your team. By applying the skill of perspective, then as well as managing emotions, you're building resilience and equipping yourself to excel, both in the face of immediate challenges and over the long term.

Managing emotions through a perspective adjustment lets you embrace the realities of life and leadership. By recognising fairy tales for what they are and recalibrating your expectations to reflect the real world, you maintain emotional balance and remain focused on your goals. This skill set empowers you to navigate challenges with clarity, which keeps you on track for sustained success in the most-trying circumstances.

Emotions as helpful signals, not instructions

Another key skill to master is **emotional translation**. Emotions should be considered to be helpful signals rather than instructions we must follow. Models such as dialectical behaviour therapy (DBT) demonstrate that emotions such as anxiety, stress, sadness and shame are merely indicators, not problems to eliminate. Recognising these signals enables you to respond constructively, rather than reacting impulsively or suppressing them, which often amplifies their intensity and makes the message even harder to ignore.

Here's a breakdown of common emotional signals and what they might mean:

- **Anxiety:** Signals there are too many unknowns or risks in a situation.

- **Stress:** Indicates something overwhelming is approaching, which is often tied to workload or perceived capacity.

- **Sadness:** Reflects loss or potential loss.

- **Loneliness:** Highlights a lack of meaningful connection.

- **Envy:** Shows a desire for something others have, which reflects your personal aspirations.

- **Shame:** Indicates a misalignment between your actions and your values, which may cause issues with your group.

- **Guilt:** Signals a significant misalignment between your actions and your values, which may lead to you being removed from your group.

- **Fear:** Recognises a perceived threat to your safety or well-being.

- **Excitement:** Suggests an opportunity is forthcoming.

These emotions aren't problems to be eliminated but valuable sources of information. For example, anxiety often arises when there are too many unknowns, which signals there's a need for clarity or preparation. Stress indicates that something overwhelming is approaching and might require action to prevent you becoming overloaded. Fear is a direct response to a perceived threat, which implies there's a need for protection or caution.

By listening to these emotional signals and allowing your R-system to take the lead on planning, you create a more effective response. Addressing these emotions in a way that's consistent with your values also helps build trust between your emotional mind and your rational mind, which reduces the amount of emotional hijacks over time. Instead of reacting impulsively, you develop the ability to assess situations comprehensively and respond in a balanced, thoughtful way.

EXAMPLE IN PRACTICE: MANAGING ANXIETY VS STRESS

Let's apply this understanding to a real-world situation. Imagine you receive an email from your manager that simply says, 'We need to meet tomorrow.' This can trigger an emotional reaction, but it's important to assess whether you're feeling anxious or stressed:

- If you're feeling *anxious*, it might stem from uncertainty about the meeting. Anxiety thrives on unknowns, so in this case, the lack of information about the meeting's purpose is likely causing your emotional reaction. The solution for anxiety is to address the unknowns in a way that satisfies your E-system. For example, you could simply request an agenda or ask your manager for more context about the meeting. This small action reduces the ambiguity and helps calm your E-system by providing clarity.

- If you're feeling *stressed*, it could indicate that you're overwhelmed at the thought of another task or responsibility, particularly if you're already managing a heavy workload. Stress signals a need to get organised and feel prepared. In this case, the solution is to use the time available to gather any relevant information, organise your thoughts and ensure you can communicate unambiguously during the meeting. Preparing helps you feel more in control and better equipped to manage the meeting alongside your other responsibilities.

Taking a stress action to address anxiety

Let's assume you feel anxious about the manager's vague email and unsure about the meeting's purpose. Instead of addressing the *unknowns* by seeking clarification, you decide to spend hours preparing a comprehensive update on all your projects, gathering data and organising materials in case it's a performance review or presentation.

Outcome:

- You waste time and energy preparing for scenarios that may not even happen, which could intensify your anxiety.
- Your E-system remains unsatisfied because the root cause – *uncertainty* – wasn't addressed. You're still left wondering, 'What's this meeting about?'
- This could leave you feeling even more overwhelmed, drained and potentially unprepared if the meeting turns out to be about something entirely unrelated to what you prepared for.

Taking an anxiety action to address stress

Now imagine you're feeling *stressed* because your workload is already overwhelming, and the thought of another meeting feels too much. Instead of addressing the *workload* and *preparation*, you send an email to your manager requesting an agenda to reduce the unknowns.

Outcome:

- Although getting the agenda may reduce some uncertainty, it doesn't solve the real issue: *time pressure* and a *lack of preparation*.
- You still feel stressed because you haven't taken the necessary steps to organise your tasks or get ready for the meeting. This means that, in the meeting itself, you might struggle to communicate clearly or feel unprepared, which reinforces the stress.
- Your E-system remains on alert because you haven't taken action to manage the overwhelming workload that triggered the stress in the first place.

Not recognising the correct emotional signal can elicit ineffective coping strategies. If you mistake stress for anxiety, you might focus on gathering unnecessary information instead of reorganising your time. Conversely, if you confuse anxiety with stress, you may overwork yourself when the real issue is the situation's ambiguity. Misinterpreting these emotional messages not only leads to unhelpful actions but also causes the E-system to amplify the signal, effectively 'turning up the volume' to make the message clearer.

For example, if you feel anxious about an unclear project scope but interpret it as stress from your workload, you might respond by working harder for longer hours. Instead of alleviating the emotion, this action leaves the root issue – *ambiguity* – unaddressed. As a result, your E-system intensifies your anxiety, instigating greater discomfort, sleeplessness or even physical symptoms – all in an effort to push you toward resolving the real problem. Correctly identifying emotional signals allows you to address their root causes, guaranteeing a constructive response that keeps you aligned with your goals and values.

Stage 3: Plan and action

A successful plan begins with assessing the current situation accurately, envisioning where you need to be and identifying the steps that offer the highest probability of reaching that goal. The foundation of this process is *clarity*: seeing the situation as it truly is, free from emotional bias or wishful thinking. Once you have a clear understanding of your starting point and destination, your focus shifts to crafting a logical series of actions that bridges the gap between those points and prioritises the steps with the biggest potential impact.

This process is investigated further in *Chapter 10: Decision-Making Under Pressure*, which provides practical tools for managing complexity and uncertainty. However, the essence remains consistent: a well-crafted plan requires both realism and forward-thinking. By staying grounded in the facts while aiming for a defined goal, leaders can chart a path that lines up with their values and guarantees progress, even in challenging circumstances.

The referee's whistle

Research into penalty-taking has revealed that the time a player takes to respond after the referee's whistle significantly impacts their success rate. Players who rush to begin their run-up straight after the whistle – within 200 milliseconds – have a success rate of only around 57%. In contrast, those who pause, compose themselves and take more than a second to start their approach score over 80% of the time. This brief pause allows the player to focus and choose their own program of actions to run through, rather than impulsively reacting to the external cue of the whistle.[27]

We can use this as a powerful metaphor for managing our E-system. The referee's whistle is a signal – indicating they're ready – but it doesn't dictate the penalty-taker's next move. A skilled player recognises that, after the whistle, it's for them to define the terms of the kick. Similarly, our emotions act as the whistle that's signalling something requires attention. However, just as a skilled player doesn't react immediately, we don't need to follow the emotional command impulsively.

Instead, we can pause, recognise the emotional signal and choose how to respond deliberately by engaging our R-system to run our own program through our own P-system. This approach allows us to act intentionally in a way that's in line with our goals and values, rather than being dictated to by the immediate urgency of our emotions. By practising this skill, we learn to maintain our composure and control, even in high-pressure situations.

Process vs outcome in managing emotions

Throughout this book, we've considered a process versus outcome focus in various contexts, and now we'll turn to how it can enhance emotional management. Having an outcome focus means we're focusing on something that's always largely outside our control. For example, if we focus on the outcome – scoring a goal – this isn't in our control because the goalkeeper could save the penalty, even if we take a perfect shot. Our E-system is sensitive to, and therefore triggered by, concentrating on things outside our control. This makes us vulnerable to frustration or stress as we prepare to perform or execute a task. In contrast, having a process focus (for example, focusing on the process of running to the ball smoothly and striking it cleanly) grounds emotions in effort and personal responsibility, which fosters resilience through emphasising what we can control, such as: preparation, communication and decision-making. This mindset reduces emotional volatility, encourages reflection and sharpens objective improvements by valuing adhering to high standards of practice over external results. Shifting focus from outcomes to processes allows leaders to maintain composure, regulate their emotions more effectively, and guide their teams with greater clarity and confidence.

One key factor to consider is that when we're under pressure, our physical and mental states differ significantly from when we're first developing and practising a process. Under pressure, the brain and body engage stress responses, including heightened adrenaline levels, reduced access to rational thinking and increased emotional reactivity. This means that even the most well-designed process – which has been practised under calm conditions – may falter if we fail to account for the physiological and cognitive shifts that occur in high-pressure situations. Leaders must prepare proactively for this disparity by building strategies to bridge the gap between practice and implementation under stress. This might include simulating high-pressure scenarios during training, incorporating stress management techniques (such as mindfulness or controlled breathing) and simplifying processes so they remain executable even when clarity of thought is compromised. By acknowledging and planning for these physiological realities, leaders can optimise their ability to deliver effectively under pressure and thus guide their teams steadily and precisely, even in the most challenging circumstances.

We can better manage the disconnection between practice and performance under pressure by creating balance in either of two ways: increasing the pressure during practice sessions to better simulate high-stakes scenarios or reducing the pressure on 'game day' to align the scenario more closely with familiar conditions. More practically, leaders can create two distinct processes to navigate pressure effectively: a practical process and an emotional process. The practical process consists of a disciplined, step-by-step approach to maintain focus and adaptability in the moment. It structures your actions to ensure that, even in the midst of stress, you're anchored in procedures that free your mind to respond dynamically to unfolding situations.

On the other hand, the emotional process is designed to manage and lower your emotional state under pressure. This could include steps such as these: (1) setting your desired outcome to regain clarity, (2) normalising and accepting the situation to avoid overreacting, (3) separating reality from the fairy tale by letting go of any catastrophic or unrealistic thoughts, (4) stepping back to gain perspective using a scale of 1–10 (1 = not severe at all, 10 = extremely severe) to assess the severity of the situation, (5) identifying the most helpful next action, and (6) delivering that action with focus and presence. Combining a structured practical approach with an intentional emotional plan helps leaders build the resilience and clarity needed to perform at their best, even under intense pressure.

Although this plan includes more steps than might be practical to recall and implement under pressure, it illustrates the possible steps of an emotional plan. By experimenting with these elements in your own practice, you can refine and internalise the steps that work best for you.

Example 1: A footballer taking a penalty in a match

Practical process

1. **Position the ball properly:** Place the ball in a consistent position that you've practised during training, which anchors you in a familiar routine.

2. **Set your stance:** Position yourself at the same distance and angle from the ball you always use. Avoid overthinking or making last-minute changes.
3. **Visualise success:** Picture the ball hitting the exact target spot in the net.
4. **Execute the kick:** Focus entirely on your process – your approach, your contact with the ball and your follow-through. Trust the mechanics you've practised.

Emotional process

1. **Set your outcome:** Set your outcome as taking the best shot you're capable of, not actually getting a goal, as guaranteeing you'll score a goal is outside your control.
2. **Normalise and accept the pressure:** Acknowledge that the pressure is part of the game, and even the best players sometimes miss. This isn't life or death – it's just football.
3. **Separate the reality from the fairy tale:** Avoid imagining catastrophic outcomes or glory-driven expectations. Focus on the task at hand, not on the consequences.
4. **Step back for perspective and identify shifts:** On a scale of 1–10 (1 = not intense at all, 10 = extremely intense), assess how intense the moment feels (for example, it may feel like a 6). Then consider what an 8 would look like (for example, there could be less time left or there could be a bigger goal deficit) and what a 4 would look like (for example, a penalty during a regular league match). Recognising these shifts allows you to recalibrate your perspective and realise that, even though the moment is high pressure, your practical skill set and abilities haven't changed.
5. **Choose the next helpful action:** Focus on *executing your practical process,* not the *outcome.* For example, set your stance and visualise your success.
6. **Deliver with focus:** Clear your mind, relax and deliver.

LEVEL 3: CHAPTER 9 – MANAGING EMOTIONS

Example 2: A professional delivering a high-stakes pitch to an investor

Practical process

1. **Prepare your materials:** Ensure your slides, notes or any visual aids are organised and ready well before the pitch.
2. **Rehearse your delivery:** Practise key sections of your pitch, including opening remarks, closing remarks and anticipated questions.
3. **Set up your environment:** Arrive early to test any technology, organise materials, and familiarise yourself with the room or virtual set-up.
4. **Adapt where needed:** Be flexible if questions or interruptions arise, while relying on your structure to guide you back on track.

Emotional process

1. **Set your outcome:** Your goal is to clearly communicate your value proposition, not to guarantee the investor's decision.
2. **Normalise and accept the pressure:** Recognise that feeling nervous is normal and means you care about the outcome. Even seasoned professionals feel this way.
3. **Separate reality from the fairy tale:** Avoid imagining worst-case scenarios (for example, 'They'll think I'm incompetent') or overly romantic outcomes ('This pitch will change my life'). Stay grounded in what you can control.
4. **Step back for perspective and identify shifts:** On a scale of 1–10 (1 = totally insignificant, 10 = extremely significant), assess how significant the pitch feels (for example, it may feel like an 8). Then identify what a 10 would look like (for example, pitching to a global investor capable of transforming your company) and what a 6 would look like (for example, pitching to a smaller stakeholder in a less critical setting). This exercise helps you adjust your

perspective to recognise that, although the stakes are high, the situation is manageable.
5. **Set the next helpful action:** Go back to your practical plan. For example, focus on delivering the next section of your pitch with clarity and composure.
6. **Deliver with focus:** Take a deep breath, look directly at your audience and communicate your ideas one step at a time, as rehearsed.

Addressing both the practical and emotional aspects in tandem lets individuals in high-pressure situations implement their processes with greater composure and effectiveness, which improves outcomes while managing internal stress. Although these emotional-regulation skills may seem simplistic in theory, anyone who's tried to execute them under real pressure will know that applying them consistently is both challenging and transformative. As discussed earlier, when you become more overwhelmed, your E-system inhibits the functioning of your R-system, which can elicit impulsive reactions rather than making decisions thoughtfully.

This is precisely why the P-system is vital – it allows you to respond effectively under pressure. The more frequently and rigorously you run and refine these procedural routines, the more seamlessly they'll activate when needed, which generates consistent, composed actions even in high-stress situations. Your ultimate goal when delivering under pressure is to stay out of both your E- and R-systems by operating through well-rehearsed and natural P-system actions. This approach helps you maintain presence and control, allowing you to function at a high level without becoming overwhelmed or bogged down in excessive analysis.

When leaders deliberately practice high-pressure decision-making and emotional regulation, they strengthen specific neural pathways in their brains. This practice contributes to a process known as 'myelination': developing a fatty sheath around neural pathways, which improves the speed and efficiency of neural communication. However, much like when an athlete performs a skill for the first time, these emotional strategies may have little noticeable impact initially – or even after the first 10 attempts.

The key lies in commitment and deliberate practice. Over time, as these strategies are consistently trained in controlled or simulated environments, they become more natural and effective. This neurological refinement enables leaders to rely on their 'mental muscle memory', which facilitates automatic and composed responses during high-stakes situations. Through consistent effort, emotional regulation transitions from being a theoretical concept to being a deeply ingrained skill, which allows leaders to navigate stress with clarity, focus and resilience.

Mind-system dynamics:
How we can get our systems to work together

The roles of the three main systems in our brains – the E-system, R-system and P-system – have unique, conflicting and complementary functions. These systems are neither inherently good nor bad, nor are they categorically useful or not useful. Each has a specific role that, when managed deliberately, helps us handle emotions effectively and perform under pressure.

The E-system functions as a warning mechanism that alerts us to potential threats or the need for action. Once such an alert is triggered, the P-system executes preprogrammed responses to address the emotional warning and identify a practical course of action. These responses are established by the R-system, which builds them based on logical reasoning, alignment with goals and values, and a focus on long-term success. Depending on the E-system warning's level of emotional intensity and the P-system's programming, the R-system may step in to normalise the situation, thus bringing perspective and balance before any action is executed by the P-system.

It's crucial to understand each system's boundaries. For instance, the E-system shouldn't engage in planning or problem-solving, as it lacks the capacity for rational analysis. Similarly, the R-system must avoid engaging in detailed analysis during the skill-execution phase, as this phase is where the P-system – which is responsible for executing learned skills and automated processes – operates most effectively.

Like with any skill, managing these systems necessitates deliberate practice and effort. With time and focus, we can learn to manage these systems effectively, which enables us to operate with emotional intelligence and perform consistently under pressure.

CONCLUSION

Managing emotions is a foundational skill for effective leadership, which impacts decision-making, team dynamics and long-term success. Emotions aren't obstacles to suppress but signals to understand and harness. By recognising the interplay of the brain's E-, R- and P- systems, leaders can shift from reacting impulsively to offering intentional, value-driven responses. This self-management strengthens clarity, builds trust and fosters a calm, composed presence that inspires confidence in others.

The abilities to normalise situations, accept what's within and beyond our control, gain perspective, and identify helpful actions are practical tools that help reduce emotional overwhelm and focus on constructive outcomes. These skills may appear simple in theory, but they're challenging to master, which requires deliberate practice and consistent effort to apply them under pressure.

Unrealistic expectations, or fairy tales, can create emotional disappointment when they don't match reality. Adjusting these expectations and embracing imperfection allows leaders to respond to challenges with resilience and empathy, which fosters an environment in which performance and collaboration thrive. By programming the P-system with thoughtful questions, preplanned responses and realistic perspectives, leaders can establish habits that are in line with their long-term goals, even in high-pressure moments.

LEVEL 3: CHAPTER 9 – MANAGING EMOTIONS

Managing emotions isn't just about personal self-control; it's about creating a culture of accountability, calm and purpose. When leaders model emotional intelligence, they empower their teams to approach challenges with the same composure and focus. This builds trust, strengthens relationships, and cultivates an environment in which individuals and teams can perform at their best. By mastering these emotional skills, leaders position themselves and their organisations for sustained, meaningful performance and success.

10
Decision-Making Under Pressure

Making decisions under pressure is one of the most challenging yet vital aspects of leadership. Whether it's during high-stakes negotiations, under pressure from staff or to achieve tight timelines, leaders must often make informed choices with limited time and little support. Effective decision-making in such situations requires clear thinking, rational assessment and a structured process. This chapter delves into the dynamics of decision-making under pressure and offers tools such as the SODA (situation, options, decision, action) loop to guide leaders through such scenarios.

It's important to understand that pressure is a highly personal experience. What feels overwhelming to one leader might not faze another. For example, some may find a tough conversation or a conflict-resolution situation extremely stressful, while others navigate it more comfortably. The feeling of pressure is often shaped by individual experiences, emotional triggers and confidence in handling specific tasks. Leaders must recognise their own thresholds for pressure while knowing it manifests differently for everyone.

However, better decision-making under pressure not only leads to more-effective outcomes but can also prevent future issues that would consume additional time and resources. By making clear, well-considered decisions early on, leaders can avoid the cascading effects of rushed choices, which reduce the need to address avoidable crises later. This proactive approach frees up time for both the leader and the team, which allows them to focus on strategic initiatives rather than firefighting constantly. It also fosters a more sustainable work environment in which pressure is managed rather than perpetuated.

Leaders who are equipped to manage their emotions and biases in high-pressure situations are better positioned to prevent stress and uncertainty from clouding their judgement. In such moments, where emotions can easily take control, having the ability to regulate and respond rather than react is indispensable for making rational, balanced decisions. This reflective capacity enables leaders to pause, consider multiple perspectives, and make certain their choices meet with their immediate needs, values and long-term vision.

The realities of decision-making under pressure

We've looked deeper into how stress affects the brain and decision-making in *Chapter 9: Managing Emotions*, which also discusses strategies for mitigating these effects. However, it's important to note that research shows stress biases us toward 'safe' or habitual decisions, even when they're suboptimal; stress undermines real-time situational reassessment.[28] When an individual experiences stress, it disrupts the balance of systems in their brain and prioritises emotional reactivity over clear thinking. This imbalance can be advantageous in life-and-death situations, when quick, instinctive reactions are critical. However, in high-stakes decision-making scenarios that require careful thought and measured judgement, this shift can hinder reaching effective outcomes, which can lead to impulsive or emotionally driven choices.

This underscores the importance of managing stress and using structured approaches for decision-making. Employing tools such as the SODA loop lets leaders counteract the negative effects of stress and time pressure, which facilitates maintaining clarity and making decisions that are both thoughtful and contribute to their long-term objectives.

Key factors that cause pressure in leadership

The following are some key factors that put pressure on leaders:

- **Time constraints:**
  - Tight deadlines and urgency in decision-making.
  - Limited time to prepare for or respond to unexpected challenges.
- **High stakes:**
  - Decisions with significant financial, reputational or operational consequences.
  - Fear of failure or decision paralysis due to the potential impact.
- **Public perception:**
  - Scrutiny from stakeholders, teams or external audiences.
  - Pressure to meet expectations or maintain a specific image.
- **Problem complexity:**
  - Multilayered issues with no obvious solutions.
  - Balancing competing priorities and navigating ambiguity.
- **Team dependencies:**
  - Relying on team performance for critical outcomes.
  - Ensuring alignment and maintaining morale during high-pressure situations.
- **Unpredictability:**
  - Managing sudden changes, crises or unforeseen challenges.
  - Adapting plans without sufficient time or resources.

- **Others' heightened emotions:**
  - Dealing with heightened emotions such as anger, fear or frustration from team members, stakeholders or customers.
  - Navigating conflicts or emotionally charged situations while maintaining composure and focus.

The SODA loop:
A practical decision-making tool

The ability to perform under pressure is a vital leadership skill, and the capacity to make decisions swiftly and confidently can determine success or failure. In high-pressure situations, emotions often run high, which pushes leaders to react impulsively or focus only on immediate problems while neglecting potential opportunities. Yet every high-stakes decision presents both challenges and possibilities. A leader's task is to remain composed, evaluate both aspects, and make decisions consistent with their values and long-term objectives.

The SODA loop offers a structured approach that helps leaders stay grounded in rational thought, even when they acknowledge their emotional reaction. It provides a well-defined framework for navigating decision-making phases, particularly in high-pressure scenarios.

The SODA loop – which was inspired by the OODA loop (observe, orient, decide, act) developed by US Air Force Colonel John Boyd for rapid decision-making in dynamic environments such as air combat – brings a similar approach to leadership. The faster that leaders can assess a situation, consider options, make decisions and act, the more effectively they can outmanoeuvre challenges and seize opportunities.

Different natures react to pressure in distinct ways. For example, leaders who favour Red energy (associated with urgency and action) may feel compelled to decide quickly – sometimes at the expense of evaluating all options thoroughly. This can lead to impulsive decisions that prioritise immediate action over long-term consequences. In contrast, leaders who favour Green energy (focused on harmony and consensus) may hesitate while striving to find a solution that satisfies everyone, thus potentially delaying the necessary action. This is what makes self-awareness and knowing your natural preferences fundamental to developing your skill set under pressure.

The SODA loop helps balance these contrasting tendencies by providing a structured process that accommodates both urgency and perspective. It guides leaders through the course of evaluating the situation, exploring options, making decisions and taking action. Importantly, it recognises that, once a decision has been made, a new cycle begins that allows leaders to adapt and refine their approach continuously as they traverse dynamic situations.

Naturally, some decisions must be made in a split second, meaning instinct and experience are paramount. However, even in high-pressure situations, there are often moments – sometimes just five minutes – where pausing to apply this framework can make all the difference. The SODA loop helps leaders maximise every second available and makes certain that decisions are not only swift but also well-considered, which increases the likelihood of effective outcomes being achieved, even under intense pressure.

How to use a SODA loop

Situation: Identifying where you are, where you want to be, what path you're on and where it will take you

The first step in effective decision-making is to assess meticulously both your **current reality** and your **desired future state**. This involves looking honestly and objectively at your present circumstances – identifying both challenges and opportunities – while also clarifying your target outcome. At this stage, the goal isn't to solve the problem immediately or make a quick decision but to fully understand the gap between your current position and where you want to be.

Two key questions for this phase are 'Where are we now?' and 'Where do we want to be?' Establishing your current reality requires making an objective assessment without letting emotions cloud your judgement. This might involve evaluating your team's performance, available resources or the alignment of priorities.

This clarity provides a reference point for decision-making that will make sure every choice moves you closer to your desired outcome. Additionally, it moves you from your E-system to your R-system and reveals potential obstacles (such as resource limitations or misaligned goals) while highlighting opportunities (such as leveraging strengths or building strategic partnerships). By thoroughly understanding both the current situation and future goals, leaders can navigate decision-making with greater focus and effectiveness.

Once this is established, you've defined the **situation**.

Options: Generating possible courses of action

Once you've identified your situation and destination, the next step is to generate **options** to bridge the gap between the two. It's imperative not to limit yourself to a single solution or default to the first idea that comes to mind. Effective decision-making necessitates having at least two options, so you must explore multiple courses of action that can move you toward your goal.

Leaders should ask, 'What are the possible ways to move forward?' This phase encourages creative thinking to consider both conventional and unconventional solutions. It's equally important to evaluate what to avoid. Identifying potential risks and actions that could worsen the situation is as vital as comprehending the paths to success. Leaders must consider what the risks are and what outcomes they want to avoid.

A fast indicator of being trapped in reactive, emotional thinking is the perception that only two choices are available. This black-and-white thinking limits problem-solving. By generating several options and factoring in potential risks, you allow for a more comprehensive evaluation and also trigger your brain moving to its R-system. This ensures you are not reacting impulsively but are making more-informed decisions. Engaging your team in this process can also uncover hidden opportunities or overlooked risks. The best path forward often becomes apparent through thoughtful deliberation of the options and potential pitfalls.

In this phase, there's a need to balance the future with present challenges. Weighing the pros and cons of each option and recognising what to avoid gets you better positioned to choose a path that's heading toward your goal while sidestepping any actions that could hinder your progress. However, if the pressure stems from a time constraint, it's important to maintain a sense of urgency throughout this process.

Decision: Choosing the best path

After investigating your options, it's time to make a **decision**. This involves evaluating the risks and rewards of each course of action. Having experience in decision-making helps leaders recognise patterns and predict outcomes. However, in high-pressure situations, it's equally important to rely on data, analysis and trusted advisors. Effective decision-making should also account for balancing the results your team is aiming to achieve and the currency they're looking to generate – whether that currency is financial gain, team morale, innovation or customer trust. By aligning the decision with both tangible outcomes and the values driving your organisation, you can make certain it supports long-term success while addressing immediate challenges.

Leaders must balance speed with accuracy. It's often necessary to make decisions rapidly under pressure, but taking a moment to reflect on the risks and opportunities can prevent costly mistakes. Leaders should ask themselves this: 'What's the best course of action based on the available information? What are the potential consequences? And am I willing to accept those risks?'

The best option is sometimes the one that minimises risk while still advancing toward the desired outcome. Understanding both what you want to achieve and what you want to avoid helps you make a more balanced and more informed decision. Often, the final decision will be a combination of multiple options.

Action: Moving forward with confidence

Once a decision has been made, the next step is taking **action**. In high-pressure situations, this often needs to happen swiftly, but speed shouldn't come at the cost of precision or thoughtful execution. Leaders must ensure their teams are on board with the decision, along with everyone understanding their roles and responsibilities. Without clear direction, action can lead to confusion and wasted time, which ultimately jeopardises the desired outcome.

Implementation plays a critical role in achieving the desired outcome. A sound decision may still fail if it's poorly executed. For example, if an engineer decides to use a hammer to drive in a nail but damages nearby materials due to a lack of focus, the issue lies not in the decision to use a hammer but in its execution. This is a crucial distinction. Leaders must balance evaluating the quality of execution with humbly reconsidering the original decision if the outcome isn't achieved.

Skilled leadership acts decisively while remaining open to adjustments. The execution must be focused and competent, and leaders should accept accountability for both the decision and its implementation. This creates an environment in which learning and adaptation are part of the process, which ensures progress is made even under pressure.

Organisational agility: Failing fast and failing safely

Ultimately, in 99 out of 100 cases, the worst decision a leader can make is no decision at all. Indecision leads to stagnation and missed opportunities, and it erodes confidence within the team. When a decision has been made and executed, it immediately creates a new reality that can be evaluated, adapted and acted upon. In contrast, a team stuck in search of the 'perfect' solution risks being left behind while others adapt and evolve in real time.

Organisational agility is the ability to adapt quickly and effectively in response to changing circumstances, challenges and opportunities. To foster this agility, a vital skill for leaders is creating circumstances in which their teams can *fail fast and fail safely*. This approach encourages experimentation, reduces the fear of failure and accelerates learning cycles.

'Failing fast' means acting decisively, testing ideas or strategies, and gathering insights swiftly. 'Failing safely' makes certain the risks are contained and any setbacks are seen as opportunities for growth rather than threats to the team or organisation. This mindset transforms failure from being a source of fear into a powerful tool for innovation and continuous improvement.

The 'agility cycle' process – **learn, adjust** and **go again** – empowers teams to adapt dynamically. Each iteration provides valuable feedback that enables the team to refine their approach, build resilience and move closer to achieving their goals. By embracing this cycle, organisations can outpace their competitors who remain paralysed by overanalysis or hesitation.

The skill lies in balancing decisiveness with reflection. Leaders must set the tone for action, which makes sure their teams feel supported to experiment, learn from missteps and keep moving forward. This not only strengthens organisational agility but also builds a culture of trust, innovation and continuous improvement.

Managing emotions during decision-making

Emotional reactions arising during high-pressure decision-making is natural. However, effective leaders learn to recognise these emotions and manage them without allowing them to dictate their choices. Emotions are useful signals that often alert leaders to the significance of a situation, but they must be balanced with rational thought to ensure decisions are in harmony with long-term goals.

This approach helps leaders remain grounded and focused on the bigger picture, even when emotions are running high. Acknowledging that emotions are signals rather than commands allows leaders to listen to them without being controlled by them.

Building confidence in decision-making

As leaders gain experience, they become better at noticing patterns in decision-making, assessing risks and predicting outcomes. This experience helps leaders to build confidence in their ability to make decisions under pressure. However, confidence isn't just a result of experience; it's also a product of preparation.

Learning from high-pressure decisions:
The role of experience in the SODA loop

One of the most valuable aspects of decision-making under pressure is the opportunity to learn from each experience. Nevertheless, not all leaders benefit equally. An experienced leader who lacks humility or the self-esteem to reflect critically on their decisions won't gain as much from their experiences. In contrast, skilled leaders who are committed to learning from every opportunity will benefit from each decision they make, because they're evolving constantly. This openness to learning lets them refine their approach for future challenges, which builds resilience, improves decision-making skills and helps them navigate similar high-pressure scenarios with greater confidence and clarity.

SODA loop stages

Situation: Experience sharpens perception

In the first stage of the SODA loop, it's essential to assess the situation accurately. Leaders with experience in high-pressure environments tend to be better at quickly identifying key issues, recognising patterns and understanding the nuances of complex situations. Over time, they develop intuition for reading situations accurately, even when under immense pressure.

For example, seasoned leaders can rapidly gauge the severity of a crisis, assess any potential risks and filter out unnecessary distractions. They learn to spot hidden opportunities within challenges, and they understand aspects of the broader context – such as stakeholder interests, resource constraints and external impacts. Their ability to read the room becomes more refined, which allows them to gather relevant information faster and make better-informed assessments.

Importantly, experienced leaders who have the humility to reflect on past decisions are less likely to fall victim to cognitive biases such as overconfidence or confirmation bias. Instead, they leverage their knowledge to maintain objectivity, which ensures they fully understand the present reality before moving on to the options. This sharper situational awareness lays the foundation for more-effective decision-making.

Options: Experience expands possibilities

When generating options, experienced leaders draw from a wealth of past encounters and strategies. This broad experience aids their consideration of a wider range of potential solutions and approaches. Years of handling similar situations mean skilled leaders can think more creatively and adaptively by weighing options that less-experienced or less-reflective leaders might overlook. Moreover, seasoned leaders develop a keen sense of the potential pitfalls to avoid, which means their decisions not only consider opportunities but also anticipate challenges that could derail progress. This ability to balance innovative thinking with risk awareness helps them guide their teams toward effective solutions while sidestepping avoidable setbacks.

Furthermore, experience teaches leaders to think beyond conventional solutions. They develop the ability to envision innovative strategies or hybrid approaches that combine elements of different options. Rather than viewing options as binary, experienced leaders often explore middle-ground solutions that address both the immediate needs and long-term objectives. Crucially, they also learn to align these options with their team's desired results and the specific currency that's relevant to their organisation. This ability to connect options to tangible and intangible goals ensures their decisions are both practical and impactful, which drives success across multiple dimensions.

Leaders who reflect on their decision-making process consistently expand their ability to generate and evaluate a broader range of options. They can quickly assess the viability, risks and potential benefits of each choice, making certain no opportunity is overlooked and decisions are made with a full understanding of the available pathways.

Decision: Experience builds confidence and judgement

The decision-making stage is where the benefits of experience become most visible. Leaders who have navigated high-pressure situations build stronger judgement, which allows them to make decisions with more confidence and speed. Experience helps leaders balance their gut instincts with analytical reasoning, thus they know when to trust intuition and when to rely on data.

Importantly, experienced leaders who embrace humility also become more comfortable with uncertainty. They understand that perfect information is rarely available in high-pressure environments and delaying a decision can sometimes be more damaging than making an imperfect choice. This understanding allows them to act decisively, which helps them avoid analysis paralysis while still warranting that their choices are thoughtful and line up with their long-term goals.

Humility is key here. Leaders who reflect critically on their decisions are willing to revisit and adjust their choices when necessary. They understand that even well-considered decisions may miss the mark, and they remain open to changing course if the outcomes suggest a reassessment is needed. This balance between confidence and flexibility defines effective leadership under pressure.

Action: Experience enhances execution

The more experienced a leader is at executing tasks, the more effectively they'll carry them out. Execution is a skill that sharpens with practice, which enables leaders and teams to deliver plans with precision, clarity and focus. Experience in execution teaches leaders how to streamline workflows, communicate responsibilities clearly and maintain alignment with overarching goals. This makes more likely that plans are carried out as intended, which increases the likelihood of success.

A common mistake in high-pressure situations is incorrectly criticising the plan or decision itself when the real issue is subpar execution. Even the best strategies can falter if they're poorly implemented. Leaders with solid execution experience understand this distinction and are expert at diagnosing where the breakdown occurred. They can identify whether an issue stems from the quality of the decision or from lapses during implementation. This clarity allows them to respond appropriately by refining their execution methods rather than prematurely discarding a sound plan.

The cycle of continuous improvement

The beauty of the SODA loop is its continuous nature. After taking action and observing the results, the loop begins again, which helps leaders reflect on what went well and where improvement is needed. Leaders who are committed to learning from every decision make this reflection process more meaningful by identifying patterns, diagnosing errors and spotting opportunities for growth.

By embracing experience as a tool for learning – reflecting critically on both successes and missteps – leaders refine each phase of the SODA loop. Over time, they become more adept at assessing situations, generating options, making decisions and executing them effectively. This engenders a leadership style that's more resilient, adaptable and better equipped to handle the challenges of high-pressure environments.

> **PUTTING THE SODA LOOP INTO ACTION: ENSURING A HIGH-QUALITY, PROFESSIONAL MEETING**

Let's walk through how to apply a SODA loop to a high-pressure scenario. You have an important meeting scheduled with key partners, and the venue cancels at the last minute. Your goal is to be at a meeting that's slick, organised and gives your partners confidence in your organisation's professionalism.

Situation: Assess the current reality

First, assess the situation thoroughly. You have a vital meeting with your key partners, and the venue has just cancelled unexpectedly. The meeting is essential for building confidence in your organisation's professionalism, and any last-minute mishaps could damage that perception. It's important to acknowledge both the immediate problem – the lack of a venue – and the potential damage to your organisation's credibility if the meeting isn't handled smoothly.

Acknowledging the urgency while maintaining composure is key. The objective is to keep the meeting running smoothly and professionally, despite this logistical setback.

- **Situation:**
  - **Where you want to be:** Successfully hosting a meeting that reinforces your organisation's professionalism and builds confidence with your key partners.
  - **Where you are:** You have no venue for a meeting that's due to start in four hours.

Options: Generate potential solutions

Next, consider potential options to safeguard that the meeting will remain professional and well-organised:

- **Possibilities:**
  - **Alternative venue:** Can you find another location quickly that will maintain the professionalism required for this meeting and facilitates the currency you're aiming to generate? For example, securing a nearby hotel or conference centre could uphold your organisation's reputation and ensure the results of the meeting aren't compromised.
  - **Virtual option:** Would switching to a virtual meeting (for example, using Zoom or Microsoft Teams) make certain that the meeting still happens without any logistical disruptions, thus preserving the outcomes and relationships you're aiming to achieve? Using a familiar

LEVEL 3: CHAPTER 10 – DECISION-MAKING UNDER PRESSURE

platform can help maintain confidence and demonstrate agility, which may enhance trust – a key currency for ongoing partnerships.

- Hybrid option: If some attendees are local and others aren't, could a hybrid format – one in which some participants attend in person while others join remotely – support the results you're working toward? This solution balances accessibility and efficiency while demonstrating adaptability, which could generate organisational currency of goodwill and credibility.

- Postpone with professionalism: If no other options are viable, could the meeting be rescheduled in a way that protects the currency of trust and respect? Offering compensation for the inconvenience or providing a clear explanation for the delay can make sure the results are deferred, not lost, while still preserving partner confidence in your professionalism and reliability.

- **What to avoid:**
  - **Substandard venue:** Selecting a venue that feels unprofessional or inadequate can erode elements of your organisational currency, such as trust or credibility, and may fail to inspire your partners to have confidence in you and your organisation. A poor venue choice could hinder you achieving the meeting's desired results.

  - **Technical issues with virtual meetings:** Using a virtual platform your team is unfamiliar with has higher risks of technical glitches or confusion, which could make the meeting feel disorganised. This could result in lost credibility and diminished confidence, which harms your ability to generate the results and trust you need to move forward.

  - **Disjointed hybrid format:** Poor coordination between in-person and virtual attendees can create an inefficient or fragmented meeting experience. This lack of cohesion could cause disengagement, which reduces the likelihood of achieving your key results and potentially costs your organisation relational and reputational currency.

- **Appearing unreliable due to postponement:** Rescheduling without professionalism or clear communication risks your organisation appearing unreliable. This could harm your currency of trust and reliability, which makes it harder to achieve results in future engagements and maintain strong relationships.

Decision: Choose the best course of action

It's time to make a decision based on the available options. Remember that your primary goal is to ensure the meeting runs smoothly and your partners leave with increased confidence in your organisation's professionalism.

For example, if you find a nearby venue that can accommodate the meeting, this might be the best option as it keeps the event on track with minimal disruption. Alternatively, if an online or hybrid meeting better fits the attendees' locations and technical set-up, that might be a smarter choice, and it demonstrates your flexibility while maintaining the organised, professional experience you're aiming for.

Having confidence in your decision is key. Communicate the new plan to your team and key partners clearly and decisively, which makes certain everyone understands the changes and what's expected of them.

It's also important to remember that you don't need to handle everything yourself. A team that knows its strengths and prides itself on delivering under pressure will step up when needed. With skilled delegation and strong team dynamics, a situation like this can be handled swiftly and smoothly. Assign tasks based on your team members' capabilities, and trust them to execute them effectively. Leveraging your team's strengths lets you maintain focus on the bigger picture while ensuring each aspect of the new plan is managed to a high standard.

LEVEL 3: CHAPTER 10 – DECISION-MAKING UNDER PRESSURE

Leaders who delegate well foster confidence not only in themselves but also within their teams, which empowers everyone to contribute to the solution. This both helps in managing the immediate challenges and strengthens team cohesion and resilience for future high-pressure scenarios.

Action: Execute the plan with a focus on professionalism

Now, it's time to execute the plan with precision and clarity, while keeping professionalism at the forefront of every move. This is your opportunity to show your partners how well your team handles pressure as they turn a potential setback into a demonstration of competence and leadership.

The key actions include the following:

» **Communicate clearly:** Immediately inform all attendees about the change in venue or meeting format. Provide clear instructions on the new location, login details for a virtual meeting or any other necessary logistics.

» **Establish logistics:** To facilitate the meeting running smoothly and maintaining its professional image, address any key logistical concerns such as parking arrangements or traffic issues for the new venue. Communicating these details upfront demonstrates thorough planning and enhances your professional image.

» **Set up hospitality:** If the new venue offers the chance to do so, ensure that hospitality – such as refreshments, signage and a welcoming atmosphere – is set up smoothly. These small touches can make a big difference in reinforcing the professional tone of the meeting.

» **Prepare the new space:** If a new venue has been secured, make certain it's set up professionally, with all the required equipment made ready. If the meeting is virtual, confirm that all technology is working seamlessly beforehand.

» **Keep the team aligned:** Communicate with clarity. Make sure your team is clear on their roles, whether it's helping set up the new venue or troubleshooting tech issues during a virtual meeting.

By executing the action plan confidently and addressing logistics and hospitality, you demonstrate to your partners that your organisation remains capable and professional, even under pressure. This impression reinforces their confidence in you, which is essential in high-stakes scenarios.

A new situation
» **If the meeting was a success**
  ▸ **Build on the momentum:** Evaluate how the meeting's success can drive further progress. Did the outcomes align with the team's objectives and the organisation's currency?
» **If the meeting was unsuccessful**
  ▸ **Reassess and regroup:** Develop a new plan to address the gaps. Should the team reconvene for a follow-up meeting? Could alternative formats or approaches – such as additional preparation, smaller focus groups or external facilitation – solve the issues?

Begin the cycle again
Whether the meeting was a success or fell short, a new situation emerges that demands thoughtful assessment and action.

Use the SODA loop to evaluate the options available:

» **Success scenario:** Focus on sustaining and amplifying the positive results to ensure the next steps are in line with your long-term objectives.

» **Unsuccessful scenario:** Prioritise learning from the shortcomings, adapting your approach and moving forward swiftly with a new plan.

By treating both success and failure as starting points for the next cycle of reflection and decision-making, you guarantee continuous improvement and demonstrate the agility and resilience that define strong leadership.

CONCLUSION

Effective decision-making under pressure is one of the most vital skills a leader can develop. It requires the abilities to balance logic and emotion, acknowledge challenges while focusing on solutions, and act decisively in the face of uncertainty. The SODA loop provides a structured approach that equips leaders to navigate high-stakes scenarios with clarity and confidence. By adopting this framework, leaders can maintain focus on long-term goals while addressing the immediate demands of high-pressure environments.

Pressure – by its nature – tests a leader's ability to stay composed, assess situations accurately and make sound decisions. Leaders who succeed under such circumstances are those who understand their emotional triggers, manage stress effectively and use structured tools to guide their thought processes. Recognising the impact of stress on the brain allows leaders to counteract its negative effects, which makes certain that decisions are rational and line up with organisational objectives.

The ability to balance urgency with thoughtful reflection separates reactive managers from proactive leaders. Leaders who engage their teams in generating options foster creativity and collective problem-solving, which ensures no perspective is overlooked. They focus not just on the immediate solution but on building an agility culture in which challenges are seen as opportunities for growth.

Moreover, being committed to reflecting and learning after every decision – whether successful or not – facilitates continuous improvement. Leaders who embrace the iterative nature of the SODA loop refine their judgement, strengthen their teams and adapt effectively to new situations.

In the fast-paced environments leaders often face, decisiveness coupled with adaptability defines success. Making deliberate choices, executing with precision and remaining open to feedback helps leaders not only navigate high-pressure situations but also create a foundation for sustained organisational growth and resilience. Decision-making under pressure becomes more than just a challenge – it's an opportunity to lead with confidence and vision.

11
Team Dynamics

Effective leadership isn't just about making decisions and driving strategy; it's about bringing a team together and helping them become greater than the sum of their parts. Transforming any team hinges on two key elements: first, the creation and consistent messaging of a meaningful team purpose, or the *why*; and second, ensuring every individual understands their unique role in contributing to that purpose, which includes both their strengths and the strengths of their teammates. When combined, these elements create alignment, cohesion and high performance.

To put this into context, imagine a team composed of four individuals, each with a distinct dominant preference but little self-awareness: one is high Red – action-oriented but inconsiderate; another is high Yellow – innovative but unreliable; the third is high Blue – methodical but unable to deliver results; and the fourth is high Green – focused on consensus and keeping everyone in mind but hesitant to move projects forward. Each team member brings something valuable to the table, but their considerable individual blind spots limit their overall individual contribution to about 6 or 7 out of 10.

Without a unifying purpose and clarity around roles, this team would likely struggle to align their efforts with each other or the organisation. Their flaws and frustrations would undermine the group's potential. However, a leader who understands the importance of the two transformative elements of purpose and role clarity could reshape this team entirely. By defining and consistently communicating a shared purpose that inspires and motivates, the leader makes sure every member knows the broader goal they're working toward. At the same time, by helping each individual to understand their unique contribution and how it connects to the team's mission, the leader fosters alignment and collaboration.

The transformation arises from this balance: consolidating the team's efforts around a compelling purpose while empowering individuals to leverage their strengths in fulfilling their roles. When every team member not only knows their own strengths but also appreciates their teammates' contributions, the number of blind spots is reduced and collaboration is enhanced. The result?

Imagine this team collaborating cohesively: despite their individual blind spots, their combined strengths elevate their effectiveness to an exceptional level. The action-oriented Red would drive results, which makes sure tasks are tackled head-on. The innovative Yellow infuses creativity, which sparks new ideas and energises the group. The methodical Blue creates structured plans to turn ideas into actionable steps, while the consensus-seeking Green ensures all voices are heard, which nurtures harmony and buy-in.

With mutual respect and trust, the team together could achieve what none of them could alone. They would act as mirrors for each other's blind spots. For instance, the Red's impatience would be tempered by the Green's consideration, which would make certain that decisions are well-rounded. The Yellow's potential to overcommit would be grounded by the Blue's focus on practicalities and deliverables. Similarly, the Green's hesitancy would be countered by the Red's decisiveness, while the Blue would ensure that bold actions are executed methodically.

LEVEL 3: CHAPTER 11 – TEAM DYNAMICS

By leveraging their strengths and working collaboratively, this team could move from a fragmented collection of individual efforts to a cohesive, high-performing unit operating at a level of 8 or 9 out of 10.

The first step in this transformation is crafting and communicating the team's *why*. A meaningful purpose acts as the team's anchor, which provides clarity and direction even in challenging moments. It connects the team's work to a bigger mission to make certain every individual understands how their efforts contribute to something larger than themselves. When the purpose is obvious and compelling, it becomes the foundation for unity, which drives alignment and resilience in the face of adversity.

It's equally important to make sure each team member understands their specific role and how it supports the team's purpose. This requires instigating self-awareness so individuals can recognise their own strengths and weaknesses while appreciating the value of their teammates' contributions. By bringing roles into line with individuals' strengths and encouraging collaboration, the leader reduces friction and amplifies their collective performance. Teams thrive when every member knows not only what they bring to the table but also how their teammates' strengths complement their own.

As a hugely simplified example, consider a football team in which each player is assigned a specific role based on their abilities and strengths. The manager builds the team around a shared purpose – winning the match – and ensures every player understands how their role contributes to this outcome. For example, the striker's role might focus on scoring, while the defender's role is to prevent attacks. However, each player also understands and values their teammates' contributions to their shared objective. This clarity allows the team to adapt during high-pressure moments: a defender might need to score a last-minute goal during a set piece, just as a striker might need to track back and defend to save the game. The purpose – the *why* – remains the constant that makes certain the individual contributions line up with the team's collective objective.

This chapter will explore how leaders can achieve this transformation by focusing on two key elements: defining and embedding the team's purpose and then ensuring clarity around individual roles. We'll discuss tools such as CliftonStrengths®, Insights Discovery® and Patrick Lencioni's Working Genius,[29] which all provide valuable insights into team members' preferences and strengths. These tools help leaders place the right people in the right roles while developing an understanding of how individual efforts contribute to the team's mission.

Excelling at managing team dynamics effectively begins with two critical elements: defining a meaningful purpose and connecting individuals to their specific roles. A clear and compelling purpose unites the team, which fosters alignment and motivation. Role clarity empowers individuals to leverage their strengths while recognising and valuing the contributions of others, which enhances collaboration and minimises friction. When these elements are in place, teams transcend their fragmented efforts and transform into cohesive, high-performing units that are capable of delivering exceptional results.

The importance of understanding team dynamics

A successful team isn't just a collection of talented individuals; it's a cohesive unit that works together toward a shared goal, with each member making the most of their unique combination of skills and strengths to contribute to the collective effort. However, although differences in abilities and perspectives can enhance a team's overall performance, they can also lead to misunderstandings, inefficiencies or conflict if they're not managed properly.

Team dynamics are the unseen forces that shape how a team interacts, communicates and performs. These include interpersonal relationships, behaviours, group norms and team culture. They influence collaboration, conflict resolution and decision-making. A skilled leader understands that even talented individuals may struggle if team dynamics are misaligned.

When team dynamics are *managed skilfully*, a range of positive outcomes emerge:

- **Enhanced self-esteem:** Building a team member's self-esteem and self-worth goes beyond mere productivity. When individuals feel valued, they're more motivated and committed, which is a meaningful achievement in itself.

- **Openness to feedback and accountability:** Team members with trust and increased self-esteem experience less self-doubt and are less territorial. This openness fosters smoother operations within a skilled and balanced team, which enables better collaboration and shared responsibility.

- **Courage under fire:** When individuals know their value and trust their teammates, their ability to perform under pressure improves significantly. Having confidence in both themselves and others enhances performance during high-stakes situations.

- **Enhanced collaboration:** Team members collaborate more fluidly, thus sharing ideas and expertise without unnecessary friction. This seamless cooperation drives innovation and efficiency.

- **Increased trust:** A high level of trust allows individuals to rely on one another as they're confident their peers will provide support when challenges arise. This shared trust strengthens team cohesion.

- **Accountability and ownership:** Having well-defined and well-understood roles and responsibilities empowers each person to understand their contribution to the larger goal, which elicits a stronger sense of ownership over tasks and outcomes.

- **Adaptability under pressure:** A well-managed team is agile and able to respond to unexpected challenges with unity and focus, which prevents disarray in high-pressure situations.

- **Creative and personal freedom:** Leaders encouraging creativity and respecting personal autonomy lets team members bring their unique ideas and perspectives to the table. This freedom not only fuels innovation but also enhances job satisfaction and individuals' senses of purpose within the team.

In contrast, when team dynamics aren't managed deliberately, various issues can arise:

- **Conflict and friction:** Differences in working styles or misunderstandings can escalate into unresolved conflicts that disrupt progress and damage relationships.

- **Lack of communication:** Poor communication leads to confusion, inefficiency and errors, because individuals will struggle to bring their efforts into line with each other and the organisation.

- **Reduced morale:** If team members feel isolated or unsupported, morale drops, which in turn affects overall productivity and engagement.

- **Inefficiency:** When dynamics aren't optimised, the team can suffer from duplicated efforts, unclear priorities or missed deadlines, all of which detract from the team's overall performance.

- **Unhealthy competition:** Excessive or mismanaged competition between team members can create division, reduce collaboration and hinder the team's ability to achieve their collective goals.

- **Territorialism:** If individuals become overly protective of their own areas of work, it can lead to a lack of knowledge sharing, collaboration and innovation, which limits the team's effectiveness.

LEVEL 3: CHAPTER 11 – TEAM DYNAMICS

- **Dishonesty:** A lack of honesty within the team undermines trust, creates uncertainty, and can give rise to poor decision-making as individuals withhold or distort critical information.

- **Backstabbing:** When team members undermine or sabotage each other to advance their own interests, it generates a toxic environment that damages relationships, reduces morale and disrupts team cohesion.

Managing team dynamics is especially crucial in high-pressure environments. Under pressure, a team's existing weaknesses can be magnified. Some individuals thrive in these conditions while others may feel overwhelmed. However, it's not uncommon for those who excel under pressure to become bored or restless from the routine of day-to-day operations. As the team leader, it's your responsibility to manage this. Team members' varied responses to pressure can create friction or disrupt cohesion if not addressed. For example, a normally collaborative team might fragment if one member feels underappreciated for their efforts or another fails to meet expectations under stress.

As a leader, you must adapt your leadership style to these dynamics to make certain the team remains cohesive and focused in challenging circumstances. This might involve facilitating open communication, offering support to struggling team members or redistributing tasks based on how individuals are coping with the pressure. By staying attuned to the emotional and operational needs of your team, you as their leader can ensure the group remains productive and committed when tensions are high.

It's crucial to recognise it's often too late if you wait to address these dynamics when there's a pressurised moment. As a leader, you have the biggest influence over how your team functions well before the high-pressure situations arise. Establishing a climate of openness and appreciation for the team's diverse strengths is essential for laying the groundwork for resilience under stress. When team members feel heard, valued and recognised for their contributions in everyday circumstances, they're more likely to support one another and maintain cohesion when the pressure mounts.

EXERCISE: VISION CREATION FOR SMALLER TEAMS

The following simplified process helps small teams develop a meaningful and actionable vision. A more detailed example is provided in *Chapter 13: Culture Creation*.

Kilter Team Dynamics Process Framework

Building a high-performing team is a strategic process that requires intentional actions, clear communication and a focus on team culture. This framework is broken down into the key steps necessary to establish a cohesive, productive team:

Step 1: Establish what your team needs from you – and what they don't

Start by understanding what your team expects from you as a leader. They need the following:

» **A clear vision and direction:** Help the team get in line with a clear, inspiring vision that provides focus and meaning. Establish a co-minded purpose – one that connects with their deeper motivations and goes beyond simple rewards. This purpose should feel meaningful and should resonate with both individual and collective aspirations, while recognising that success can lead to more security, career growth and promotion opportunities.

The most simple but impactful way to create a team vision is asking the team this: 'What do we want people to say about us? What do we not want them to say about us?'

» **Support to overcome challenges:** Offer assistance and encouragement to navigate obstacles while cultivating resilience and problem-solving skills.

» **Clarity around goals, roles and responsibilities:** Ensure everyone understands their contributions and how they fit into the bigger picture, thus avoiding confusion and inefficiency.

» **Compassion:** Demonstrate empathy and understanding for individual team members' needs, which nurtures trust and emotional safety within the group.

» **Integrity:** Lead by example through demonstrating honesty, transparency and ethical decision-making; this builds credibility and trust within the team.

» **Balance direction, mentoring and coaching:** Combine unambiguous guidance with opportunities for personal and professional growth, which empowers team members to develop their skills while achieving the collective goals.

What they don't need:

» **Micromanagement that stifles their initiative:** Excessive control can limit team members' ability to think independently, which reduces engagement and innovation.

» **Ambiguity in leadership:** A lack of clear direction or inconsistent messaging can lead to confusion, inefficiency and disarray among the team.

» **Disconnection:** A lack of meaningful engagement or understanding between you, as a leader, and your team members can create feelings of isolation, which reduces morale and trust.

» **Manipulation:** Using deceptive or coercive tactics to achieve goals undermines trust, damages relationships and creates a toxic work environment.

Listen actively to understand how they prefer to work, and lead by empowering them, not by controlling their every move.

Step 2: Learn their strengths

To unlock your team's full potential, you need to go beyond their practical skills (although those are important). Identify the following:

- » **Practical skill set:** Understand your team members' technical competencies and job-specific knowledge.

- » **Personal natures and character types:** Recognise individuals' personality traits and how they influence teamwork.

- » **Leadership potential:** Identify natural leaders and those who can grow into leadership roles.

- » **Project contribution:** Determine what part of a project each member contributes to the most naturally – whether it's ideation, execution or completion.

Step 3: Define the purpose of your team and establish its core values

Clearly establish the team's co-minded purpose, vision and values, which will guide all actions:

- » **The purpose – your *why*:** Define a collective purpose that's meaningful and resonates on a deeper level. This purpose should inspire the team to work toward something greater than individual tasks or short-term rewards. However, don't ignore practical benefits such as higher security, chances for promotion and recognition; show how fulfilling the purpose supports both personal and professional growth.

- » ***What* success looks like:** Describe the team's potential and what it will look like when operating at its highest level. Define success, not just in terms of results but also regarding how well the team embodies the core values.

- » ***How* you'll achieve this:** Break down the strategy into actionable steps, which ensures values such as integrity and enjoyment are woven into daily activities and team behaviours. The way you approach projects and challenges should reflect these values, which reinforces the team culture.

By establishing team values early, they become the foundation for the roles, norms and decisions that follow. A co-minded purpose guarantees alignment, while shared values such as *integrity* and *enjoyment* create the foundation for motivation, resilience and trust.

Step 4: Assign roles and responsibilities based on individuals' strengths

Now you understand your team members' strengths and character types, allocate roles as follows:

- » **Align roles with strengths:** Leverage individuals' talents when allocating responsibilities. Set up each team member for success by placing them in roles where they can thrive.

- » **Strategic considerations:** Assign roles based on both current abilities and leadership development pathways. (There's more on strategy and leadership development in *Level 4*.)

- » **Support team goals:** Select roles that not only line up with individuals' strengths but also contribute to the team's collective objectives. Structure each role to support the overall strategy and drive progress toward shared goals.

Step 5: Create space for open communication

Effective processes and measurable outcomes rely on a culture of open communication. Team members need to feel they can share concerns, ideas or feedback without hesitation. More than anything, three elements bond a team together: overcoming significant challenges, sharing moments of laughter and enjoyment, and connecting on a deeper, more meaningful level.

A culture of open communication could consider these elements:

- » **Safe spaces for feedback:** Foster a culture in which feedback flows freely. Create opportunities, such as regular one-to-one meetings, for team members to provide and receive feedback in a safe, judgement-free environment. These spaces also allow people to connect on a human level, thus gaining an understanding of what's important to each other beyond their professional roles.

» **Bonding through challenges and enjoyment:** The shared experience of facing something incredibly challenging together – whether it's a demanding project or navigating pressure – forges stronger connections. Equally, enjoying moments together builds camaraderie and a sense of belonging. Both challenges and enjoyment create the kind of relationships that lead to lasting team cohesion.

» **Avoid gossiping or talking behind people's backs:** Refrain from discussing team members behind their backs unless it's part of planning a direct and constructive conversation with them. Gossip erodes trust, creates division and engenders a culture of paranoia in which individuals may feel insecure about what's being said about them. Addressing issues directly and respectfully is essential for maintaining a healthy, transparent and cohesive team environment.

The **Kilter Team Dynamics Process Framework** centres on building a team with a strong co-minded purpose and every individual connected to a role that leverages their strengths and is consistent with the shared mission. Establishing a purpose that resonates beyond simple rewards, while still acknowledging the tangible benefits of success, engenders deep motivation and alignment. Role clarity and open communication complete the foundation for creating a cohesive, high-performing team that's capable of achieving extraordinary results.

Identify your norms and build your culture

Define the behaviours and norms that will create a strong, resilient team culture:

» **Team norms:** Agree on the behaviours that have fostered a productive and supportive environment. Hold each other responsible for positive interactions, accountability and mutual respect in day-to-day operations. Consider what you want your currency to be and reinforce this deliberately.

» **Persevere through slow days:** Make sure the team can maintain focus during less-intense periods; recognise that how they act during slower times impacts how they perform when the pressure increases.

» **Balance the language and energy for your culture:** Agree the language you'll continue to use, which sets the tone for your team's mindset. Positive language focused on enthusiasm, purpose and commitment can cultivate resilience, while aggressive, results-driven language may create pressure and leave individuals feeling vulnerable. Both sides of the spectrum are needed, but balance is key. The language you choose should be in line with the culture you want to create. Whether it's extreme or moderate, it will likely be effective if it's consistent and matches with your actions, strategy and other cultural decisions.

» **Performance under pressure:** Create a culture that lets the team perform at its best when the stakes are high. A strong culture acts as an anchor, which helps the team stay unified and effective, especially under stress. While building trust and relationships takes time, nothing galvanises a team like going through tough situations and sticking together. Overcoming challenges as a unit cultivates resilience, strengthens bonds and creates a shared sense of purpose that endures beyond the crisis.

Tool for finding your team's strengths

Both the Insights Discovery® and CliftonStrengths® tools, which we've already discussed, are excellent for identifying individuals' strengths and preferences. These tools help leaders understand how their team members approach relationships, decision-making and personal growth. However, when it comes to understanding how individuals contribute to a project – from the original idea to full completion – Patrick Lencioni's Working Genius model provides a practical framework for team dynamics and project management.

The Working Genius model identifies six types of work activities that people naturally gravitate toward: **wonder** (asking probing questions and exploring possibilities), **invention** (generating innovative ideas), **discernment** (evaluating and providing critical feedback), **galvanising** (rallying the team and driving momentum), **enablement** (supporting others) and **tenacity** (ensuring tasks are completed with precision).[30] By understanding these work activities, leaders can better align their team members with roles that fit their strengths, which results in higher engagement, job satisfaction and productivity.

When leaders assign tasks strategically based on individuals' strengths, they create a more efficient and harmonious working environment. For example, someone who excels in generating ideas may struggle with detailed execution, and those who are brilliant at driving projects to completion may not enjoy early stage brainstorming.

Aligning team members with the right roles

To explore how team dynamics can drive the project's success, we can examine six distinct steps that showcase the power of collaboration:

1. **Sparking the idea**
2. **Generating solutions**
3. **Refining the concept**
4. **Energising the team**
5. **Supporting the process**
6. **Driving the project to completion**

Let's consider a project where the goal is to revolutionise travel by inventing the first luggage with wheels (please note, an existing real product has intentionally been chosen for this example to help you concentrate on the process, not the product). A cross-functional team has been assembled, and each person's unique strengths will play a vital role in the project's success.

Step 1: Sparking the idea

A team member who excels at thinking broadly and imagining new possibilities identifies a gap in the market. They question why travellers still carry heavy suitcases, and so they propose adding wheels to suitcases to simplify the experience, which sparks the beginning of the project.

Contribution: Their ability to think innovatively identifies an untapped opportunity, which lays the foundation for the concept of wheeled luggage.

Step 2: Generating solutions

Another team member, who's known for their creativity and ability to develop practical solutions, starts brainstorming designs. They explore various ways to attach wheels to luggage and sketch multiple configurations to determine what will work best.

Contribution: Their resourcefulness allows the team to translate the initial idea into tangible solutions, which is the groundwork for production.

Step 3: Refining the concept

A team member who's skilled at analysing and improving ideas evaluates the prototypes. They assess the balance of the suitcase and test different wheel placements to make certain it meets the practical needs of travellers.

Contribution: Their critical thinking ensures the final design is refined and fit for purpose, which prevents potential flaws making it to market.

Step 4: Energising the team

Once the final design has been approved, another team member with a natural gift for motivating others takes over. They bring energy to the team, align all departments and facilitate the production process moving forward smoothly.

Contribution: Their enthusiasm and leadership keep the team focused and on track, which helps the project progress through the crucial production phase.

Step 5: Supporting the process

During production, a team member with strong organisational and supportive skills gets the process running seamlessly. They coordinate between departments and provide the necessary resources to keep everything on schedule.

Contribution: Their coordination and support make sure the logistical side of the project flows without disruptions, which allows the team to focus on project execution.

Step 6: Driving the project to completion

As the product nears launch, a team member with a natural drive to complete tasks steps in. They oversee the final stages of production to make certain the luggage is ready for distribution and that all deadlines are met.

Contribution: Their determination guarantees the project is completed on time and with attention to detail, thus delivering a high-quality product to the market.

The next stage: Reinventing the wheels!

After the successful launch of the first wheeled luggage, a team member once again begins to think creatively. They ask, 'What if we added four wheels instead of two?' sparking the next wave of innovation and leading to the creation of modern spinner luggage.

Progressing flexibility through the phases

Throughout the project, each team member's strengths were utilised at the appropriate stage:

1. Big-picture thinking identified the opportunity.
2. Creativity brought the solutions to life.
3. Analytical skills refined the product.
4. Motivation drove the team forward.
5. Organisational support ensured smooth collaboration.
6. Determination saw the project to its successful conclusion.

By focusing on individual strengths while maintaining flexibility, leaders ensure projects progress smoothly, teams remain balanced and organisations are well-positioned to handle future challenges.

Back to inventing the first luggage with wheels – when strengths clash in the wrong phases

In this example, an organisation is developing the first luggage with wheels, but the project is derailed as team members apply their strengths at the wrong stages, which leads to confusion and setbacks.

Critiquing too early

The project starts with a team member suggesting ideas to improve travel. However, another team member, who's skilled in evaluation and critique, steps in too early. They assess every suggestion before the ideas have a chance to develop fully, saying things such as 'That won't work at airports,' or 'Travellers won't buy that design.' Evaluating ideas prematurely stifles creativity before the team can explore viable options. The team becomes hesitant to move forward, due to being unable to consider new approaches without critique.

How it pulls the project back: Overanalysis and critique during the idea-generation phase hinder creativity, which makes it difficult for the team to explore new concepts and solutions.

Distracting during execution

When the project enters the final stages, another team member with a knack for generating new ideas gets restless. Instead of letting the team focus on executing the current design, they propose additional features, such as a retractable handle or a motorised version. These new ideas, although creative, come too late in the process to be implemented effectively. The focus shifts away from completing the product, and deadlines are missed, which frustrates those working to see the project through to the finish line.

How it pulls the project back: Introducing new ideas during execution causes unnecessary distractions, which prevents the team from completing the project and delaying its launch.

The result: Pulled in different directions
Rather than progressing smoothly from concept to conclusion, the project is constantly stalled as team members step into their roles in the wrong phases:

- Premature critique stifles creativity during the idea-generation stage.
- New ideas introduced during execution delay completion and frustrate the team.

The result is a project that's pulled in different directions by team members working out of sync. This misalignment leads to delays, confusion and a lack of focus, which makes it difficult to finalise and launch. Beyond the practical challenges, the team members may walk away from the project feeling frustrated and believing their colleagues are impossible to work with – perhaps viewing some as too negative or others as flighty. In reality, if the team had been more aware of when and how to apply their individual strengths and had gained a clearer understanding of the strengths each person brought to the table, the entire project could have turned out differently. The same team, with the same skills, could have delivered a successful outcome by working more cohesively and aligning their strengths effectively.

Fostering collaboration and managing conflict

Collaboration is the lifeblood of any high-performing team; however, collaboration can be challenging when team members have different working styles, motivations and preferences. A leader's ability to cultivate collaboration while managing potential conflicts is crucial to maintaining team cohesion, especially when the team are under pressure.

Fostering collaboration

Effective collaboration doesn't just happen – it needs to be nurtured. Leaders can promote collaboration by creating an inclusive environment in which every team member feels valued and heard.

This starts with clear communication and setting expectations around how the team will work together. Leaders should encourage open dialogue, active listening and mutual respect, which are the foundations of strong collaboration.

In a collaborative environment, team members are more likely to share ideas, offer feedback and support one another – even in challenging times. Leaders should also ensure team members are not siloed in their roles but have opportunities to work cross-functionally. This helps the team to see the bigger picture and understand how they individually contribute to reaching the larger goal. It also cultivates an appreciation for other people's strengths and perspectives, which encourages team members to value diverse approaches rather than becoming frustrated by their differences.

Managing conflict

Conflict is inevitable in any team, particularly when working under pressure. Differences in working styles, personality clashes or disagreements over strategy can lead to tension if not addressed promptly. Leaders must be proactive at identifying and managing conflict before it escalates.

A key part of managing conflict is understanding the root cause. Conflicts often arise not from fundamental disagreements but from misunderstandings or miscommunications. Leaders should encourage their team members to express their concerns openly, and the leaders can then facilitate constructive conversations to resolve issues.

One proactive solution to managing conflict is agreeing as a team what constitutes appropriate and inappropriate ways of addressing it. While there's no single *right* way to handle conflict, some approaches will work better than others for a specific team dynamic. By establishing shared expectations – such as addressing disagreements directly rather than gossiping or escalating things unnecessarily – the team creates a framework for respectful, solution-focused communication. This shared understanding helps prevent misunderstandings and facilitates a cohesive approach to managing disagreements.

Adapting leadership style to team dynamics

An essential aspect of a leader managing team dynamics is adapting their leadership style to suit the needs of their team. Different situations and different team members require different approaches. A more directive leadership style may be needed when quick decisions are necessary, whereas a coaching or empowering approach might be better suited to nurturing long-term development and collaboration.

Skilled leaders are flexible and adjust their style based on the dynamics of their team and the challenges at hand. Understanding the preferences, strengths and weaknesses of each team member aids leaders in providing the right kind of support and guidance to help the team perform at its best.

One of the toughest challenges in leadership is joining a new team. In such situations, leaders must balance being authentic with being aware of the unique needs of the team or organisation they're stepping into. Although it's important to be yourself as a leader, it's equally crucial to recognise different teams necessitate different types of leadership, especially in the initial stages of joining a team.

For example, a team that has been through difficult times may be demoralised and in need of a leader who can inspire confidence and make them believe in themselves again. On the other hand, a high-performing team that's already firing on all cylinders might not need motivation; rather, they may need someone to steer the ship, keep things on track and avoid disrupting their flow. In some cases, a team may have developed bad habits or dysfunctions that oblige a leader to be more courageous and decisive and to address problems head-on, perhaps with seemingly less compassion but with more focus on discipline and change.

A skilled leader doesn't demand the team adapts to the leader's style; instead, they bring their authentic self to the table while remaining adaptable to what the team needs most. This requires a nuanced understanding of the team's current state, culture and challenges. Carefully observing and assessing the team's strengths, weaknesses and dynamics helps leaders tailor their approach to provide the right balance of support, direction and vision. This level of judgement demands a high degree of skill, along with a careful balance of courage and compassion – much as effective communication does. Courage is necessary to make tough decisions or address difficult issues, while compassion ensures those decisions are empathetic and considerate of the team's well-being. This delicate balance allows leaders to build trust, foster growth and guide their teams through both opportunities and challenges.

Skilled and balanced leadership is about flexibility and authenticity. Leaders must remain true to who they are and simultaneously adapt their style to fit the team's needs, whether they're joining an organisation in need of a morale boost, steering a well-oiled machine or addressing deep-rooted issues. Having the ability to adapt without losing what's at your core is what distinguishes a truly effective leader.

CONCLUSION

Managing team dynamics effectively is at the heart of successful leadership. A cohesive and high-performing team doesn't arise by chance; it's the result of deliberate and skilful leadership that aligns individuals' strengths with collective goals while fostering a culture of trust, collaboration and adaptability. By understanding and leveraging each team member's unique contributions, leaders can transform diverse talents into a unified force capable of achieving exceptional results.

A key aspect of managing team dynamics is building self-awareness within the team. Leaders who help team members recognise their strengths and blind spots empower them to contribute more effectively, which reduces friction and enhances meaningful collaboration. This self-awareness – combined with focusing on team culture and shared values – lays the foundation for trust and mutual respect, which are essential for navigating challenges and maintaining unity under pressure.

Leaders must also cultivate flexibility within their team. Although it's vital to align roles with strengths, a team must be adaptable, with its members being willing to step outside their defined responsibilities when the situation demands it. This adaptability helps the team remain resilient and focused, even in high-stakes or fast-changing environments.

Effective leaders don't just respond to problems as they arise; they shape team dynamics proactively by creating a culture of open communication, clear processes and shared accountability. They understand that a well-balanced team thrives on both individual contributions and the collective spirit that emerges when everyone is working toward a common purpose.

By blending empathy, strategic thinking and adaptability, leaders can cultivate high-performing teams that are also resilient, motivated and capable of achieving sustained meaningful success. This skilful management of team dynamics elevates both individual and organisational potential, which ensures long-term progress and security.

LEVEL 4

12
Strategic Leadership

Strategic leadership is the art of balancing immediate, complex challenges with a vision for long-term success. Effective leaders know that addressing today's problems is only part of the equation; they must also anticipate future needs and opportunities. This progression – from reactive problem-solving to proactive leadership and, ultimately, to strategic thinking – is crucial for sustainable growth across all sectors, including education, sports and hospitality.

One key to becoming a balanced strategic leader is having the ability to stay true to the values and mission of the organisation while preparing for the future landscape. Strategy isn't merely about adapting to fit the future; it's about growing and positioning the organisation so it can contribute to the future in meaningful ways that are consistent with its goals and core principles. Strategic leaders make certain that their actions today lay the groundwork for tomorrow, which lets their organisation seize opportunities when they present themselves and play a purposeful role in the future without compromising its identity.

For example, in the sports sector, managers must focus on not only the team's immediate performance but also player development, team cohesion and long-term tactical planning. Restaurant managers face the dual challenges of managing daily operations while preparing for future changes in consumer preferences and industry trends.

The ability to select a meaningful future goal and craft a purposeful path to achieve it is another vital aspect of strategic leadership. This involves more than following trends, adopting popular frameworks or getting in line with fleeting public opinions. Instead, leaders must base their goals on having a deep understanding of their organisation's mission and values, plus the unique contributions it aims to make in the world. A leader's strategy should be one that is visionary and original, charts a course that responds to external changes, and inspires the necessary innovation and transformation. By resisting the urge to merely follow external influences, strategic leaders assert true leadership, which makes certain their goals and strategies are grounded in purpose and authenticity and are in line with the long-term aspirations of their organisation. This is a fundamental difference between leading and following.

This chapter sets out how strategic leadership can move past reactive and proactive leadership to create long-term success. Strategic leaders prepare their teams for future challenges by fostering a forward-looking mindset and equipping them with the skills and agility to adapt.

A significant element that guides both strategy and culture is a clear and meaningful vision. Vision serves as the guiding light that aligns strategic efforts and cultural practices, which makes sure an organisation remains focused on its long-term aspirations at the same time as adapting to today's challenges. In *Chapter 13: Culture Creation*, we'll explore how to create a vision that's inspiring, actionable, and provides the foundation for meaningful, resilient and sustainable progress.

Strategy defined

A **strategy** is a comprehensive plan that's been designed to achieve a specific long-term goal while considering the steps necessary to reach the goal and any potential challenges along the way. A key component of strategy is *identifying obstacles or threats* that might hinder progress and outlining ways to *overcome* or *mitigate* them. A good strategy doesn't just set the goal; it prepares for what could go wrong to ensure the organisation is equipped to navigate challenges without losing sight of the objective. In addition, an excellent strategy will predict opportunities in the future and turn today's efforts into tomorrow's wins.

When developing a strategy, effective leaders consider the following important questions:

- **What specific goal are we trying to achieve?**

  Defining the objective clearly will elicit alignment and focus across the organisation. A well-articulated goal serves as the foundation for all subsequent planning and decision-making.

- **What strengths or advantages do we have that can support us in achieving this goal?**

  Recognising internal capabilities, resources and/or unique opportunities enables leaders to leverage these assets effectively. Strengths such as skilled personnel, an established market presence or technological superiority can be key drivers of success.

- **What obstacles or threats could prevent us from reaching this goal?**

  Identifying potential challenges allows leaders to anticipate barriers and prepare proactive solutions. This step makes sure risks are managed, rather than left to chance.

- **How can we overcome these obstacles or mitigate these risks?**

  Using targeted actions to address each threat identified helps leaders develop resilience and adaptability. This process transforms potential vulnerabilities into manageable challenges. Elite-level leadership goes a step further by seeking ways to turn obstacles into advantages.

- **What's our plan of execution?**
  A strategy is only as strong as its implementation. Leaders must outline a clear, actionable roadmap that includes specific tasks, the parties responsible, timelines and measurable outcomes. This facilitates accountability and progress toward the goal while providing enough flexibility for adjustments as circumstances evolve.

From reactive to proactive and from proactive to strategic

This section explores these three stages of leadership – **reactive**, **proactive** and **strategic** – using the example of school leaders navigating a recruitment crisis due to a shortage of new teachers entering the profession. Each leadership development stage is illustrated through the experiences of three leaders, who are facing this challenge in different ways: one reactive, one proactive and one strategic.

Reactive leadership: Managing issues as they arise

In the early stages of leadership, much of a leader's time is spent in a *reactive leadership mode*. This means dealing with issues as they arise, and often under pressure. For a school leader, this could involve responding to sudden teacher shortages, staff absences or unexpected changes in student enrolment. Reactive leadership is about problem-solving in the moment, using emotional management and decision-making skills to address immediate crises.

Let's consider the example of Leader A, a school head teacher who's currently facing a recruitment crisis due to a shortage of new teachers entering the profession. When the school is unexpectedly left without a key teacher, Leader A takes swift action. They have a good relationship with the local community and are able to fill the vacancy temporarily by promoting a highly skilled teaching assistant or bringing in a local teacher they know through their connections. This is an example of *effective* reactive leadership: Leader A deals with the problem effectively in the short term and ensures the students aren't left without a teacher.

However, reactive leadership is only about solving today's problems. While Leader A successfully manages the immediate crisis, they're likely to find themselves in similar situations again unless they develop more proactive strategies. This type of leadership – though important – neither addresses the root causes of the teacher shortage nor prevents future crises.

Proactive leadership: Anticipating and preventing issues

Proactive leadership involves anticipating challenges before they develop fully and then taking action to prevent them. Instead of waiting for crises to occur, proactive leaders are constantly scanning the environment to look for early warning signs and then putting systems in place to avoid potential problems.

In the case of the teacher-recruitment crisis, Leader B – another school principal – has taken a proactive approach. Over the past few months, Leader B has recognised that teacher shortages were becoming more common. Instead of waiting for vacancies to arise, they set up networking opportunities with local universities and teaching colleges, attended career fairs and built relationships with trainee teachers. As a result, Leader B has created a pool of contacts comprising talented educators they can reach out to when a vacancy opens. Additionally, they've established strong ties with local educational recruitment agencies.

When the recruitment crisis hits, Leader B doesn't need to scramble to find a replacement. They've already laid the groundwork by building relationships with qualified teachers, which makes certain they can fill vacancies quickly and without disruption to their students. This proactive leadership approach means Leader B can avoid many of the short-term issues that would have caused significant disruptions in Leader A's school.

Proactive leadership not only helps prevent problems but also fosters a sense of preparedness and resilience. However, although proactive leaders are excellent at addressing near-term challenges, another level of leadership takes this approach even further: **strategic leadership**. This involves thinking long term and solving both today's problems and those of the future. Strategic leadership goes beyond merely anticipating future threats; it creatively turns those threats into opportunities by bringing them in line with the strengths, vision and purpose of the team. This ability to reframe challenges as avenues for growth often requires a spark of creativity, but ultimately, it's a skill that can be honed and developed through deliberate practice and experience.

Strategic leadership: Planning for the future

Strategic leadership involves looking even further ahead to address long-term challenges by making decisions today that will prevent future problems. A strategic leader isn't just focused on this week or the next few months; they're thinking about how their actions now will impact the school or organisation for years to come.

In the recruitment-crisis example, Leader C takes a strategic approach. Two years ago, they noticed a significant drop in the number of student teachers entering local universities and teaching programmes. On realising this would likely result in a future shortage of qualified teachers, Leader C took immediate action, even though the effects wouldn't be felt for some time.

Leader C built strong relationships with universities and teaching colleges, which was partly through offering their school as a placement site for student teachers and ensuring that those students received training that went above and beyond. They invested in a robust mentorship programme, which made certain new teachers received excellent guidance and support from experienced staff. This not only made sure the school was a desirable place for new teachers to train at but also that those who completed their placements there were highly skilled and well-prepared for the demands of teaching.

In addition to focusing on new teacher recruitment, Leader C recognised that this shortage of teachers would probably result in a future shortage of leaders within the school system. To address this, they began to invest in leadership development programmes for their existing staff. They offered professional development opportunities focused on leadership skills to create clear pathways for staff who exhibit the potential to take on leadership roles in the future.

While Leader A is focusing on solving today's crisis and Leader B is preventing short-term issues, Leader C is addressing the problems of next year and beyond. Their decisions today – around recruitment, leadership development and school culture – are setting their school up for long-term success, which ensures they'll have a regular supply of top-tier teachers and future leaders, even as the broader recruitment crisis continues.

By adopting this approach, Leader C has taken the opportunity to transform their school into a destination of choice for ambitious professionals and aspiring leaders. This careful cultivation of a strong, supportive culture and a clear pathway for professional growth means the school will become a place for talent seeking both stability and opportunity. If this strategy is executed skilfully, Leader C will mitigate the staffing crisis and turn it into a strategic advantage that positions their school as a trailblazer in talent retention and development. In doing so, they safeguard that their school's reputation will thrive by attracting and retaining exceptional educators who share their vision and values.

Using data and milestones to chart progress

Strategic leaders understand that, to achieve long-term goals, it's crucial to set clear, measurable milestones. Leaders can use data-driven insights and performance markers to monitor progress, make informed decisions and course correct as needed. This approach not only transforms abstract visions into achievable, concrete plans but also plays a pivotal role in maintaining team motivation, instilling faith in external stakeholders, calming anxieties and enhancing overall cohesion. Whether you're leading a sports team, a business or a school, using data to break down large objectives into smaller, actionable steps helps ensure the organisation stays on track while fostering a unified and confident environment for all involved.

One of the most effective ways to *use data strategically* is by setting a specific future goal and then reverse engineering the steps required to reach that goal. For example, a track cycling team competing in a team pursuit might predict the winning time for the Olympic Games four years from now, based on trends and historical data. With this target in mind, they would then set themselves incremental time goals for each year leading up to the Olympics. These milestones would give the team an obvious indication whether they're progressing fast enough to hit their ultimate target, which allows them to adjust their training schedules, tactics and equipment as necessary. By tracking performance data throughout their training cycle, the team can ensure that they're steadily moving toward their goal.

Similarly, in an educational context, a school might set its long-term objectives around the level of provision to offer its students. For example, a school could aim to develop a curriculum with a strong focus on specialist subjects over the next four years. To achieve this, it would need to be determined which subject specialists are required and how many top-tier teachers will need to be developed or recruited. Alongside this, the school could track attendance data as a marker for student engagement, with incremental goals set each year to monitor improvement. This data monitoring not only helps to keep the school accountable but also makes future successes more tangible for both teachers and administrators.

However, it's important to note that, although data can be a powerful tool for strategic leadership, it comes with a health warning. Over-relying on data and statistics without understanding the broader context can narrow the focus and pull the organisation away from its core vision. For instance, a business might become overly obsessed with cutting costs based on financial metrics, while neglecting employee morale, which results in a high staff turnover and diminished productivity. Similarly, a school that focuses solely on test scores might overlook the wider development of its students, which could engender burnout among teachers and disengagement among students. Data should inform decision-making, but it should always be balanced with the organisation's values and its leader's long-term vision.

For team members who are highly sensitive to anxiety, setting clear data-driven milestones can help reduce uncertainty about the future. When employees or athletes understand the specific targets they're working toward, the unknown becomes less daunting, which allows them to focus on what they can control. In this way, data can provide structure and clarity, which helps to alleviate stress and builds their confidence in their ability to succeed. Knowing that progress is measurable can reassure and motivate teams to push forward, even during challenging periods.

For executive leaders and investors, data-driven milestones are invaluable for making the future more tangible. When leaders can plainly show how current performance aligns with future targets, they inspire their team's confidence in the organisation's strategic direction. This visibility often facilitates more freedom and access to resources, as stakeholders can see how their investment is being used to drive long-term growth. However, many key metrics take significant time to materialise fully, so a crucial leadership skill is identifying and tracking the leading indicators that signal progress before the final outcomes emerge.

For example, winning matches and climbing the league table may take a football team an entire season to achieve. However, metrics such as increased possession, improved shot accuracy and a higher number of shots on target can act as early indicators of a team's progress and potential for success. Similarly, in an educational setting, the final test scores may take a full academic year or more to improve. However, intermediate metrics such as increased pupil engagement, improved behaviour patterns, higher attendance rates and more participation in classroom activities can provide early indications of a positive trajectory. A skilled leader – whether that's in sports, education or elsewhere – monitors these factors and uses them to demonstrate progress, which reinforces stakeholder confidence while maintaining momentum toward the final goal.

Data and milestones act as essential tools in a strategic leader's toolkit. They provide clarity, facilitate progress tracking, and give both team members and external stakeholders confidence that the organisation is moving toward its goals. However, leaders must ensure that data remains only a guide – not the sole focus – by integrating it with the organisation's overall mission and values. By using data wisely, strategic leaders can focus and motivate their teams to drive toward sustained success while adapting to the challenges that arise along the way.

Combining responsive, proactive and strategic leadership

It's important to note that *strategic leadership doesn't replace responsive or proactive leadership; it builds on them.* Skilled leaders strive to excel in both proactive and responsive leadership, as they understand that each plays a vital role in their success. Even the most strategic leaders will face situations that require immediate, responsive problem-solving, and they'll still need to take proactive steps to prevent issues from arising. Strategic leadership, however, focuses on integrating these approaches to make certain the actions taken today resolve the immediate challenges, prevent tomorrow's crises *and* build a foundation for long-term success.

An essential part of effective leadership, particularly at Level 3 of the Kilter Leadership Taxonomy, is the ability to react in the moment. The fast-paced nature of leadership means unexpected challenges will always arise, and having the ability to respond quickly and effectively is crucial. However, there are two distinct points to acknowledge in how immediate responsive leadership ties into broader strategic thinking.

Firstly, those who have planned and prepared strategically often have the most *freedom to act in the moment*. For leaders to respond to unforeseen events with greater agility, they must have anticipated potential challenges and created flexible systems and structures. Strategic foresight gives leaders a well-prepared foundation that allows them to handle crises without being overwhelmed or forced into purely defensive reactions. By having contingency plans or adaptable frameworks in place, leaders can face the immediate challenges while staying in harmony with their long-term goals. This readiness is a sign of a leader who's mastered the balance between acting on the present situation and staying focused on the future.

Secondly, the skill set used to act in the moment has often been developed and honed over time, through strategic foresight. The ability to make fast, effective decisions doesn't happen by chance; it's the result of experience, practice and thoughtful preparation. Leaders who spend time considering possible scenarios and mentally rehearsing responses are better equipped to make sound decisions under pressure. This strategic foresight sharpens a leader's instincts, so when they need to react quickly, they can do so confidently and with a higher probability of success. Practising decision-making in low-stakes situations and building a repertoire of responses helps leaders to prepare themselves for high-stress moments when rapid action is required.

For *all leaders*, this ability to shift between responsive, proactive and strategic leadership is particularly valuable. They must rise to daily operational challenges, take proactive steps to mitigate future issues and think strategically to position their institutions for long-term success. The best leaders are those who can move deliberately between these leadership modes, which makes certain they're not only managing the present but also preparing their organisations to excel in an unpredictable future.

Creating a vision – or defining the *why* for your organisation – is like mastering any other leadership skill. For some, envisioning and articulating a meaningful and purposeful vision comes naturally, while others' strengths may lie in different areas of the Kilter Leadership Taxonomy. Regardless of where your natural abilities lie, frameworks exist that can guide you in strengthening your capacity to craft and communicate an inspiring vision. Like any skill, it can be honed with intentional practice and a structured approach.

One extremely important area to consider when creating a strong vision is making certain it resonates with your team's E-systems and R-systems. When your team is in a stable, rational place, they typically require less support in driving the vision forward. However, when they're experiencing an emotional state – such as disappointment, frustration or fatigue – they're more likely to disengage from the vision. A powerful vision must therefore connect with both their logical aspirations and their deeper emotional motivations.

Kilter Strategic Framework

There are many different strategic frameworks available. Here's the **Kilter Strategic Framework**, which has been designed to balance the full needs of a strategy and of a team:

1. **Start with the *why*:** Every strategy begins with seeking to understand the purpose behind it: why are you and your team pursuing this goal? This foundational question clarifies the mission, values and reasons for embarking on this path. It ensures all future actions remain aligned with a meaningful purpose.

   Key questions: Why is this important to you? What is motivating this journey?

2. **Define what you want to achieve:** Once the *why* has been established, the next step is to articulate the specific goal you want to accomplish. This should be a clear, measurable objective that's in line with the overarching purpose.

   Key questions: What's the specific goal you're aiming to achieve? What does success look like?

3. **Assess where you are vs where you want to be:** It's crucial to evaluate the current position relative to the goal. This involves identifying strengths, weaknesses, and gaps in resources or capabilities.

   Key questions: Where are you now? What gaps need to be addressed to reach your goal?

4. **Explore different possibilities and identify unique advantages:** Consider various strategic options for moving from the current position to the desired state while leveraging the team's unique strengths or capabilities. This step includes exploring potential pathways to success and identifying competitive advantages that could set the team or organisation apart.

   Key questions: What approaches or strategies can you employ to reach the goal? How can you leverage your team's unique strengths and capabilities to gain an advantage?

5. **Identify considerations and risks:** As part of strategic thinking, it's important to recognise any potential risks and pitfalls. This step focuses on seeking to understand what should be avoided to prevent failure or misalignment with the core values.

    Key questions: What risks, threats or obstacles should you avoid as you move forward? Are there ways these could be turned into advantages?

6. **Evaluate logistical and resource-based constraints:** Assess the logistical and resource constraints that may impact the implementation of any strategic approach. These could include financial limitations, time constraints or availability of human capital.

    Key question: What constraints or limitations (resources, time or skills) must you work within?

7. **Filter through the values and return to the *why*:** It's vital to filter the strategic options through the organisation's values to make certain they line up with the initial *why*. This will warrant that the strategy remains grounded in your purpose and ethical standards.

    Key questions: Is this strategy consistent with your core values and your *why*? Will this move you away from your vision?

8. **Establish metrics and milestones:** Once the strategy has been chosen, identify measurable metrics to track progress and create milestones to ensure progress toward the goal is on track. Metrics provide accountability and help assess success.

    Key questions: How will you measure progress? What milestones can you set to check your progress against?

9. **Communicate clearly and monitor progress:** The final phase involves communicating the strategy clearly to all stakeholders and setting up systems for ongoing monitoring

and adaptation. Regular check-ins and transparent communication make sure the strategy remains relevant and progress remains on course.

Key questions: How will you communicate the strategy to make certain everyone is aligned? How will we monitor progress and make necessary adjustments?

A strengths-based approach to strategy

As discussed in previous chapters, we each have natural strengths and preferences that mean we naturally contribute to different strategy areas. However, it's important to note that multiple needs exist at every stage of a strategy. A strengths-based approach encourages leveraging each individual's natural abilities while acknowledging that a successful strategy must address diverse challenges throughout its lifecycle.

Here's how the Kilter Strategic Framework integrates all personality types by building on the strengths-based approach:

1. **Start with the *why*:**

    Red: Provides direct, decisive input to ensure the purpose is clear and focus is maintained.

    Yellow: Engages and inspires the team by connecting the strategy to a larger vision.

    Green: Makes certain the purpose resonates with people and is in line with shared values.

    Blue: Brings precision and logic to the table to make sure the purpose is well-defined.

    At this stage, while some individuals may lead through vision or analysis, others contribute by helping the purpose connect with the team's values or by providing the decisiveness needed to move forward.

2. **Define what you want to achieve:**

    Red: Pushes for a clear, actionable goal.

Yellow: Adds creative and ambitious ideas for what success can look like.

Green: Makes sure the goal is achievable and realistic for the team.

Blue: Breaks down the goal into measurable, practical elements.

A strengths-based approach here recognises that both ambitious visionaries and practical, analytical thinkers contribute to refining the goal.

3. **Assess where you are vs where you want to be:**

    Red: Highlights critical gaps and areas for improvement.

    Yellow: Focuses on growth opportunities and possibilities.

    Green: Encourages collaboration in seeking to understand challenges.

    Blue: Conducts detailed analysis to pinpoint the current status.

    At this stage, each personality's strength – whether it's decisive action, optimism, collaboration or analytical depth – ensures a comprehensive understanding of the current situation can be reached.

4. **Explore the possibilities and identify the unique advantages:**

    Red: Explores bold, action-oriented options and drives the team to leverage their competitive advantages.

    Yellow: Fosters creative brainstorming while identifying innovative opportunities for differentiation.

    Green: Makes certain the approaches remain practical and people-focused, which cultivates collaboration as a unique asset.

    Blue: Evaluates feasibility, conducts data-backed analysis and pinpoints where the team has an edge.

Combining exploration with identifying the team's unique advantages ensures both creativity and practicality are balanced, which allows the team to innovate while leveraging their existing strengths effectively.

5. **Identify the considerations and risks:**

    Red: Tackles risks head-on with a focus on solutions.

    Yellow: Maintains positivity while identifying hidden opportunities within the risks.

    Green: Makes certain that the impact on people is taken into account.

    Blue: Conducts thorough risk assessments to mitigate the threats.

    Balancing optimism and caution makes sure risks are addressed without stifling creativity.

6. **Evaluate the logistical and resource-based constraints:**

    Red: Focuses on overcoming constraints decisively.

    Yellow: Finds creative ways to utilise limited resources.

    Green: Ensures constraints don't overwhelm the team and resources are distributed fairly.

    Blue: Plans meticulously and tracks resources.

    While logistical challenges need practical solutions, having different perspectives on overcoming them facilitates both creativity and realism.

7. **Filter through values and return to the *why*:**

    Red: Offers decisiveness while bringing actions in line with values.

    Yellow: Engages the team's passion, which keeps values at the heart of the strategy.

Green: Makes certain the approach remains people-centred and consistent with the group's shared values.

Blue: Verifies that actions align logically with the core values and purpose.

Here, the team's diverse strengths allows the final approach to stay grounded in both purpose and values.

8. **Establish metrics and milestones:**

    Red: Drives the team toward ambitious milestones.

    Yellow: Keeps the team motivated with enthusiasm and focused on the larger vision.

    Green: Ensures the milestones are achievable and set with the team's well-being in mind.

    Blue: Breaks down the milestones into measurable, trackable progress points.

    Each strength contributes to the milestones being inspiring, achievable and easily measurable.

9. **Communicate clearly and monitor progress:**

    Red: Communicates with authority, which drives accountability.

    Yellow: Keeps communication positive to facilitate engagement and energy.

    Green: Fosters open dialogue and ensures that communication strengthens collaboration.

    Blue: Sets up structured systems to monitor progress with data-driven updates.

    Diverse strengths make certain both clear, motivating communication and systematic progress tracking are provided, which keeps the team aligned and focused.

CONCLUSION

Strategic leadership is the culmination of reactive and proactive leadership, and it offers a pathway to long-term success, which comes through deliberate planning, adaptability and foresight. Although reactive leadership addresses those challenges with an immediate impact and proactive leadership anticipates near-term risks, strategic leadership elevates these approaches by aligning today's actions with a vision for tomorrow. It requires leaders to balance present demands with future opportunities, which will ensure the organisation thrives in a complex, ever-changing landscape.

Key to this process is having a clear strategy – one that's rooted in purpose, informed by data and built upon the strengths of the team. Through frameworks such as the Kilter Strategic Framework and by using a strengths-based approach, leaders can craft strategies that not only achieve specific goals but also inspire innovation, collaboration and resilience. This involves leveraging the diverse abilities of their team members, identifying unique advantages and maintaining alignment with core values to guide decision-making.

Strategic leaders also understand that progress isn't linear. Metrics and milestones are essential tools for monitoring success, but true strategic leadership goes beyond numbers. It integrates data with mission-driven leadership, which makes certain that progress is both measurable and meaningful. By tracking key indicators, addressing obstacles with creativity and maintaining clarity of purpose, leaders can keep their teams focused, motivated and confident.

Strategic leadership is about transformation: it turns crises into opportunities, strengths into competitive advantages, and visions into reality. It prepares organisations to adapt, innovate and grow, which creates a sustainable foundation for success. Excelling across the reactive, proactive and strategic modes of leadership helps skilled leaders navigate uncertainty with confidence, which drives their teams toward a future that aligns with their highest aspirations and values.

13
Culture Creation

Every action is a brick in the wall

Culture creation is one of a leader's most important responsibilities. An organisation's culture consists of the shared values, beliefs, attitudes and behaviours that influence how work gets done. It's the invisible force that permeates daily interactions and long-term decision-making. A thriving culture fosters innovation, collaboration and accountability, while a toxic culture can undermine even the best strategies and systems. It's important to understand that leaders don't choose whether to create a culture – a culture will naturally emerge as a product of their decisions, actions and priorities.

Every action a leader takes and each decision they make – whether deliberate or unconscious – adds to this cultural structure. These small actions build up over time, like individual bricks forming a larger wall, shaping the values and behaviours that permeate the organisation. To build a thriving culture, leaders must be intentional about forming it by consciously choosing which behaviours to reinforce and which to address – whether it's saying yes or no to a request, praising or punishing particular behaviours, or choosing what to tolerate or ignore. Leaders who fail to pay attention to the culture they're creating risk unintentionally fostering behaviours that are misaligned with their personal or their organisation's values or long-term goals. Conversely, those who take deliberate action to reinforce positive behaviours and address negative ones can build a strong, cohesive culture that aligns with both their and their organisation's vision.

At a fundamental level, culture creation is simple, but it isn't a straightforward process: it's like walking a tightrope. On one side is the need to encourage belonging and inclusivity, and on the other is the necessity for selection and accountability. Leaders must create an environment in which employees feel they belong and are valued, while also ensuring a high level of performance is maintained. Similarly, leaders who push for excellence must also avoid the pitfall of creating a high-stress, burnout-inducing environment. Balancing these competing demands requires skill and thoughtful decision-making because every decision impacts the organisation's overall culture.

What takes months and years to build can be damaged in a moment and completely destroyed in an incredibly short amount of time. A lapse in leadership integrity can erode trust, undo progress and dramatically shift the tone of the workplace. This fragility underscores the importance of having consistent, intentional leadership that protects and nurtures the culture while recognising the profound responsibility of maintaining it over time.

Returning to the area of *process vs outcome*, we'll look at the cultural implications of this. As leaders shape culture through the behaviours they model and the actions they prioritise, if they choose to focus on **processes** rather than just **outcomes**, this sends an obvious message to the organisation about what's valued. Processes are within the team's control, but outcomes can be influenced by external factors. By placing the emphasis on processes, leaders empower their teams to focus on executing their skill set in the moment, which ultimately leads to better outcomes and higher performance over time. On the other hand, focusing exclusively on outcomes can create a culture of pressure in which short-term results are prioritised at the expense of long-term growth and sustainability.

It's important to note that there's no one-size-fits-all approach to creating culture. Every organisation is unique, and developing the right culture requires a consistent, deliberate and skilled approach that's tailored to the team's specific needs and values. Ultimately, every action a leader takes shapes the culture – whether deliberately or unintentionally – and it's their responsibility to ensure the 'bricks' they lay contribute to the right foundation.

What organisational culture is

Before examining how leaders can create and shape culture, it's essential to define what we mean by **'organisational culture'**. 'Culture' refers to the collective values, beliefs and behaviours that determine how people within an organisation interact with each other, make decisions and achieve goals. It's the environment that shapes employees' daily experiences, which influences everything from their productivity to their sense of belonging.

Culture is often described as being an organisation's personality. It sets the tone for how employees communicate, how they approach their work and how they relate to one another. A *strong, positive culture* fosters an environment in which employees feel supported, motivated and engaged, which drives productivity and innovation. In contrast, a *toxic culture* can lead to disengagement, high staff turnover and even unethical behaviour, which undermine the organisation's long-term success.

For leaders, understanding the components of culture is the first step in shaping it. Organisational culture is driven by several key factors:

- **Vision:** A vision provides a clear and inspiring goal that the organisation is aiming to achieve. It serves as a unifying force that aligns efforts across teams and guides decision-making. A meaningful vision reflects the organisation's aspirations, motivates employees and sets the direction for long-term success. Leaders must make certain the vision is actionable, grounded in shared values and communicated consistently.

- **Values:** These are the core principles guiding an organisation's actions and decisions, which serve as its moral compass. These beliefs influence strategy, ethics and daily operations. However, having designated values that are ignored in practice can be more damaging than having none at all. Leaders must make sure their values are consistently reflected in their actions and decisions.

- **Norms:** These are the unwritten rules that govern behaviour within the organisation. Norms establish what's considered acceptable and guide how employees collaborate, communicate and solve problems.

- **Symbols and rituals:** These are the tangible expressions of culture. Symbols might include company logos or office design, and rituals could involve awards, team-building exercises or regular celebrations of successes. These expressions help solidify an organisation's cultural identity.

- **Behaviours:** These are the day-to-day actions of employees and leaders, which reflect the organisation's values. Leaders in particular set the standard for behaviour through their decisions, actions and responses to both successes and failures.

- **Language:** This is the way people within the organisation communicate with one another. It includes both the formal language used in meetings and reports and the informal jargon or phrases that are unique to the company. Language shapes how employees connect and express ideas, and it contributes to a shared sense of identity.

Organisational culture isn't *static*; it evolves over time as the company grows, adapts to changes, and responds to internal and external challenges. However, a leader's role is to guide and shape this evolution to ensure the culture remains consistent with the organisation's mission, vision and values. This necessitates deliberate action, clear communication and the constant reinforcement of the desired behaviours. Leaders must be conscious of the messages they're sending – whether that's through formal channels (such as meetings and speeches) or through everyday decisions (such as recognising effort or addressing misconduct). Every interaction contributes to the ongoing development of the organisation's culture.

Organisational culture is the foundation upon which long-term success is built. It influences employee engagement, retention and performance, as well as the organisation's ability to innovate and adapt. A leader who actively shapes the culture fosters a positive, values-driven environment in which employees are aligned with the organisation's goals and feel empowered to contribute to its success. However, there's no universal definition of what constitutes a *good* culture – it depends on the organisation's goals, values and context. The executive leader, who holds the most control, plays a pivotal role in determining the culture. With a highly developed skill set and intentionality, they can shape the culture as they choose so as to bring it into line with their vision for success.

EXERCISE: VISION CREATION

Creating a vision comes naturally to some and feels like an intuitive and inspiring process. For others, however, it can feel daunting, especially when faced with the challenge of aligning diverse perspectives or articulating long-term aspirations. This exercise is designed to scaffold the process by offering a structured approach to make certain every team – regardless of their starting point – can craft a meaningful and actionable vision.

This team exercise can help you create a meaningful vision, regardless of whether you naturally excel in visionary leadership:

1. **Start with values and aspirations:** Begin by asking your team, 'What do we want people to say about us?'

    This question taps into the group's values, encourages forward thinking and engages the team's E-system. It highlights what they aspire to be recognised for and allows them to envision the positive legacy they want to build.

2. **Identify what to avoid:** Follow this by asking, 'What don't we want people to say about us?'

   This question complements the first by activating the team's emotional responses around values and aspirations, as well as addressing their fears or concerns. It creates a clear understanding of the behaviours or outcomes the team should avoid.

3. **Translate this into a vision statement:** Use the answers to these two questions to craft a vision collaboratively that reflects both what the team wants to achieve and what they aim to steer clear of. This helps guarantee the vision resonates emotionally and is forward-looking.

4. **Define supporting behaviours:** Next, ask, 'What behaviours will get us to where we want to be?'

   This question focuses the team on actionable, positive behaviours that are consistent with the desired vision.

   Then ask, 'What behaviours will take us to where we don't want to be?'

   Identifying and discussing these behaviours helps the team define the actions and habits that will either support or hinder the vision.

5. **Group behaviours into values and norms:** From these behaviours, group the recurring themes into values and norms. These become the building blocks of the organisation's culture that link the vision to everyday actions and expectations.

By following this structured process, as a leader, you can guide your team in crafting a vision that's both meaningful and practical. Whether or not visionary thinking is your natural strength, using this approach will ensure the vision reflects your organisation's collective values and aspirations, while being deeply rooted in actionable behaviours.

LEVEL 4: CHAPTER 13 – CULTURE CREATION

EXAMPLE IN PRACTICE: CYCLING TEAM VISION

Here's a step-by-step example of how a cycling team could create meaning and a purposeful vision.

Step 1: Identify what they want people to say about them

The team brainstorms and decides they want people to say this:

- They're *fast*.
- They're *brave*.
- They *never give up*.
- They *come back even when it seems impossible*.
- They *stick together no matter what*.
- They're *absolute pros*.
- Even though they're amazing, they're still *humble*.

Step 2: Identify what they don't want people to say

The team reflects on what they want to avoid and identifies they don't want people to say this:

- They're *quitters*.
- They're *lazy*.
- They're *arrogant*.
- They're *in it for themselves as individuals*.
- They *crack under pressure*.

Step 3: Translate this into a vision

From this discussion, they craft their vision:

> *We want to be as good as the world's best cycling teams.*

This vision reflects their aspirations to reach the highest standards while staying true to their values of resilience, teamwork and humility.

Step 4: Define the behaviours that will help them achieve this vision

The team identifies the behaviours that align with their vision:

- » **Being disciplined in training:** Committing to rigorous preparation and consistent effort, knowing it's the foundation of success.
- » **Being honest with each other:** Offering constructive feedback and support to facilitate continuous improvement.
- » **Looking out for how they can help each other:** Fostering teamwork by prioritising the team's goals over individual ambitions.
- » **Focusing on the process, no matter the result:** Staying committed to executing their strategy and approach, even when good results don't come immediately.

Step 5: Define the behaviours that would move them away from their vision

The team also identifies the behaviours that would derail their vision:

- » **Cutting corners:** Compromising on effort or preparation, which causes long-term underperformance.
- » **Arguing in front of other teams:** Showing disunity, which damages their reputation and morale.
- » **Talking behind each other's backs:** Erodes trust and creates a toxic environment.
- » **Relying on motivation:** Depending on fleeting emotions rather than cultivating discipline and resilience.
- » **Giving up when things aren't straightforward:** Losing focus or quitting when challenges arise.
- • **Blaming others and making excuses:** Avoiding accountability, which undermines the team's ability to learn and grow.

Step 6: Group the behaviours into values and norms

The team organises their behaviours into these values and norms:

- **Values:** Discipline, teamwork, honesty, perseverance, professionalism and humility.

- **Norms:** Be on time, look to help the team, encourage one another, communicate openly, take responsibility and prioritise process over results.

Through this exercise, the cycling team creates a vision that's both inspiring and actionable. They know what they're striving for, how they'll get there and what pitfalls to avoid. This vision and framework will guide their actions and culture to make certain they're aligned with their goals at every stage of their journey.

The leader's role in shaping culture through communication

A leader's role in shaping culture extends far beyond making decisions and creating strategies. It's about communicating the organisation's values and expectations clearly and consistently. What leaders choose to say and do – and perhaps, more importantly, what they choose to monitor and measure – sends strong signals about what the organisation stands for and how success is defined.

The power of everyday messaging

Culture isn't built through one-time declarations or occasional speeches. It's constructed through the day-to-day messages leaders communicate to their teams. These messages are conveyed through both formal and informal channels – meetings, emails, speeches and one-on-one conversations – and through the leader's actions and behaviours.

For instance, if a leader talks continuously about the importance of innovation but consistently shuts down new ideas or punishes missteps, the unspoken message becomes clear: innovation isn't truly valued. Conversely, if a leader encourages risk-taking and praises those who attempt new approaches (even if they fail), the message is that innovation is a core part of the culture. Naturally, balance is key; leaning too far in either direction can create issues. Overemphasising risk-taking without accountability may lead to chaos, while excessive caution stifles creativity. Striking the right balance helps innovation thrive within a structured and supportive environment.

Celebration and sanction

How leaders respond to success and failure is vital in shaping culture, particularly when their reactions attach further values to the event. For instance, if sanctions or rewards emphasise external perceptions (such as prioritising public image over genuine effort or practice), the cultural message shifts. In such cases, individuals may internalise the idea that appearances or short-term outcomes matter more than long-term development or integrity. This can undermine trust and resilience within the team as team members may feel their intrinsic efforts are secondary to external opinions. Conversely, when leaders balance their responses and maintain emotional steadiness after wins and losses, they convey the message that performance matters but doesn't solely define a person's value. This consistency fosters a culture of trust and belonging, which enables individuals to focus on improving their skills and contributing sustainably to the organisation's success.

Leaders must be intentional in reinforcing key cultural messages every day. Whether it's in large meetings or casual corridor conversations, they should consistently communicate the organisation's values and link those values to the team's daily actions. These consistent messages help employees align themselves with the organisation's goals, which makes certain culture is not just an abstract idea but a lived reality.

What's measured and monitored becomes culture, so focus on processes

One of the most powerful ways leaders shape culture is through what they choose to measure and monitor. What leaders emphasise –

whether that's processes or outcomes – fundamentally impacts how employees behave and what they prioritise in their efforts.

Focusing too heavily on *outcomes* can create a culture in which employees feel pressured to deliver results at any cost, which often leads to shortcuts, burnout or unethical behaviour. Outcomes are frequently influenced by external factors beyond the team's control, such as market conditions or economic shifts. If success is measured purely by outcomes, employees may feel demoralised if targets aren't met, despite them following best practices.

Instead, leaders can focus on monitoring and measuring *processes*, which are within the team's control. 'Processes' refers to the specific methods, actions and systems employees use to achieve their goals. When leaders prioritise and monitor processes – such as collaboration, communication, problem-solving and customer engagement – they help build a culture that emphasises excellence in execution and continuous improvement. Striking a balance in this monitoring is key as it elicits the right emphasis and focus without overwhelming the team. By balancing attention across the critical processes, leaders create an environment in which improvement feels achievable, which fosters both engagement and sustained high performance.

Measuring processes allows leaders to make sure employees are following best practices and engaging in behaviours that are consistent with the organisation's values. Over time, robust processes naturally lead to better outcomes. And even if outcomes don't improve immediately, the processes can be evaluated and refined without placing undue pressure on employees.

EXAMPLE IN PRACTICE: SALES TEAM AT WORK

The following example shows the outcomes for a sales team with different degrees of focus on outcomes or processes:

- **Too much focus on process:** A sales team rigorously follows their engagement strategies and diligently completes all the steps in their scripts and internal procedures. However, they fail to adapt their approach when customers raise new concerns, which causes sales to stagnate despite their disciplined adherence to processes.

- **Too much focus on results:** Being under pressure to meet revenue targets, a sales team prioritises closing deals at all costs. They cut corners on customer engagement, oversell products and fail to build long-term relationships. Although they might hit short-term goals, customer dissatisfaction leads to a decline in both trust and repeat business.

- **Correct balance:** A sales team follows well-established engagement strategies while remaining adaptable to meet customer needs. Leaders monitor both processes (such as message refinement and collaboration) and outcomes (such as revenue targets and customer retention).

Leaders who focus on *processes* and maintain *consistency* in their messaging – both in celebration and chastisement – create a culture that values discipline, commitment and resilience over short-term results (which can engender short-cuts and dishonesty). By emphasising what employees can control, rather than fixating on outcomes that may fluctuate, leaders build a culture in which people feel valued for their contributions and motivated to perform at their best.

Strategic culture creation: Building an inclusive and values-driven organisation

Creating a strong and positive culture requires strategic planning and intentional actions. Leaders must think strategically about how the organisation's culture can support its long-term goals and ensure it's inclusive, positive and values-driven.

Aligning culture with organisational strategy

One of the most critical aspects of culture creation is making sure the culture supports the organisation's overall strategy. For example, if the company's strategy focuses on innovation, the culture must encourage *creativity, risk-taking* and *continuous learning*. Leaders must cultivate an environment in which employees feel comfortable with sharing new ideas, experimenting with new approaches and learning from failures.

Conversely, if the organisation's strategy focuses on customer service, the culture must prioritise *empathy, communication* and *customer-centricity*. In this case, leaders should encourage behaviours that promote excellent customer service, such as active listening, problem-solving, and going above and beyond to meet customer needs.

In both cases, what the leader *communicates, monitors* and *measures* plays a central role in reinforcing the desired behaviours that align with the organisation's strategy.

Building a culture of inclusion

An *inclusive culture* is one in which all employees feel *valued* and *respected*, regardless of their background, experience or position within the organisation. Inclusivity isn't just a moral imperative; it's also a strategic advantage. Research shows that diverse and inclusive teams are more innovative, make better decisions and are better equipped to solve complex problems.[31]

Leaders must be intentional about creating an inclusive culture by doing the following:

» **Promoting diversity:** Ensuring the organisation hires and promotes individuals from diverse backgrounds and perspectives.

» **Encouraging open dialogue:** Creating opportunities for employees to share their experiences and perspectives in a safe and supportive environment.

» **Providing equal opportunities for growth:** Making certain all employees have access to opportunities for development and advancement, regardless of their background.

By fostering an inclusive culture, leaders create an environment in which all employees feel empowered to contribute to the organisation's success.

Embedding values in daily practices

To create a values-driven culture, leaders must act in such a way that the organisation's core values are not just words on a page but are *reflected in their daily actions and decisions.*

This means embedding values into the following:

- **Recruitment and onboarding:** Making sure new employees are aligned with the organisation's values from the start through values-based interview questions, culture-focused onboarding and early mentorship. As interviews often fail to identify high-quality leaders accurately, complementary methods such as situational assessments and practical exercises can provide more reliable measures of leadership potential.

- **Performance management:** Evaluating employees not just on what they achieve but also on how they achieve it. Leaders should incorporate values into performance reviews and promotions, and thus reward employees who demonstrate they're aligned with the company's core principles.

- **Decision-making:** Ensuring organisational decisions – whether they're about strategy, partnerships or investments – are made with the company's values in mind. For example, if integrity is a core value, leaders give ethical considerations top priority in their decision-making.

Addressing challenges in culture creation

Building and sustaining a positive organisational culture isn't without its challenges. Leaders must be prepared to navigate *resistance to change,* handle *conflict* when it arises and address *toxic behaviours* that may undermine the culture they're trying to create.

Overcoming resistance to change

When leaders attempt to shape or transform organisational culture, they may face resistance from employees who are comfortable with the status quo.

To overcome resistance, leaders should do the following:

» **Communicate the vision of the new culture (and what the alternative might look like)**: Employees are more likely to embrace change if they understand how it will benefit them and the organisation.

» **Involve employees in the process:** Leaders should solicit input from employees and involve them in discussions about cultural changes. This not only makes employees feel valued but also increases their buy-in.

» **Lead by example:** Leaders must model the behaviours and attitudes they want to see throughout the organisation. If leaders aren't fully committed to the new culture, the employees are unlikely to accept it.

The impact of added pressure and the importance of the *why* in culture

The VIPs' impact

One of the most damaging actions a leader can take is to *drastically change behaviours or processes when VIPs visit.* Whether it's for an inspection, audit or executive visit, altering the usual way of working or implementing short-term measures that don't reflect normal daily practices sends a strong, negative cultural message. Employees learn quickly that consistency isn't valued and authentic performance only matters when someone external is watching. This both undermines trust and encourages a culture of superficiality in which employees feel compelled to act differently to impress external figures, rather than focusing on achieving genuine excellence for those they work for every day.

Making short-term changes for inspections can create a 'checklist mentality' in which employees focus on simply meeting criteria rather than embodying the organisation's values and goals. For example, if a school only focuses on cleanliness, curriculum adherence and/ or student behaviour when inspectors are visiting, it tells staff that these areas are only important with respect to external perception, not as part of the ongoing culture. This approach can lead to *cognitive dissonance* among employees, who see their leaders preaching one thing but prioritising something entirely different when outside scrutiny is involved. Over time, this weakens the leaders' credibility and damages employee engagement.

Moreover, a culture built on impressing external parties undercuts authenticity and creates stress. Employees may feel pressured to meet unrealistic standards during these periods, which often leads to burnout, confusion and disengagement.

That said, it's reasonable and sensible to pay extra attention to details during an inspection or visit, as neglecting to do so can be wilfully disrespectful. Such instances can be likened to a first date: you want to be genuine because changing your whole persona simply to impress your date could kick off a relationship you're not genuinely suited for. Conversely, showing up dressed in a sloppy way could offend someone who might actually be a great match. Similarly, organisations should aim for authenticity while demonstrating respect and pride in their work during such occasions. The best organisations strive to operate at high standards consistently, regardless of who's watching, which promotes transparency and integrity in all their actions.

Returning to the power of the *why* in cultural development

Central to shaping any culture is understanding and communicating the *purpose* behind an organisation's actions – its *why*. A strong, well-communicated *why* gives employees a clear sense of purpose and direction, which motivates them to contribute meaningfully to the organisation's mission. When the *why* is powerful, it becomes the culture's foundation, which influences how employees work, collaborate and make decisions.

However, if the organisation's *why* is *short-term, uninspiring* or *externally driven*, the culture will reflect this. For example, if employees feel their main purpose is to meet quarterly sales targets, impress inspectors and/or generate positive reports for leadership, their engagement and motivation will suffer. This approach focuses on *external validation* rather than *intrinsic values*, which leaves employees uninspired and more likely to disengage.

In contrast, when the *why* is tied to a *deeper, more meaningful mission*, the culture is transformed. If an organisation's purpose is framed around *serving the community, improving lives* or *making a significant societal impact*, employees can see how their work contributes to a larger goal. For example, a school's *why* could be about nurturing future generations and eliciting a love of learning, rather than simply scoring well on inspections. Or a retail organisation's *why* could be about providing value and creating strong relationships with the community it serves, instead of focusing solely on revenue targets.

Inspiring a strong why creates a sense of ownership and pride. Employees are motivated by the impact they can have and are therefore more likely to go above and beyond in their work. This deeper connection to the organisation's purpose fosters resilience, creativity and a culture of continuous improvement. It also brings individuals' goals in line with organisational success, which creates a unified, motivated workforce.

Leaders must continually communicate the organisation's *why* and tie it to daily actions. Although a clear and compelling reason for being helps employees focus on long-term excellence, balance is key. Successful inspections and achieving quarterly targets are still essential for sustaining and validating an organisation's performance. A strong *why* provides consistency, which helps make sure short-term pressures (such as preparing for evaluations or meeting targets) are in harmony with the organisation's values and behaviours. This balance prevents external demands from eroding the foundations of a healthy, productive culture while leveraging them as opportunities to demonstrate excellence.

Handling conflict and toxic behaviours

Conflict is a natural part of any workplace, but when left unresolved or compounded by toxic behaviours, it can erode even the strongest organisational culture. A *toxic blame culture* is particularly damaging. In such environments, employees may be more focused on outperforming or undermining each other than on collaboration or collective success. This behaviour breeds distrust, stifles innovation and leads to a culture in which people are reluctant to take responsibility for their mistakes due to fearing they'll be punished or scapegoated.

In a blame culture, individuals may speak publicly about *compassion* and *integrity*, but their actions suggest otherwise. They might engage in *backstabbing, gossip* or *withholding information* in an attempt to gain a personal advantage over their colleagues. This misalignment between words and actions is one of the warning signs of a toxic environment, in which there's often a façade of values that aren't lived in practice. Team members learn quickly that success in this culture is based on politics, not performance, and they may adopt similar behaviours to protect themselves. Over time, this erodes morale, disengages employees and diminishes trust across teams. Leaders have a vital role in addressing this type of toxic behaviour and preventing it from spreading.

Here are some key strategies leaders can use to combat a toxic blame culture and foster a healthier, more inclusive environment:

» **Encouraging open communication:** In a toxic culture, communication is often distorted or withheld altogether, with employees being afraid to voice their concerns or share feedback for fear of retribution. Leaders must create an environment in which *open, honest communication* is not only encouraged but expected. This involves establishing feedback channels, promoting psychological safety, and facilitating team members expressing their concerns without fearing personal or professional consequences. A proactive leader can encourage this openness through regular one-to-one check-ins, anonymous feedback systems and open forums for discussion. Leadership *transparency*, where their successes and failures are shared candidly, helps build trust and demonstrates that everyone – leaders included – is accountable for their actions.

» **Addressing toxic behaviours early:** Toxic behaviours such as *gossiping, bullying* and *undermining others* must be addressed swiftly and decisively. Leaders who tolerate or overlook these behaviours send the message that such actions are acceptable, which allows them to spread unchecked. The longer toxic behaviours persist, the harder they become to root out, and they can cause long-term damage to the organisation's culture. A good leader will recognise when these behaviours emerge and then take action – whether that's through direct conversations, mediation or disciplinary measures.

» **Ensuring accountability with compassion:** In toxic blame cultures, accountability often turns into finger-pointing. Employees are quick to shift responsibility to avoid consequences, which elicits dysfunction and low morale. Leaders must make certain that accountability is upheld *with compassion*. This means creating an environment in which employees are encouraged to own their mistakes and learn from them, rather than fear retribution. Compassionate leadership involves supporting employees when things go wrong and focusing on learning and growth rather than blame. Leaders who model integrity and empathy help to reshape a culture of fear into one of mutual respect.

» **Reinforcing integrity in actions, not just words:** Leaders who speak about values such as *integrity* and *compassion* but fail to demonstrate these qualities in their behaviour will rapidly lose credibility. In a toxic culture, employees will see through empty words, especially if the leaders themselves engage in behaviours that contradict their stated values. Leaders must consistently act in ways that reflect the values they promote, whether by addressing issues head-on, holding themselves accountable, or recognising and rewarding positive behaviours within their teams.

For instance, if a leader stresses the importance of teamwork but rewards individual achievements at the expense of collaboration, the true cultural message becomes clear. Leaders should warrant that their actions – whether through recognition, feedback or decision-making – are consistent with the values they want to see reflected across the organisation.

» **Balancing performance with well-being:** Toxic blame cultures often place an overwhelming emphasis on *performance at any cost*, which engenders burnout, high turnover and ethical compromises. Leaders must balance the need for high performance with *employee well-being*. This means recognising that employees aren't machines; pushing for results without considering their mental and emotional health leads to long-term damage.

Leaders should regularly check in on their team's workload and stress levels, make certain that employees have the resources they need to succeed, and promote a culture in which it's acceptable to ask for help. When employees feel supported, they're more likely to engage in healthy, sustainable performance.

How culture impacts long-term success

A strong, positive organisational culture has far-reaching effects on the long-term success of the organisation. *Employee engagement, retention, innovation* and *performance* are all closely linked to culture. A positive culture enhances employee satisfaction and loyalty, which in turn reduces turnover and improves productivity. It also promotes a sense of ownership and accountability, which encourages employees to take the initiative and contribute to the organisation's success.

Moreover, a thriving culture *attracts top talent*. In a competitive job market, talented individuals are more likely to join and stay with organisations that have a strong, positive, values-driven culture. Companies with positive cultures also tend to have better relationships with their customers and stakeholders, as employees are more engaged, motivated and aligned with the company's mission.

Ultimately, the culture a leader creates will determine the organisation's ability to *adapt, innovate* and *thrive* in a constantly changing environment.

Setting personal visions or smaller-team visions

Although creating an organisation-wide vision is ideal, not all leaders are in a position to shape the overarching vision for their organisation. In such cases, it's highly advisable as a leader to set your own personal vision or craft visions for your smaller teams. These visions, when consistent with the broader organisational goals, can still serve as powerful guiding forces for your leadership and your team's actions.

CONCLUSION

Organisational culture is the foundation of long-term success, and it influences everything from employee engagement to innovation and adaptability. This chapter has highlighted the pivotal role leaders play in shaping and sustaining culture. Culture isn't an abstract idea; it's built through the daily actions, decisions and priorities of leaders. Each choice – whether intentional or unconscious – contributes to the values and behaviours that define the organisation.

A strong, positive culture balances inclusivity, accountability and high performance. Leaders must skilfully manage the tension between encouraging excellence and avoiding burnout, plus between fostering belonging and maintaining accountability. Culture is also fragile – what takes years to build can be damaged in moments by inconsistency or a lapse in integrity. This underscores the importance of deliberate leadership that aligns every action with the organisation's true values and goals.

Culture is shaped by messaging, decision-making, and what leaders choose to measure and monitor. Whether they're focusing on processes or outcomes, leaders must maintain balance to guarantee sustainable success. A culture that prioritises authenticity and consistent high standards, rather than superficial efforts to impress external parties, is one that fosters trust and resilience. By bringing cultural practices in line with the organisation's purpose, leaders create an environment in which employees are motivated to perform at their best.

Deliberate culture creation requires a skilled, intentional approach that's tailored to the unique goals and values of the organisation. Leaders who actively shape their culture are better equipped to navigate challenges, inspire their teams and achieve sustained success. By consistently reinforcing the desired behaviours and values, they ensure their organisation remains focused, united and prepared for the future.

14

Leadership Structure and Pathways

Developing future leaders is critical for any organisation's long-term sustainability and success. In a rapidly changing world, organisations that don't prioritise leadership development will risk stagnating and falling behind. The task of identifying, nurturing and empowering the next generation of leaders requires strategic foresight and planning, as well as a commitment to creating clear leadership pathways. These pathways should provide individuals with opportunities for growth, mentorship and hands-on experience, which equip them with the skills and confidence needed to take on future leadership roles.

It's also a strategic skill to select a leadership structure that provides the organisation with a competitive advantage. Ensuring the organisation's most impactful areas are led by skilled and deliberate individuals amplifies overall success. These leaders may bring drive or innovation to their roles, and the ability to create such impactful positions – and to equip the right people to fill them – can be developed deliberately through experience and effort. A strong leadership framework that's been tailored to an organisation's unique goals and needs can be transformative.

This chapter builds on the principles studied in previous discussions on developing others, team dynamics, and strategic leadership shifting the focus toward developing people in a structured and strategic way. In this context, leadership pathways are not just about identifying high-potential employees but about creating an environment in which their unique strengths are harnessed, their skills are front-loaded and their development is intentional. We'll explore how to craft leadership pathways strategically using tools to support every step of an individual's development journey. Finally, we'll address the challenge of avoiding the **Peter Principle**,[32] which makes certain that individuals are promoted based on their readiness for leadership, rather than just their proficiency at the skills serving their current role. We'll also consider how the organisation's culture plays a crucial role in shaping these future leaders.

The importance of leadership pathways

Leadership pathways are structured opportunities for the individuals within an organisation to develop the skills, knowledge and experiences necessary to assume more-senior leadership roles in the future. These pathways are essential because they thoroughly prepare future leaders to meet the demands of their roles. When an organisation prioritises developing future leaders, it fosters a culture of continuous improvement, which is vital for maintaining long-term success. Furthermore, when current team members see others being promoted internally, it can boost motivation significantly as it demonstrates that the organisation is invested in growth and advancement. This practice also attracts talent, as potential employees recognise a workplace that's committed to development and offering obvious opportunities for career progression.

Strategic leadership pathways address more than just immediate talent needs; they consider the organisation's long-term sustainability by preparing individuals to handle evolving challenges. Leaders who create these pathways don't just wait for talent to emerge – they actively identify potential early on, nurture growth and provide opportunities for the practical application of learned skills. This helps avoid the pitfalls of promoting individuals too soon or without the proper preparation, which is known as the Peter Principle; this occurs when individuals are promoted to positions they aren't equipped for, which often leads to wide-scale organisational inefficiencies.

Creating leadership pathways based on strengths and commitment

To build effective leadership pathways, organisations must first understand and leverage the unique strengths of their people. Rather than focusing solely on minimising weaknesses, the emphasis should be on recognising and nurturing the exceptional qualities individuals bring to the table. Leadership development is most successful when it creates opportunities for people to lead in areas where they naturally excel, which reflects their potential and the value they consistently offer.

Once these strengths have been identified, it's important to communicate to them that promotion won't simply be based on talent or individual performance in certain areas; it also requires demonstrated commitment to the broader fundamental skills that are integral to the team or organisation. For instance, a highly creative designer or a talented presenter and speaker could still cause long-term issues if their wider behaviours are blame-focused, unreliable or misaligned with their organisation's values.

Promotion should therefore be contingent on not only showcasing an individual's talents but also demonstrating the behaviours that will move their organisation toward its vision, such as reliability, accountability and integrity. This makes sure those moving into leadership roles are fully prepared to embody the organisation's principles, which engenders a positive and resilient culture. However, it's important to note that many of these skills – such as reliability, self-awareness and accountability – can be developed over time with effort and dedication. Organisations must create environments in which individuals are supported in developing these competencies, even if they aren't initially their strongest areas. Additionally, it's important to note that promotion and selection give the clearest and strongest messages from leaders, which signals what the organisation truly values and expects from its people. It's crucial that these opportunities are seized upon to reinforce the standards and culture that are consistent with the organisation's strategic vision.

EXAMPLE IN PRACTICE: THE IMPACT OF PROMOTION DECISIONS IN A SCHOOL CONTEXT

A school is considering two teachers for promotion to head of department. The first candidate is highly experienced and delivers strong academic results. However, they're known for creating a negative atmosphere, engaging in gossip and criticising colleagues publicly. Although they're skilled in their own teaching, their behaviour undermines team morale and collaboration.

The second candidate is less experienced but has the potential to be equally strong in teaching. They consistently meet deadlines, handle high-pressure situations effectively and approach challenges with positivity. They avoid workplace politics and act as a calming influence during conflicts, which nurtures teamwork and collaboration.

Promoting the experienced candidate may seem like the obvious choice based on their expertise, but the long-term cultural impact must be considered too. Rewarding negative behaviours sends a signal that such conduct is acceptable, which erodes trust, collaboration and morale over time.

Choosing the less experienced candidate would prioritise positive behaviours – such as reliability, respect and accountability – and reinforce a culture aligned with the school's values. While this may present short-term challenges, it sets a standard for constructive team dynamics, which boosts trust, cohesion and long-term performance.

Promotion decisions communicate what the organisation values. Choosing the experienced but negative candidate could harm morale and teamwork, while promoting the less experienced but positive candidate demonstrates a commitment to fostering a healthy, collaborative culture. This approach ensures long-term success and remaining in harmony with the organisation's vision. Additionally, imagine the impact on performance if the team were made up of and led by individuals like the second candidate. A team built on reliability, accountability and positivity would cultivate an environment of trust and collaboration, which would lead to higher levels of engagement, resilience and innovation. Over time, this culture would not only improve staff satisfaction but also deliver stronger, more consistent results, which would create a foundation for sustained excellence across the organisation.

Front-loading skills to avoid the Peter Principle

One of the biggest challenges in leadership development is avoiding the Peter Principle – a concept introduced by Laurence J. Peter and Raymond Hull in their 1969 book *The Peter Principle: Why things always go wrong*.[33] The Peter Principle describes the tendency for individuals to be promoted based on their success in their current roles rather than their suitability for meeting the demands of the new position or their potential for leadership. Over time, this results in individuals being elevated to roles for which they lack the necessary skills or behaviours to perform effectively.

This principle's consequences are far-reaching and often lead to frustration, inefficiency and poor performance at multiple levels within an organisation. However, its impact extends beyond individual underperformance; it creates a systemic effect that can ripple across the organisation, which erodes culture, collaboration and overall results. In this discussion, we'll examine the wider systemic consequences of promoting individuals based solely on technical performance, rather than on how they align with organisational values and their potential to grow into leadership roles. By exploring this through the lens of the Peter Principle, we'll highlight the importance of front-loading leadership skills to ensure individuals' readiness and alignment before promotion decisions are made.

SCENARIO: A CHAIN OF INCOMPETENCE

A technology company is growing rapidly. A front-line software developer excels in technical execution and consistently delivers high-quality work. Her manager, on seeing her technical prowess, promotes her to a *team leader* position. However, this new role demands leadership capabilities – such as effective communication, developing others and finding creative solutions – that the developer hasn't yet had the opportunity to build. As a result, she struggles to manage her team. She continues to focus on technical tasks while neglecting her leadership responsibilities, which decreases morale and productivity within her team.

At the next level, her line manager had similarly been promoted based on their past performance as a successful project manager. Although he excels at personal responsibility, building strong relationships and effective communication, leadership at this level also requires the ability to make good decisions under pressure, develop his team and enable them to work to their full potential as a cohesive unit. Unfortunately, this team leader struggles with team dynamics and emotional management, which causes collaboration inefficiencies and group underperformance. This further compounds the issues, as the team – despite their individual strengths – fails to achieve their collective potential and misses key targets.

Above him, the organisation's deputy CEO was promoted based on their strong financial background. However, in this role, broader responsibilities – such as long-term strategic decision-making for a changing market, strategic forethought and culture development – are essential. The deputy CEO struggles in these areas and focuses narrowly on short-term financial metrics rather than adapting to market shifts or fostering a resilient and innovative organisational culture. As a result, although the company's financial health may appear stable in the short term, it fails to position itself for future success, with the culture deteriorating, employee turnover spiking, and opportunities for innovation and growth being missed.

This scenario reveals the systemic impact of the Peter Principle, which illustrates how misaligned promotions can weaken an organisation at every level. A company that bases promotions solely on technical expertise rather than leadership readiness evolves into a fragmented and ineffective entity. A technically proficient workforce becomes mismanaged when skilled contributors are elevated into leadership roles they're ill-equipped to handle, which elicits disengagement and inefficiency.

At the team level, a lack of effective management results in poor coordination, decreased morale and unmet objectives. Without a focus on cultivating leadership, the company develops isolated silos of technical work rather than cohesive, high-performing teams. Middle management, while operationally competent, fails to foster resilience or drive growth, which creates a bottleneck in innovation and execution.

At the executive level, the absence of strategic vision and adaptability leaves the organisation ill-prepared for market shifts and competitive pressures. With culture development having been deprioritised, the company experiences a decline in employee engagement and retention, which erodes institutional knowledge and agility. Misaligned promotions at this level undermine the organisation's ability to inspire, innovate and align its workforce with shared goals.

Preventing the Peter Principle:
A strategic leadership pathways approach

To avoid the negative impacts of the Peter Principle, organisations must take a proactive and structured approach to leadership development. This means not only identifying potential leaders early in their careers but also actively teaching them the core skills and competencies outlined in the organisation's leadership taxonomy.

Once these areas have been developed, it's crucial to provide individuals with opportunities to *apply* these skills in real-world settings. This could include leading small projects, managing teams on a temporary basis or taking ownership of cross-functional initiatives. By giving employees the chance to put their learning into practice, organisations can evaluate their capacity and readiness for the next level of leadership.

For instance, if reliability and accountability are core competencies in the organisation's key leadership skill set, employees should be given specific responsibilities that test these attributes – such as managing a project timeline or resolving team conflicts. If self-awareness and communication are essential, potential leaders could be placed in situations where they must give feedback, facilitate meetings or lead team discussions. These real-world experiences provide a controlled environment in which individuals can practise and refine their leadership skills; this offers insights into their capabilities beyond their current technical expertise.

As individuals progress along leadership pathways, it's crucial for them to adapt their leadership styles to meet their evolving needs, as outlined in Level 2 of the Kilter Leadership Taxonomy. For new leaders, a directive style builds their confidence and foundational skills, which should be followed by a coaching style that cultivates their problem-solving and independence. Finally, a delegative approach allows capable leaders to take on greater responsibility with minimal oversight. Communication and relationships are critical at each stage, as this makes certain that leaders remain connected to their teams while fostering open mindsets that embrace instruction, support and progress. This approach helps leaders transition effectively through the development phases while keeping their teams engaged and forward focused.

The three replacements rule

In interviews, finding fantastic leaders can be incredibly challenging because leadership is more about what someone can do than what they can explain or discuss in an interview setting. Jocko Willink, a former Navy SEAL and leadership expert, emphasised this challenge when asked how to identify good leaders during an interview process. He pointed out that leadership is a skill set that's delivered through action, not just conversation. However, he did suggest a powerful question to help uncover strong leaders: 'Which three people are ready to replace you if you get this role?'[34]

Asking this question helps interviewers gain insight into whether a candidate is actively developing those around them. Outstanding leaders don't just excel in their current role; they also recognise the importance of empowering others to grow. Leaders who can readily identify at least three people who have been prepared to step into their shoes are the ones who have been investing in the development of their team. They aren't just focused on personal success but are proactively creating opportunities for others to succeed.

Building a strong, future-ready team

In a healthy, future-oriented organisation, this approach to leadership – developing successors – is crucial. Leaders who actively cultivate the skills of those below them make sure the organisation remains resilient and capable of handling change. This idea forms the foundation of the three replacements rule: every leader should be actively developing at least three people who could step into their role if they're promoted, transferred or otherwise unavailable.[35]

This practice encourages several important dynamics within a team:

- **Active development:** Leaders regularly provide mentorship, coaching and feedback to their successors, which makes certain that the team's capabilities continue to grow.

- **Opportunities for growth:** By focusing on the next generation of leaders, the leaders offer opportunities for hands-on experience and professional development, which gives team members the chance to step up and lead in small but impactful ways.

- **Focus on strengths:** A good leader knows their team's strengths and tailors their development opportunities to maximise these strengths, which prepares their team members to take on more responsibility over time.

When an organisation utilises this approach, it creates a culture of continuous leadership development. Every leader at every level is investing in their team, which makes certain the organisation can handle growth, change and unexpected leadership gaps. It also ensures promotions are smooth transitions because future leaders have already been prepared for their new roles through deliberate guidance and real-world experience.

By making the three replacements rule part of your leadership culture, you not only strengthen your current team but also future-proof your organisation, which makes sure that it remains agile, capable and resilient throughout any changes in leadership.

Creating opportunities for leadership development

Effective leadership development goes beyond formal training programmes; it requires creating *practical, real-world opportunities* for future leaders to develop their skills. Leadership isn't solely an academic pursuit; it's cultivated through experience, decision-making and managing others. As a leader, it's your responsibility to ensure the individuals you're developing are well prepared for the leadership challenges they'll face.

Several approaches can be used to facilitate leadership development:

- » **Mentorship/coaching:** Pair emerging leaders with experienced mentors/coaches who can offer valuable guidance, share insights from their own experiences and advise on navigating complex leadership scenarios.

- » **Cross-functional projects:** Assign emerging leaders to work on projects that involve multiple departments. This approach lets them work across different teams, which exposes them to diverse perspectives and helps them develop a broader skill set.

- » **Challenging assignments:** Offering larger responsibilities – such as leading a new initiative, managing a budget or overseeing a team – can push emerging leaders beyond their comfort zones, which allows them to learn how to handle higher levels of accountability and decision-making.

» **Job rotations:** Rotating emerging leaders through various roles within the organisation provides them with a more comprehensive view of the business while also helping them gain a wider range of the competencies needed for leadership roles.

» **Shadowing:** Enable emerging leaders to observe senior leadership during strategic decision-making processes or critical meetings. Shadowing offers insights into leadership dynamics at higher levels and provides a deeper understanding of complex decision-making.

These experiences not only help emerging leaders to build both their confidence and essential leadership skills but they also provide them with a clear path for growth. When individuals see structured opportunities for development, they're more likely to remain engaged, motivated and committed to advancing their leadership capabilities.

Moreover, it's vital for you, as a leader, to consider the specific developmental needs of the emerging leaders you're guiding. It could be that they require opportunities to build resilience by tackling challenging projects, or they may need to enhance their ability to lead and develop others. Regardless of the focus, it's essential that you communicate effectively with the teams they're joining, which will make sure that expectations are aligned and the learning process is supported by the entire organisation.

A skilled leader is one who recognises their own role in the development process. If the emerging leader doesn't fully develop the desired skills, it's important to assess the support and preparation provided, rather than attributing any shortcomings solely to the individual. By owning the development process, you can refine the guidance and opportunities offered to ensure future success.

Emerging leaders' growth and success is a shared responsibility. By managing their development thoughtfully and making certain they have the resources and guidance needed, you contribute to building a leadership pipeline that will benefit both the individual and the organisation.

Aligning leadership development with organisational strategy

Strategic leadership development isn't just about nurturing individual growth; it's about ensuring leadership growth is inextricably linked with the organisation's *overall strategy*. By bringing the leaders' development in line with the organisation's long-term objectives and vision, the leaders are better prepared to contribute meaningfully to both *immediate goals* and *future growth*.

This necessitates leaders adopting a *balanced approach* to development, which makes sure individuals aren't simply advancing their personal strengths in isolation but are enhancing the organisation's collective capabilities. Leadership development efforts should therefore be tied directly to the company's broader goals, whether that's driving innovation, improving operational efficiency, expanding into new markets or undergoing a significant change, such as a digital transformation.

Making promotion criteria transparent

One of the most impactful ways to align leadership development with organisational strategy is to make sure the promotion criteria are clear, consistent and transparent. Teams are far more likely to accept bold decisions around promotions when the success criteria are well-defined and communicated. This clarity empowers individuals to focus on developing the skills that contribute directly to the organisation's success, while fostering a culture of accountability and trust.

For example, team leaders must demonstrate skills in responsibility, building strong relationships and communication, developing others, delegating tasks proactively while maintaining quality, and turning efforts into results. Senior leaders must show they're able to manage emotions effectively, make sound decisions under pressure and manage team dynamics skilfully. Executive leaders, in turn, must be able to produce strategic visions, establish actionable plans, identify and foster a culture that supports this vision, and create sustainable pathways to secure long-term success. By basing promotions on these clearly defined criteria, organisations send a strong signal about the behaviours and competencies they value, which cultivates a values-driven culture that supports sustained success.

Embedding organisational values in leadership development

Leadership development should also be a key driver of cultural alignment within the organisation. Leaders play an essential role in shaping and reinforcing the organisation's values, and those values should be embedded in the leadership pathways. For instance, if collaboration, sustainability or customer-experience are central to the company's mission, leadership development programmes must reflect the appropriate values to make certain emerging leaders not only understand them but also model and promote them within their teams.

Embedding these values into leadership training and development facilitates organisations cultivating a consistent leadership ethos that's consistent with the company's long-term vision. This also helps to create leaders who'll continue to strengthen the organisational culture, regardless of how external challenges or internal dynamics evolve.

Leadership structures

One of strategic leadership's key skills is the ability to identify areas where targeted improvements will yield the most significant impact, even if these areas lie outside the conventional focus of existing roles within the organisation. This often requires prioritising emerging needs over traditionally high-profile roles, which allows the organisation to adapt and innovate in response to changing circumstances. However, this shift must be balanced with an awareness of the foundational roles that, if neglected, could lead to declining standards and long-term setbacks.

In educational settings, for instance, high-profile roles typically focus on core subjects such as maths and English, which are considered indicators of academic achievement and are integral to students' foundational knowledge. However, a skilled school leader may determine that the areas with the most potential for meaningful improvement are strengthening pedagogical approaches and behavioural-regulation support. These areas address underlying issues such as student engagement, effective learning strategies and emotional regulation, which significantly influence overall student success.

Although prioritising these areas can drive impactful changes across the school, it's essential not to lose sight of the importance of core-subject roles. Neglecting maths and English, for example, would risk diminishing the very skills students rely on for success in both further education and the workforce. A drop in standards within these subjects could elicit widespread academic gaps, lower outcomes and reduced student confidence, all of which potentially affect the school's reputation and future enrolment rates.

Balancing role creation and core responsibilities to achieve a sustainable impact

After identifying high-impact areas, a strategic leader must carefully balance creating new roles with maintaining support for established ones. For example, when focusing on improving teaching standards and behavioural regulation, introducing roles such as behavioural specialists and teaching coaches can significantly enhance classroom management and teaching effectiveness. These positions are intended to address vital areas that indirectly elevate performance across all subjects, including core areas such as maths and English.

However, introducing these new roles must not come at the expense of existing resources allocated to foundational subjects. A skilled leader generates a balanced structure in which traditional and innovative roles work collaboratively to support the school's broader mission. By maintaining robust support for maths and English teachers, the leader strengthens the school's academic foundations while also cultivating a learning environment that meets the diverse needs of students.

> **HEALTH WARNING: POTENTIAL CONSEQUENCES OF NEGLECTING CORE-SUBJECT STANDARDS**

If roles focusing on core subjects such as maths and English are deprioritised in favour of new initiatives, the long-term consequences can be detrimental to the school's success. Declining standards in these foundational subjects can hinder students' development of essential academic competencies, which negatively affects their performance in other areas and limits their future educational opportunities. Furthermore, diminished outcomes in maths and English could damage the school's reputation, which results in lower student numbers, dissatisfaction among parents, and potentially reduced funding or resources from the educational authorities.

These risks highlight the importance of balancing innovation with a steadfast commitment to core functions. Although addressing the emerging needs in pedagogy and behavioural support is vital, it must be done in a way that reinforces the academic standards that are underpinning educational success. Leaders who are naturally inclined toward creativity and innovation must temper this bias by focusing clearly on the key performance areas their team must deliver in. Achieving this balance ensures that the new initiatives complement, rather than detract from, the team's core responsibilities.

Creating strategic leadership structures

Creating roles and structures within a leadership team is a critical yet complex decision-making process. These decisions shape the organisation's ability to respond to current challenges and anticipate future opportunities. Whether they're prompted by external forces or internal foresight, such decisions can be made reactively, proactively or strategically. Each approach carries different implications for the organisation's effectiveness and resilience.

Reactive, proactive and strategic approaches to role creation
The manner in which leadership structures and roles are created reflects the organisation's ability to navigate challenges and leverage opportunities. To illustrate, consider a charity organisation that's deciding to create a digital media lead role that aims to strengthen the charity's digital presence and engagement with stakeholders.

The following approaches could be taken:

» **Reactive decision-making:** A reactive approach is creating this role when the need for it arises from a pressing, unanticipated issue. For example, the charity may have experienced a sharp decline in online donations due to outdated marketing strategies and missed opportunities to engage younger donors on social media platforms. On recognising these failures after the fact, the organisation hastily creates the digital media lead role to help recover from the setbacks. Although this approach addresses the immediate issues, it often results in rushed decisions and limited foresight, which potentially leads to misaligned expectations or insufficient support for the new role.

» **Proactive decision-making:** In contrast, a proactive approach involves identifying potential challenges before they escalate into crises. For instance, the charity might notice a gradual decline in engagement metrics and anticipate that the current digital efforts are inadequate for reaching a tech-savvy audience. As a result of monitoring these trends, the organisation creates the digital media lead role before the issue impacts donations significantly. This proactive move smooths implementation and integration, which allows the organisation to stay ahead of emerging challenges.

» **Strategic decision-making:** A strategic approach goes further by integrating broader trends, organisational goals and industry foresight. For example, the charity might observe patterns in donor behaviour, such as the rise of mobile-first engagement, increased reliance on video storytelling and growing preferences for interactive digital campaigns. By acknowledging these shifts and bringing the vision in line with them, the charity not only creates the digital media lead role but also redefines its entire communications strategy to include emerging technologies such as artificial intelligence and analytics. This strategic move positions the organisation to do more than addressing the current needs: this allows the charity to thrive in a rapidly evolving digital landscape.

The skills needed for structuring strategic leadership

The effective structuring of leadership roles demands a nuanced understanding of the organisation's current and future needs combined with the ability to identify solutions that will address those needs effectively.

This requires the following:

» **Reading the organisation's current state:** Leaders must have a clear understanding of the existing challenges, gaps and opportunities the organisation is experiencing. This involves assessing team performance, workflow bottlenecks and the external factors influencing organisational outcomes.

» **Anticipating future needs:** Foresight is essential for strategic structuring. This means analysing trends, gathering stakeholder insights and understanding where the organisation is heading. A charity leader, for instance, might predict that donor engagement will shift toward gamification or blockchain-based transparency, which prompts an early reorganisation to address these possibilities.

» **Judging the right solutions:** Leadership structuring necessitates evaluating potential solutions – whether it involves creating new roles, breaking down silos or realigning departments. Leaders must weigh the trade-offs, bring the solution in line with organisational goals, and consider both short-term impacts and long-term sustainability.

The balance between creation, consolidation and adaptation

Structuring strategic leadership doesn't always mean creating new roles or departments. It sometimes involves streamlining existing structures to improve impact.

Here are some examples:

» **Creating new roles or departments:** When some needs are entirely unmet or new opportunities emerge, leaders must innovate confidently. For instance, creating a community insights manager role to harness data-driven approaches for stakeholder engagement.

» **Breaking down or grouping departments:** In other scenarios, merging overlapping functions can maximise efficiency, while breaking down overly broad departments can help teams focus on specific priorities. For example, splitting a combined fundraising-and-marketing team into two distinct departments might allow for deeper expertise and more-transparent accountability.

» **Adaptation for resilience:** Structures must be dynamic, adapting to changes in either the environment or the organisation's mission. Leaders who embrace this adaptability ensure their teams remain agile and equipped to meet evolving demands.

> **EXAMPLE IN PRACTICE: STRATEGIC CREATION OF A TECHNOLOGIES LEAD ROLE IN A PRIMARY SCHOOL**

In a primary school, the integration and development of design technology (DT) and computing are increasingly important, especially with the growing emphasis on science, technology, engineering and maths (STEM) education. However, these subjects often present challenges for new or inexperienced subject leaders due to their technical demands, the need for specialist resources and the pressure of inspections. To address these challenges and create a cohesive strategy for technological education, schools can establish a *technologies lead* role to oversee both DT and computing.

Role creation – from reactive to strategic

The primary school decides to introduce a technologies lead role to oversee the DT and computing curricula. This role aims to enhance both subjects by providing experienced leadership, fostering cross-curricular opportunities and mentoring individual subject leads. We'll explore three different approaches to creating this role: one made reactively in response to immediate pressures or gaps, one made proactively to address the anticipated needs and opportunities, and one made strategically as part of a broader, longer-term plan that's aligned with the school's vision and goals.

Each approach illustrates the variation in impacts on the success and sustainability of the role from the three decision-making styles.

Why the role was created

- **Reactive creation:** In the past, the school had separate leaders for DT and computing, both of whom were new to leadership. During an inspection, the school received feedback that DT lacked cross-curricular coherence and computing wasn't meeting the requirements of the national curriculum. After the inspection, the school created the technologies lead role to recover and bring both subjects in line under stronger leadership.

- **Proactive creation:** On recognising that both DT and computing were being led by relatively inexperienced staff, the school anticipated the potential challenges in meeting curriculum standards. Before any formal issues arose, they introduced the technologies lead role to support these subject leaders proactively and ensure alignment with evolving educational demands.

- **Strategic creation:** With a broader vision, the school leadership team examined trends in STEM education and identified the need for a cohesive strategy that integrated

DT and computing with other subject areas such as science. The technologies lead role was created not only to oversee these subjects but also to drive innovation, develop new high-quality leadership, connect with external partners and future-proof the school's approach to technological education.

Benefits of a technologies lead role

- **Expert mentoring of subject leaders:**
  - The technologies lead mentors the individual DT and computing leads, which helps them with curriculum planning, resource management and developing confidence in their roles.
  - This mentorship includes preparing subject leaders for inspections, guiding them through the scrutiny process and alleviating their stress by presenting the overarching strategies to the inspectors.

- **Cohesion and consistency across subjects:**
  - The technologies lead makes certain the teaching approaches and resource usage are consistent by creating a unified vision for technology education.
  - This role also supports the integration of DT and computing with other curriculum areas, which cultivates a cross-curricular approach to STEM learning.

- **Improved inspection readiness:**
  - During inspections, the technologies lead presents the strategic plan for DT and computing, which provides a clear vision for how these subjects contribute to the school's broader educational goals.
  - By managing the inspection pressures, the technologies lead enables the subject leaders to focus on their specific contributions, which results in less stress.

- **Driving innovation and future-proofing:**
  - By focusing on technological trends, the technologies lead identifies opportunities for innovation, such as incorporating coding workshops, robotics projects or sustainable design challenges into the curricula.
  - They also build partnerships with local industries or secondary schools to enhance resources and opportunities for students.
- **Leadership development pathways:**
  - By creating this umbrella leadership role, the school has engendered a pipeline for developing future leaders. Emerging DT and computing leaders gain leadership experience under the guidance of the technologies lead, which prepares them for wider roles in the future.

Balancing role creation with organisational sustainability

Although creating new roles can address critical needs and unlock opportunities, it's vital to strike a balance between the benefits of the new roles and the organisation's fundamental operational running to avoid any unintended operational challenges. Overextending resources, overwhelming staff or introducing complexity can detract from the intended benefits of creating the role. Organisations must consider the ripple effects of new roles on their people, processes and overall sustainability.

Assessing resource allocation and capacity

Establishing a new role often diverts resources – financial, human and operational – from existing priorities. Leaders must critically evaluate whether the organisation has the capacity to support the new role without compromising other essential areas.

The questions to consider include these:

» **Budget impact:** Does the organisation have the financial flexibility to sustain the role long-term without cutting corners elsewhere?

» **Workload balance:** How will the new role affect team workloads? Are there risks of overburdening existing staff or creating bottlenecks?

» **Support systems:** Are there mechanisms to support the individual stepping into the new role, such as mentoring, training or additional staffing?

Avoiding role creep and overlap

When new roles are introduced, there's often a risk of role creep, where responsibilities are inadvertently expanded beyond the original scope. This can lead to inefficiencies and conflicts with existing roles.

To mitigate this, leaders should do the following:

» **Define clear boundaries:** Unambiguously articulate the responsibilities and expectations of the new role to avoid overlap with other roles.

» **Regularly review and adjust:** Schedule periodic reviews to ensure the role remains focused and aligned with organisational goals.

» **Engage stakeholders:** Involve staff in the planning process to identify potential conflicts and foster collaboration.

Avoiding the trap of being 'victims of their own success'

High-performing team members are often moved quickly from one priority role to the next to leverage their skills to address pressing needs. Although their success and adaptability are invaluable to the organisation, this can unintentionally elicit frustration or burnout. These individuals may feel disheartened if their efforts to elevate their areas of responsibility are disrupted by constant reassignment. To prevent resentment, it's crucial to invest in meaningful relationships with high performers, which acknowledge their contributions and provide clarity early in their career about their long-term value to the organisation. Transparent discussions about career pathways and the importance of their work can make certain they feel recognised and supported, which helps them maintain their motivation and commitment while avoiding the pitfalls of overburdening their success.

CONCLUSION

Building a robust leadership structure and clear development pathways is fundamental to the long-term success and sustainability of any organisation. This process involves more than simply identifying high performers; it requires intentional strategies to nurture leadership potential, align individual growth with organisational values, and equip emerging leaders with the skills and experiences necessary to meet future challenges. When executed thoughtfully, leadership pathways serve as powerful tools for fostering engagement, promoting accountability and driving organisational resilience.

Effective leadership structures not only address current challenges but also position organisations to anticipate and adapt to future opportunities. Leaders who strategically design roles and pathways will make certain that key areas are supported by individuals with the right mix of technical expertise and leadership readiness. By embedding values such as reliability, collaboration and accountability into leadership criteria, organisations reinforce a culture that prioritises long-term success over short-term gains. Decisions made about leadership roles and promotions should send a clear signal about the behaviours and competencies the organisation values most, which creates a foundation for sustainable growth.

Additionally, leadership pathways must support strategic alignment by addressing both foundational and emerging needs. Balancing innovation with preserving core standards ensures new initiatives strengthen, rather than undermine, the organisation's mission. With thoughtful planning and clear communication, leaders can create structures that empower teams, promote adaptability, and cultivate a leadership culture that drives both present and future successes. This investment in leadership development lays the groundwork for a resilient and thriving organisation.

Final Reflection: From Natural to Skilled and Balanced Leadership

The Kilter Leadership Taxonomy provides a comprehensive and adaptable framework for developing leadership skills that are both deeply personal and have a broad impact. At its heart, leadership is not a static destination but an ongoing journey of growth, self-awareness and adaptability. It demands achieving a balance between responsibility, relationships, self-awareness and strategic influence – all of which are intricately connected and evolving continuously.

Leaders who excel in responsibility inspire trust and foster accountability by focusing on solutions rather than blame. They own outcomes, adapt to challenges and empower their teams to do the same. Responsibility isn't a burden; it's a powerful tool for driving progress and creating a culture of collaboration and continuous improvement. Similarly, self-awareness forms the foundation of effective leadership as it enables leaders to understand their strengths and limitations, manage their emotions, and appreciate the diverse talents of their team members.

Strong relationships are the core of leadership success. They build trust, enhance collaboration and create resilient teams capable of navigating challenges together. Reliable leaders earn respect by consistently following through on commitments, which cultivates environments in which team members feel valued and empowered. Relationships, when nurtured, serve as the best fuel for sustainable ambition and long-term success.

Strategic leadership – the pinnacle of the taxonomy – challenges leaders to align their daily actions with their organisation's long-term goals. It requires vision, adaptability and a commitment to balancing short-term needs with sustainable growth. Strategic leaders set the tone for their organisations by inspiring innovation and empowering the next generation of leaders to emerge.

Throughout the Kilter Leadership Taxonomy, one unifying principle remains constant: *balance*. Leaders must balance self-awareness with action, responsibility with empowerment, and personal growth with organisational impact. This equilibrium is what distinguishes excellent leaders from good ones, and it helps them to navigate complexity, inspire trust and achieve lasting results.

The Kilter Leadership Taxonomy equips leaders with the tools needed to make a meaningful difference – in themselves, their teams and their organisations. By embracing its principles, leaders can cultivate a mindset of humility, adaptability and purpose, which makes sure they not only meet the challenges of today but also shape a brighter future for tomorrow.

Leadership isn't about perfection; it's about progress. The Kilter Leadership Taxonomy serves as a guide to excellence in every step of that journey.

About the Author

Alan Rogers is a practising leader in education, based in the West Midlands, England. With his broad leadership experience, he has led teams and influenced culture across a range of sectors.

Alan is known for his ethical, people-focused approach to leadership, which is grounded in clarity, balance and long-term impact. His work focuses on helping leaders achieve sustainable results by developing both themselves and those they lead.

Through *Kilter Leadership*, he offers a structured, practical framework – drawn from real-world experience – that's designed to help individuals lead with purpose, develop others and build meaningful, high-performing cultures.

References

1. Buckingham, M. (2022). *Love + Work*. Boston, MA: Harvard Business Review Press.
2. Buckingham, M. (2022). *Love + Work*. Boston, MA: Harvard Business Review Press.
3. Peters, S. (2012). *The Chimp Paradox*. London, UK: Vermillion.
4. Magsamen, S. and Ross, I. (2025). *Your Brain on Art*. Edinburgh, UK: Canongate Books.
5. Called to Coach (2022, 12 December). *How to Overcome Burnout with Strengths*. Retrieved from: https://www.gallup.com/cliftonstrengths/en/406727/how-to-overcome-burnout-with-strengths.aspx
6. Willink, J. (2015). *Extreme Ownership*. New York, NY: St Martin's Press.
7. Covey, S. (2020). *The 7 Habits of Highly Effective People*. 30th Anniversary Edition. London, UK: Simon & Schuster UK.
8. Covey, S. (2020). *The 7 Habits of Highly Effective People*. 30th Anniversary Edition. London, UK: Simon & Schuster UK.
9. Willink, J. (2015). *Extreme Ownership*. New York, NY: St Martin's Press.
10. Willink, J. (2015). *Extreme Ownership*. New York, NY: St Martin's Press.
11. Guidera, W. (2022). *Unreasonable Hospitality: The remarkable power of giving people more than they expect*. New York, NY: Optimism Press.
12. Holiday, R. (2016). *Ego is the Enemy*. New York, NY: Portfolio.
13. Holiday, R. (2016). *Ego is the Enemy*. New York, NY: Portfolio.
14. Holiday, R. (2016). *Ego is the Enemy*. New York, NY: Portfolio.
15. Takahashi, H., Kato, M., Matsuura, M., Mobbs, D., Suhara, T., and Okubo, Y. (2009). When your gain is my pain and your pain is my gain: Neural correlates of envy and schadenfreude. *Science, 323*(5916), 937–939. DOI: https://doi.org/10.1126/science.1165604
16. Sinek, S. (2009). *Start with Why*. New York, NY: Portfolio.
17. Covey, S. (2020). *The 7 Habits of Highly Effective People*. 30th Anniversary Edition. London, UK: Simon & Schuster UK.
18. Covey, S. (2020). *The 7 Habits of Highly Effective People*. 30th Anniversary Edition. London, UK: Simon & Schuster UK.

REFERENCES

19. Blanchard, K., Zigarmi, P., and Zigarmi, D. (1985). *Leadership and the One Minute Manager: Increasing effectiveness through Situational Leadership.* New York, NY: William Morrow & Company.
20. Loehr, J. and Schwartz, T. (2003). *The Power of Full Engagement: Managing energy, not time, is the key to high performance and personal renewal.* Glencoe, IL: Free Press.
21. Thaler, R.H. and Sunstein, C.R. (2008). *Nudge: Improving decisions about health, wealth, and happiness.* New Haven, CT: Yale University Press.
22. Sinek, S. (2009). *Start with Why.* New York, NY: Portfolio.
23. Walsh, B. (2009). *The Score Takes Care of Itself: My Philosophy of Leadership.* New York, NY: Portfolio.
24. Peters, S. (2012). *The Chimp Paradox.* London, UK: Vermillion.
25. Peters, S. (2021). *A Path Through the Jungle.* Buxton, UK: Mindfield Media Ltd.
26. McGonigal, J. (2015). *SuperBetter.* London, UK: Penguin Press.
27. Jordet, G. (2023). *Pressure: Lessons from the psychology of penalty shootouts.* Shoreham-by-Sea, UK: Pavilion Publishing.
28. Yu, J., Nickens, T., Liu, D., and Vincenzi, D.A. (2023). *Decision-Making under Crisis Conditions: A training and simulation perspective.* Boca Raton, FL: CRC Press.
29. Lencioni, P.M. (2022). *The 6 Types of Working Genius: A better way to understand your gifts, your frustrations, and your team.* Dallas, TX: Matt Holt Books.
30. Lencioni, P.M. (2022). *The 6 Types of Working Genius: A better way to understand your gifts, your frustrations, and your team.* Dallas, TX: Matt Holt Books.
31. Mizrak, K.C. (2023). Comparative analysis of employee engagement strategies. *Premium e-Journal of Social Sciences, 7*(35), 1336–1348. Retrieved from: https://pejoss.com/index.php/pub/article/download/328/303/824
32. Peter, L.J. and Hull, R. (1969). *The Peter Principle: Why things always go wrong.* New York, NY: William Morrow and Company.
33. Peter, L.J. and Hull, R. (1969). The Peter Principle: Why things always go wrong. New York, NY: William Morrow and Company.
34. Willink, J. (2015). *Extreme Ownership.* New York, NY: St Martin's Press.
35. Willink, J. (2015). *Extreme Ownership.* New York, NY: St Martin's Press.